APOLLO

Apollo is a comprehensive study of the Greek god in all his aspects, from the first attestations of his myth and worship to his reception in modern European and American culture. Fritz Graf uses literary texts, inscriptions, and archaeological finds to develop the complex image of a young god who was central to Greek culture, both in the way the Greeks themselves perceived him and as later ages looked at the Greeks.

Apollo was the god of what the Greeks called *mousikē*, a combination of song, lyre music, and dance. He was the god of divination: as Zeus' favorite son, he had direct access to the mind of Zeus and was willing to reveal this knowledge to humans. He was the god of healing: as a healer he arrived in Rome and from there in the Western provinces of the Roman Empire. He was the god of the young male citizen and through them the protector of all citizens of a Greek city-state. He has ties to the Ancient Near East, but he is no Eastern god brought to Greece; he became important in Etruria, Italy, and the Roman West.

Literature, art, philosophy, and astrology preserved and transformed the god in the Middle Ages and the Modern Age: he became a god of poetry, the god of the planet sun, finally a symbol of pure rationality and order in opposition to the chaotic god Dionysus.

For students of Greek religion and culture, of myth and legend, and in the fields of art and literature, *Apollo* is an informative and enlightening introduction to this powerful figure from the past.

Fritz Graf is Professor of Greek and Latin, and Director of the Center for Epigraphical Studies at the Ohio State University. His research interests include the religions of the Greek and Roman world. His publications include *Greek Mythology: An Introduction* (1993), *Magic in the Ancient World* (1997), and with Sarah Iles Johnston, *Ritual Texts for the Afterlife: Orpheus and the Bacchic Gold Tablets* (2006).

Gods and Heroes of the Ancient World

Series editor Susan Deacy
Roehampton University

Routledge is pleased to present an exciting new series, Gods and Heroes of the Ancient World. These figures from antiquity are embedded in our culture, many functioning as the source of creative inspiration for poets, novelists, artists, composers and filmmakers. Concerned with their multifaceted aspects within the world of ancient paganism and how and why these figures continue to fascinate, the books provide a route into understanding Greek and Roman polytheism in the 21st century.

These concise and comprehensive guides provide a thorough understanding of each figure, offering the latest in critical research from the leading scholars in the field in an accessible and approachable form, making them ideal for undergraduates in Classics and related disciplines.

Each volume includes illustrations, time charts, family trees and maps where appropriate.

Also available:

Perseus
Daniel Ogden

Athena
Susan Deacy

Zeus
Keith Dowden

Prometheus
Carol Dougherty

Medea
Emma Griffiths

Dionysos
Richard Seaford

Oedipus
Lowell Edmunds

Susan Deacy is Senior Lecturer in Greek History and Literature at Roehampton University. Her main research interests are Greek religion, and gender and sexuality. Publications include the co-edited volumes *Rape in Antiquity* (1997), and *Athena in the Classical World* (2001), and the monograph *A Traitor to Her Sex? Athena the Trickster* (forthcoming).

APOLLO

Fritz Graf

Routledge
Taylor & Francis Group

LONDON AND NEW YORK

First published 2009
by Routledge
2 Park Square, Milton Park, Abingdon, Oxon OX14 4RN

Simultaneously published in the USA and Canada
by Routledge
270 Madison Ave, New York, NY 10016

Routledge is an imprint of the Taylor & Francis Group, an informa business

© 2009 Fritz Graf

Typeset in Utopia by
Swales & Willis Ltd, Exeter, Devon
Printed and bound in Great Britain by
TJ International Ltd, Padstow, Cornwall

Library of Congress Cataloging in Publication Data
Graf, Fritz.
Apollo / Fritz Graf.
    p. cm.
    Includes index.
    1. Apollo (Greek deity) 2. Greece—Religious life and customs. I. Title.
    BL820.A7G73 2008
    292.2′113—dc22
    2008016457

ISBN10: 0–415–31710–X (hbk)
ISBN10: 0–415–31711–8 (pbk)
ISBN10: 0–203–58171–7 (ebk)

ISBN13: 978–0–415–31710–8 (hbk)
ISBN13: 978–0–415–31711–5 (pbk)
ISBN13: 978–0–203–58171–1 (ebk)

For Sarah Iles Johnston

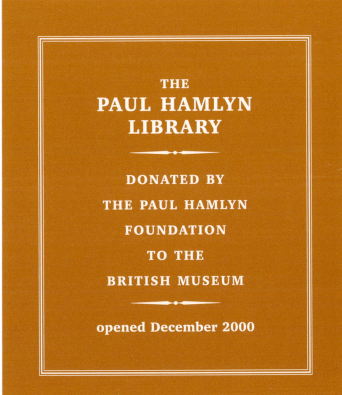

CONTENTS

SERIES FOREWORD

It is proper for a person who is beginning any serious discourse and task to begin first with the gods.

(Demosthenes, *Epistula* 1.1)

WHY GODS AND HEROES?

The gods and heroes of classical antiquity are part of our culture. Many function as sources of creative inspiration for poets, novelists, artists, composers, filmmakers and designers. Greek tragedy's enduring appeal has ensured an ongoing familiarity with its protagonists' experiences and sufferings, while the choice of Minerva as the logo of one the newest British universities, the University of Lincoln, demonstrates the ancient gods' continued emblematic potential. Even the world of management has used them as representatives of different styles: Zeus and the "club" culture for example, and Apollo and the "role" culture: see C. Handy, *The Gods of Management: Who they are, how they work and why they fail*, London, 1978.

This series is concerned with how and why these figures continue to fascinate and intrigue. But it has another aim too, namely to explore their strangeness. The familiarity of the gods and heroes risks obscuring a vital difference between modern meanings and ancient functions and purpose. With certain exceptions, people today do not worship them, yet to the Greeks and Romans they were real beings in a system comprising literally hundreds of divine powers. These range from the major gods, each of whom was worshipped in many guises via their epithets or "surnames," to the heroes – deceased individuals associated with local communities – to other figures such as daimons and nymphs. The landscape was dotted with sanctuaries, while natural features such as mountains, trees and rivers were thought to be inhabited by religious beings.

Studying ancient paganism involves finding strategies to comprehend a world where everything was, in the often quoted words of Thales, "full of gods."

In order to get to grips with this world, it is necessary to set aside our preconceptions of the divine, shaped as they are in large part by Christianised notions of a transcendent, omnipotent God who is morally good. The Greeks and Romans worshipped numerous beings, both male and female, who looked, behaved and suffered like humans, but who, as immortals, were not bound by the human condition. Far from being omnipotent, each had limited powers: even the sovereign, Zeus/Jupiter, shared control of the universe with his brothers Poseidon/Neptune (the sea) and Hades/Pluto (the underworld). Lacking a creed or anything like an organised church, ancient paganism was open to continual reinterpretation, with the result that we should not expect to find figures with a uniform essence. It is common to begin accounts of the pantheon with a list of the major gods and their function(s) (Hephaistos/Vulcan: craft, Aphrodite/Venus: love, and Artemis/Diana: the hunt and so on), but few are this straightforward. Aphrodite, for example, is much more than the goddess of love, vital though that function is. Her epithets include *hetaira* ("courtesan") and *porne* ("prostitute"), but also attest roles as varied as patron of the citizen body (*pandemos*: "of all the people") and protectress of seafaring (*Euploia, Pontia, Limenia*).

Recognising this diversity, the series consists not of biographies of each god or hero (though such have been attempted in the past), but of investigations into their multifaceted aspects within the complex world of ancient paganism. Its approach has been shaped partly in response to two distinctive patterns in previous research. Until the middle of the twentieth century, scholarship largely took the form of studies of individual gods and heroes. Many works presented a detailed appraisal of such issues as each figure's origins, myth and cult; these include L.R. Farnell's examination of major deities in his *Cults of the Greek States* (five volumes, Oxford, 1896–1909) and A.B. Cook's huge three-volume *Zeus* (Cambridge, 1914–40). Others applied theoretical developments to the study of gods and heroes, notably (and in the closest existing works to a uniform series), K. Kerényi in his investigations of gods as Jungian archetypes, including *Prometheus: Archetypal image of human existence* (English tr. London 1963) and *Dionysus: Archetypal image of the indestructable life* (English tr. London 1976).

In contrast, under the influence of French structuralism, the later part of the century saw a deliberate shift away from research into particular gods and heroes towards an investigation of the system of which they were part. Fuelled by a conviction that the study of isolated gods could not do justice to the dynamics of ancient religion, the pantheon came to be represented as a logical and coherent network in which the various powers were systematically opposed to one another. In a classic study by J.-P. Vernant for example, the Greek concept of space was shown to be consecrated through the opposition between Hestia (goddess of the hearth – fixed space) and Hermes (messenger and traveller god – moveable space: Vernant, *Myth and Thought Among the Greeks* London, 1983, 127–75). The gods as individual entities were far from neglected however, as may be exemplified by the works by Vernant, and his colleague M. Detienne, on particular deities including Artemis, Dionysus and Apollo: see, most recently, Detienne's *Apollon, le couteau en main: une approche expérimentale du polythéisme grec* (Paris, 1998).

In a sense, this series is seeking a middle ground. While approaching its subjects as unique (if diverse) individuals, it pays attention to their significance as powers within the collectivity of religious beings. *Gods and Heroes of the Ancient World* sheds new light on many of the most important religious beings of classical antiquity; it also provides a route into understanding Greek and Roman polytheism in the twenty-first century.

The series is intended to interest the general reader as well as being geared to the needs of students in a wide range of fields from Greek and Roman religion and mythology, classical literature and anthropology, to Renaissance literature and cultural studies. Each book presents an authoritative, accessible and refreshing account of its subject via three main sections. The introduction brings out what it is about the god or hero that merits particular attention. This is followed by a central section which introduces key themes and ideas, including (to varying degrees) origins, myth, cult, and representations in literature and art. Recognising that the heritage of myth is a crucial factor in its continued appeal, the reception of each figure since antiquity forms the subject of the third part of the book. The volumes include illustrations of each god/hero and where appropriate time charts, family trees and maps. An annotated bibliography synthesises past research and indicates useful follow-up reading.

For convenience, the masculine terms "gods" and "heroes" have been selected for the series title, although (and with an apology for the male-dominated language), the choice partly reflects ancient usage in that the Greek *theos* ("god") is used of goddesses too. For convenience and consistency, Greek spellings are used for ancient names, except for famous Latinized exceptions, and BC/AD has been selected rather than BCE/CE.

I am indebted to Catherine Bousfield, the editorial assistant until 2004, who (literally) dreamt up the series and whose thoroughness and motivation brought it close to its launch. The hard work and efficiency of her successor, Matthew Gibbons, has overseen its progress to publication, and the former classics publisher of Routledge, Richard Stoneman, has provided support and expertise throughout. The anonymous readers for each proposal gave frank and helpful advice, while the authors' commitment to advancing scholarship while producing accessible accounts of their designated subjects has made it a pleasure to work with them.

Susan Deacy, Roehampton University, June 2005

ACKNOWLEDGMENTS

My thinking about many of the topics I touch upon in this book goes back over many years and even decades. During this time, I have learned from many colleagues and friends with whom I have discussed single issues or whose work has helped me to shape my own answer. I especially thank Jan Bremmer, Walter Burkert, and Philippe Borgeaud, and I will always remember Christiane Sourvinou and Michael Jameson with immense gratitude. Norita Dobyns has read a draft of the manuscript and streamlined my English, and Susan Deacy has been an understanding and helpful series editor. I dedicate the book to Sarah Iles Johnston who has been for many years now an understanding and sometimes provocative companion of my life and my work.

My quotations from ancient authors do not need explanations; the translations are mostly mine, if not marked otherwise. Later authors need more documentation. Robert W. Service is quoted from *More Collected Verse* (New York: Dodd, Mead, 1955). For Dante, I quote the translation of Robert and Jean Hollander (New York: Doubleday, 2007), for Petrarch, that of Mark Musa (Indiana University Press, 1996). R.M. Rilke, *Früher Apollo* and *Archaïscher Torso Apollos*, are cited in Stephen Cohn's translation; the German original is reprinted with permission of Insel Verlag, Hamburg, the translation with permission of Carcanet Press, Manchester. Winckelmann is cited in the English translation of Alexander Gode (New York: Ungar, 1968).

LIST OF ILLUSTRATIONS

WHY APOLLO?

INTRODUCTION
Why Write a Book on A God?

Greek gods, everyone agrees, possess rounded, complex, and full-blooded personalities, not unlike the humans who worshipped them, Pericles or Sappho or Alexander the Great. There are many books on Alexander and not a few on Sappho or Pericles; but when one looks for books on one of the Olympians, one finds far fewer books than one would have thought. Certainly, Karl Kerényi's monographs on Zeus and Hera, Demeter, or Dionysus have found a wide readership, but the author's interests are shaped and limited by the underlying Jungian psychoanalysis that reduced the gods to concretizations of an archetype; the same is true for the few books that take their inspiration from Sigmund Freud. These books aside, especially English-speaking scholars have been hesitant to devote a monograph to a single god. The single volumes of Lewis Richard Farnell's *The Cults of the Greek States* use the gods as an ordering principle for information on cults, and Arthur Bernhard Cook's *Zeus* is far from being a monograph on the father of the gods; it is a compendium of rare and strange rituals. Since the days of Sir James Frazer and Jane Ellen Harrison, scholars on Greek religion have always been much more interested in rituals than in the divine recipients; myths – which would have narrated divine biographies – were thought as somehow being generated by ritual, and thus of secondary interest only.

More recent scholarship has reinforced the scholarly reluctance to focus on a single god as if he were not essentially different from Pericles or Sappho. Ritual (especially sacrifice) in its social and communal function remained at the center of research. The recipients of sacrifice were of secondary interest. Furthermore, Greek religion was understood as having a rather precarious unity: the basic unit of religion was the polis, the city-state; some scholars underscored this by writing books on *Greek Religions*. In the pantheon of two different cities, the same god could have two very different roles: in a classical paper, Christiane Sourvinou-Inwood showed how Persephone in Locri had roles that in other cities were fulfilled by Artemis or Aphrodite. Following the lead of Jean-Pierre Vernant, the Parisian scholar whose work was instrumental in reshaping research on Greek religion, a god was thought as being determined by all the other gods in the pantheon of each city, not unlike in linguistics a specific meaningful sound, a phoneme, is determined by all the other phonemes of the same language. Thus, Vernant did not write on the god Hermes, he wrote on "Hermes and Hestia" who defined each other in a complex interplay of roles and functions. With very few exceptions, only coffee table books that centered on ancient art have dared to focus on one single god.

The coffee table books, perhaps unwittingly, make an important point. Each Greek god has an iconography that is individual and recognizable; and although some local temple images might have strange and unusual features, usually the same god looked about the same whether one saw his image in a temple in Sicily, Athens, or Smyrna: the Athenian Phidias created not only the gold-ivory image of Athena on the Athenian acropolis, but also the image of Zeus in his temple in Olympia. The same is true for mythology. There were local myths; most are lost, some surface in inscriptions or in the fragments of the lost books of local historians, and they shaped the way locals thought and talked about their Zeus, their Athena, or their Artemis. Despite local traditions, the power of the stories narrated by the epic singers and, after them, on the Athenian stage was stronger than the local stories; repeated and reread through the centuries all throughout the Greek cities and far beyond, it was these stories more than anything else that shaped the way one imagined a divine personality. With the professionalization of cultic entertainment, these same stories of the gods travelled from city to city. Herodotus already had underscored the role Hesiod and Homer played in shaping a panhellenic mythology: "They have created the theogony for the Greeks, given the gods their names, defined their fields and functions and described their forms."

The Greeks, like all other worshippers, did not only perform rituals: they imagined the recipients of their prayers and sacrifices, they talked about them to each other, well beyond the limits of the city-state, and they had images made of them. The figures of gods took shape in a forcefield created by local myths and rituals on the one side, the Panhellenic stories and images on the other; from early on and increasingly over time the panhellenic pull was strong and often dominant. Given this, it should be possible to write a book on a single god. The task needs some circumspection: one has to keep in mind that, unlike with Pericles, with the gods there is a play between local and panhellenic traditions, and they may look somewhat different in different places. There is another characteristic that prevents gods from being as uniform as humans: it is the multiplicity of roles and functions they play in Greek life. This multiplicity is expressed in a multitude of cultic epithets (epicleses in scholarly terminology). Most of them are speaking: Athena Polias is the protectress of the polis, Zeus Kataibates is the Zeus who "descends," *katabainei*, in lightning; Poseidon Asphaleios is the god who guarantees the safety, *asphaleia*, of the city walls when an earthquake hits. These epithets map the roles a god plays, and these roles may be so diverse that we are almost unable to imagine a unity behind them: what has Zeus Meilichios, the "mild" Zeus who manifests himself as a gigantic snake, in common with the god of storms who rules the world?

My first five chapters unfold this diversity of the god Apollo. It manifests itself in a series of functions and fields that can be described and that often are marked by a specific epithet, and in stories that show the god acting in a specific role. The first chapter concentrates on Homer and the *Homeric Hymn to Apollo*, the earliest and immensely influential narrations of Apollo's myths and cultic roles; a central image is that of Apollo the Archer. Each of the next three chapters focuses on one specific field where Apollo's protection was vital and where he himself excelled: music, oracular divination, and healing (where he was eclipsed over time by his son Asclepius). The fifth chapter is more complex: it looks at Apollo as the protector of adolescent men and the many political roles that accrued to him in this role. In mapping the provinces of Apollo's activities, I will not even try to find a unity that would underlie the different roles; the Aristotelian enterprise to reduce multiplicity to one single origin never convinced me when dealing with Greek gods. Instead, in my sixth chapter, I will have a look at the different theories with which past scholars have tried to find a local and temporal origin for Apollo; the question still defies a clear and certain answer. My final chapter will follow Apollo through the centuries, from the Roman Empire through late antiquity to the present times. Given the amount of time and space, I will barely scratch the surface, and each reader will miss something that he might deem important. There is even less of uniformity than before, although each epoch and place is building on the insights of the preceding epoch.

KEY THEMES

1

APOLLO IN HOMER

THE GOD OF THE ILIAD

The *Iliad*, Homer's poem on the anger of Achilles and its dire consequences, starts by invoking "the plan of Zeus" in order to explain the
carnage and suffering its singer is about to narrate. But at this point, it is
not Zeus who is holding center stage among the gods, it is Apollo, and his
role is awe-inspiring and frightening, with no trace of the golden radiance that the classicism of our own time usually ascribes to him. The
story, told to explain how it all came about, is familiar, but still worth
retelling. At some point in the long siege of Troy, a certain Chryses,
priest of Apollo at Chryse somewhere in the Troad, entered the Greek
encampment, "carrying the sacred ribbons of Apollo Far-Shooter on his
golden staff" (*Il.* 1.14f.). He wanted the return of his daughter, Chryseis,
whom the Greeks had abducted during one of their raids along the coast,
and he brought with him "immense ransom" (*Il.* 1.13). Agamemnon, the
middle-aged commander-in-chief who had the girl in his tent and bed,
rudely refused – a rash and unwise act by all accounts, as his army was
well aware; Homer makes it very clear that the priest's sacred status, not
just the feelings of an elderly father, were violated. Brutally rebuked and
frightened, the old man left, going "along the whispering surf line," a
pathetic image for all the fathers whose daughters have fallen easy prey
to warriors, from Troy to Iraq and beyond. He did not go home along the
beach, however, since Chryse is about twenty-five miles to the south,
and he must have come by ship with his ransom: he needed the solitude
of the lonely shore, and not only to grieve. Out of sight, he prayed to his
god, Apollo Smintheus: "Let the Danaans [that is: the Greeks] pay for my
tears with your arrows." And Apollo reacted fast: "Down he went from
Olympus' peaks, fury in his heart, on his shoulder a bow and arrow case,
and the arrows rattled on the shoulders of the angry god while he moved.
And he arrived like the night." At a distance from the Greek army, he sat

down and began shooting his arrows into their encampment; the arrows brought illness and death, to dogs and mules first, then to the warriors. "And the corpses burnt in fire without ceasing." After nine days of unmitigated horror, the Greeks consulted their seer, Calchas, and he revealed the reason for the deadly plague: "Because of his priest whom Agamemnon dishonored." Agamemnon had to give in; Odysseus, the wily diplomat from the island of Ithaca, was dispatched to bring the girl back to her father, together with a lavish sacrifice for the god, a hecatomb, literally one hundred animals. The restitution was very formal: Odysseus handed her over to her father, the priest, at the altar of his god, Chryses prayed a second time to cancel his first prayer, the Greeks sacrificed their hundred sheep and filled the remainder of the day with yet another cult activity: "The entire day, the young men worshipped the god with song and dance, singing the paean, dancing for the Far-Shooter: he listened and enjoyed it." They ended only at sunset, and they sailed home at night. And while they were away, Agamemnon had the army perform their own rites, purifying the encampment and offering "to Apollo a perfect hecatomb of oxen and sheep on the shore" (*Il.* 1.316).

It is the most detailed ritual sequence in the entire *Iliad*; only the description of Nestor's sacrifice to Poseidon in the fifth book of the *Odyssey* comes close – and that description focuses on correct human interaction during a ritual, not on the god: the narrator of the *Odyssey* is interested in the social competence of his figures, not in any divine presence or ritual lore. Here, however, the god is at the very center, and this is emphasized from the start. It is none other than Apollo who is responsible for the fight between Agamemnon and Achilles that triggered the entire plot of the *Iliad*: "Who among the gods set them against each other in strife? Leto's and Zeus' son: angry at the king, he sent an illness over the army, an evil one" (*Il.* 1.8f.).

This initial role reflects Apollo's prominence throughout the *Iliad*. He is a major player in the action of the poem, and with the exception of Zeus, no other god is mentioned as often as he is. He is the main protector of the Trojans; as such, he has his temple on the acropolis, the Pergamos, of Troy (*Il.* 5.446 and 7.83). He protects the walls of his city, and he constantly helps the main Trojan fighters – not only the archers Paris and Pandaros, but also Aeneas and, as long as he can, Hector, and he thwarts the attacks of the Greek heroes, Diomedes, Patroclus, and Achilles. Achilles will find his death at the hands of Paris and Phoebus Apollo, as he is well aware (*Il.* 22.359). When Patroclus, having become reckless, attacks the walls of Troy, Apollo protects them, standing on a high tower, and pushes Patroclus away (*Il.* 16.700ff.); some days later, when the other gods leave the battlefield for Olympus, he goes to the city in order to protect its walls (*Il.* 21.538ff.). When Diomedes stuns Aeneas and then wounds his mother Aphrodite who shielded her unconscious son from Diomedes' attacks, Apollo takes over, drives Diomedes away and brings Aeneas to his temple; here Leto and Artemis, Apollo's mother and sister, nurse the wounded hero (*Il.* 5.344ff.). When Hector challenges a Greek, he promises to hang his armor in Apollo's temple, should he win (*Il.* 7.83), and his victory over Patroclus is decisively helped by the god (*Il.* 16.787ff.). He is no easy god to deal with: when Diomedes or Patroclus try to resist him, he pushes them back and finally threatens them with hard words, and he yells at Achilles when the hero does not recognize him immediately. It is no surprise that, in the funeral games for Patroclus, the archer Teukros loses the shooting contest because he failed to promise Apollo a hecatomb of young sheep (*Il.* 23.865). This lofty attitude, however, is reserved for his dealings with humans only: when his uncle Poseidon, a staunch supporter of the Greeks, challenges him to a fight, Apollo just shrugs: "Don't tell me that I am crazy enough to fight you because of miserable mortals" (*Il.* 21.463). The younger god had too much respect for his uncle, or was too well brought up, to fight him.

His main opponent, during the Trojan War, is his sibling Athena. Over and over again, the two can be seen counteracting each other, and not just in battle. During the games for Patroclus, Diomedes, secure of his horsemanship, is leading in the chariot race when Apollo, still angry at him, throws the whip out of his hand; Athena, observing this, picks it up, hands it back, breaks the yoke of another chariot and helps him win (*Il.* 23.383). Their fierce opposition is all the more surprising as Athena too has her temple on the Trojan acropolis; but the one time we hear of it, when Hector ordered his mother to pray to the goddess and promise her a gift, she declined to help the Trojans (*Il.* 6.269–311).

Athena, of course, has her reasons for hating the Trojans, as has Hera with whom she conspires. Years ago, at the famous wedding of Achilles' parents Peleus and Thetis, Eris, the goddess of dispute, promised a golden apple to the most beautiful goddess. Hera, Athena, and Aphrodite fought over it, and the human judge whom they finally made decide their conflict voted for Aphrodite, the goddess of love, spurning wisdom and royalty, the bribes promised by Hera and Athena. The judge was Paris, son of Priam, king of Troy, and his abduction of Helen, the dazzlingly beautiful queen of Sparta with whom Aphrodite had bribed him, triggered the Trojan War: Helen, after all, was married to a prominent Greek king. Apollo, on the other hand, has no good reason for loving the Trojans or hating the Greeks. There is only one other story that connects Apollo with Troy: a generation ago, he and Poseidon had been servants of Priam's father Laomedon for a year; Poseidon built Troy's wall and

Apollo guarded Laomedon's cattle, or they both built the wall (Homer is somewhat inconsistent here). Laomedon, however, refused to pay his divine servants, instead he threatened them and chased them away. This still rankles with Poseidon and is the reason why he hates the Trojans (*Il.* 21.446–460, see also 7.452). If anything, the story makes Apollo's strong and unique predilection for Troy even less understandable.

No surprise, then, that scholars tried to look for a reason outside the story of the *Iliad*, a reason that related to Apollo's role in Greek cult. The answer they usually came up with was a historical one: Apollo originally was not Greek but Anatolian, and his origins in Asia Minor were still remembered when the Troy myth was formed: the god champions a city of his homeland. This answer, however, is not convincing. There is no doubt that the *Iliad* itself connects Apollo with Anatolia, more precisely with Lycia, a region in the southwest of Anatolia. The Trojans were helped by a large contingent of Lycian fighters that were led by Sarpedon and Glaukos (*Il.* 2.876f.); when wounded by an arrow, Glaukos prays to Apollo, "Lord who dwells in Lycia's fat lands and in Troy," and Apollo helps (*Il.* 16.514). Apollo has a sanctuary not only in Troy, but also in Lycia, and it is well known even today. The rich sanctuary of Leto near Xanthos, Lycia's main city, was famous already in antiquity, and it is well excavated and researched; Apollo and Artemis, Leto's children, have their place there as well. Homer also sometimes calls Apollo *lykēgenés*: ancient commentators ("scholiasts") on Homer understood this as "born in Lycia," modern linguists have their doubts, and they seem justified.

There is more. It is not just Apollo who protects the Trojans: Aphrodite and Ares do the same, although nobody would regard them as Anatolian divinities. Aphrodite has Oriental connections, since her main sanctuary was in Paphos on the island of Cyprus, but Cyprus is not Anatolia: the argument sounds like special pleading, and it cannot account for Ares whom Greeks could understand as a Thracian divinity, if they talked about ethnic origins of their gods at all. Even more seriously, explanations from hypothetical origins have run out of favor with scholars. It has become increasingly clear that it is not origins that matter but roles in stories and rituals. Often enough, tensions and oppositions that exist at the same time in a text or a ritual have been expressed by the Greeks as the result of a sequence in time and history: diachronical theories of origins served as a code for expressing synchronical tensions. Modern scholars, steeped in the historicism of the nineteenth century, however, took this seriously; by now, we have learned that such theories are mostly wrong. The best-known example is Dionysus, the god who brought carnevalesque disorder into Greek cities and disrupted the well-arranged and secure order of daily city life. Already fifth-century

Athenians said that he had grown up in Anatolia; nineteenth-century scholars argued for an origin in Thrace (modern Bulgaria). Both theories run against historical facts: the god was already being worshipped in Bronze Age Crete.

Athena's protection of the Greeks in the *Iliad* has been seen as part of a wider picture: Athena is the protectress of many Greek heroes. In the *Iliad*, she especially cherishes Achilles and Diomedes, in the *Odyssey*, Odysseus. In other stories, she protects Jason, the leader of the Argonauts, or Perseus, the slayer of many monsters; yet another protégé of hers is the mighty Heracles – on a relief from the temple of Zeus in Olympia, she even helps him carry the sky. This relationship has been explained from the role she plays as a protectress of the ephebes, the adolescent young men around the age of seventeen or eighteen: in most Greek cities, they served as the city's frontier guards and standing army for a year, before becoming full citizens. The heroes are their mythical prototypes. Many heroes are young men who perform their main exploits before they reach adulthood and sometimes earn their role as adults (often kingship and a wife) through such exploits, such as Jason or Perseus: the heroes' protectress is the ephebes' protectress as well. Apollo has close ties with adolescent males as well, but these ties are very different. Only rarely is he said to be protector of a specific hero. Jason calls upon him when he sets out for his voyage and dedicates an altar to Apollo Embaterios ("He of the Embarkation") who protects those who set out to the sea, and Heracles is said to have received his bow and arrows from Apollo. But Apollo does not protect them because he protects young men: he gave Heracles bow and arrows as the patron deity of archery, and Jason invoked him as the protector of passages in Greek cult. Apollo's general connection with young men is more ambivalent. On the one hand, he protects the boys at the very moment when they turn into adults: together with the nymphs and the local rivers, he receives their hair when they cut it short as a sign of leaving their boyhood behind (Hesiod, *Theogony* 347). Achilles and Patroclus still were wearing their hair long (*Il.* 23.141), as does Apollo, the divine ephebe; and it is Apollo who protects Telemachus who is just coming of age in the main subplot of the *Odyssey* (*Od.* 19.86). But the same god is also responsible for the sudden death of young men, as is Artemis for the sudden death of young women. Telemachus, whom Apollo protects, could also become his victim: at least the suitors fervently wish that Apollo would kill him when they begin to perceive his growing independence (*Od.* 17.251). The suitors are young men at the age of military service; but their excess testosterone is not spent on campaign but in wild parties at the court of Odysseus, at the expense of his wife (or, in their reading, widow) Penelope. Penelope in turn, Odysseus' faithful but harassed wife, wishes that Apollo would kill the most vicious among them, Antinous (*Od.* 17.494); Odysseus will oblige her by shooting Antinous first when he returns, as Homer describes in a masterfully detailed scene (*Od.* 22.8–21). In a myth narrated by old Priam, Niobe queen of Thebes mocked Leto, and her children took their revenge by shooting Niobe's twelve children, Artemis the six girls, Apollo the six boys (*Il.* 24.602ff.). And when lamenting her dead son Hector, the Trojan queen Hecabe is struck that he does not look like someone killed in war, although his body has been cruelly maltreated by Achilles: rather, he looks "like one whom Apollo killed softly with his silver arrows" (*Il.* 24.578). It seems double-edged for a young warrior to be under the sign of Apollo; Athena's protection is more robust. In this light, Apollo is the fitting god for the side that eventually will lose the war and whose main defender, Hector, dies in the course of the poem when Apollo has to leave his side.

ARCHER, KILLER AND HEALER

Homer's dark image of the angry god, descending from Olympus with his bow and his quiver full of rattling arrows, sticks in one's mind. Apollo is the archer, as his sister Artemis is the archeress, and they both kill. Artemis' archery is usually confined to hunting: she is the mistress of animals, and killing animals is as much her business as nurturing them; today's hunters are still aware of the intimate connection that exists between nurturing and killing. Apollo can be a protector of hunters as well, but not very often; his archery is the more deadly art of the warrior. The mighty hunter Orion is protected (and killed) by Artemis; Apollo gave his weapon to the Lycian Pandaros (*Il.* 2.827) and to Ajax's brother Teukros (*Il.* 15.441), the two most accomplished archers on the Trojan and Greek side, and to Heracles who used archery to kill foes and monsters alike. Apollo will guide the hand of the archer Paris when Achilles is being killed, as he guided the arrow of the archer he loathes, the Greek Teukros, away from Hector (*Il.* 8.31). Human archers had better pray to him before they shoot: in the shooting contest during the funeral games for Patroclus, Meriones vows a hecatomb of sheep to the god while his opponent Teukros shoots without praying (*Il.* 23.865): this explains why Teukros missed despite being generally recognized as the better archer. One sees how divine intervention helps to save face: Teukros is a bad worshipper, not a bad archer. However, prayer and sacrifice do not always help. Before Penelope's suitors began the shooting contest that would determine who would finally get to marry her, they decided to offer a goat to Apollo (*Od.* 21.265). This did not prevent them from failing: it is the unlikely contestant, Odysseus in the guise of a lowly beggar, to whom Apollo granted the fame of victory (*Od.* 21.338. 22,7).

But in the world of Greek warrior ideology, archery is a problematic affair. A fight with spear and sword is straightforward, involves direct physical contact and needs as much courage as it needs training. The hoplite, the warrior in heavy armor, is the ideal Greek fighter. Most heroes in myth and often in cult are such warriors, and to fight in full armor in the hoplites' closed line is the task and the pride of the fully adult citizen. Archers have a special talent that others might lack, and they certainly need much training, but they are sneaky and cannot be trusted. The ambivalent Paris is an archer, a warrior who prefers the bedroom: "Back from the war? You should have died out there, beaten by a real hero, my former husband!" – thus Helen greets her abductor after Aphrodite whisked him out of battle (*Il.* 3.428f.). Wily Odysseus is perfectly capable of fighting in heavy armor, but the *Odyssey* makes him an archer too: deceit is as much Odysseus' tactic as the straightforward attack. Another archer, the Trojan Pandaros, sabotages the armistice which Greeks and Trojans are about to conclude early in the *Iliad* by shooting at Menelaos. Athena had talked him into it: like the audience who wants action, she has no use for an armistice that would end the war, and the narration. He missed Menelaos, despite his prayer to Apollo, only because Athena deflected the arrow to a less important bystander; the damage was nevertheless done, and the fighting went on (*Il.* 3.88–147). In the reality of Greek warfare, archers were either ephebes or they were foreigners, Cretans or Lycians; adolescents were nearly as marginal in the Greek city as foreigners. Again, Apollo is rather ambivalent; the hoplite's goddess is Athena, with helmet, breast armor and shield.

Apollo's arrows are as deadly as they are stealthy; sudden and unexpected death is their doing – the arrow that suddenly strikes from afar is an apt image for a sudden epidemic whose results are as terrible as its causes are unexplained. Already in Bronze Age narrations of the Eastern Mediterranean, we hear that a god is spreading a plague with his arrows. Reshep, the god of plague in the pantheon of Bronze Age Syria, shoots his arrows to send the "fires of illness"; on Cyprus where he was worshipped as well, he was identified with Apollo. Echoes of the same idea persist even in the Old Testament. "I shall heap on them one disaster after another and expend my arrows on them: pangs of hunger, ravages of plague, and bitter pestilence" – these are God's angry words to his people (Deuteronomy 32.23f.). The image has lost nothing of its threatening force.

But he who sends illness can also cure it. In the *Iliad*, healing is not the special province of Apollo, but nevertheless it is he who heals the plague. This comes about from the way the plague started: when a wrathful god is sending illness, placating him is the only successful cure. Homer's Chryses makes the mechanism admirably clear. His first prayer ("let the Danaans pay for my tears with your arrows" 1.42) triggers the plague, his second ("keep now away the terrible plague from the Danaans" 1.456) stops it. In another instance, healing is a result of Apollo's more general power as a god: when the Lycian Glaukos is wounded by an arrow of Teukros, he prays to his god Apollo, and the god immediately closes his wound and gives him his strength back. Neither makes Apollo a specialized healer. There are specialists for healing in the *Iliad*, both among mortals and among the gods. The Greek army has two heroic physicians in their ranks who at the same time are leading a military contingent, Podalirios and Machaon, "good doctors," the sons of Asclepios (*Il.* 2.729–733). They are efficient doctors; but when they are most urgently needed, when the Trojans attack the encampments, they are unavailable: Podalirios is in his tent nursing his own wounds, and Machaon is fighting. It is up to Achilles to use the herbal medicine learnt from his teacher, the wise centaur Chiron (*Il.* 11.833). The equivalent of these doctors among the Olympians is called Paean: he healed not only the wound Diomedes inflicted on Ares (*Il.* 5.899), he even cured Hades, the god of the underworld, when Heracles shot him with an arrow (*Il.* 5.401). Homer is reticent about Apollo's role in healing, whether among humans or among gods. In later mythology, Asclepios is his son and has inherited his healing power from his divine father whom he will slowly supplant as a healer. Homer mentions Asclepios only as the father of the heroic physicians in the *Iliad*, and he never alludes to his divine origin; we have to wait until the *Catalogue of Women* in the late sixth century BCE for the full myth of Asclepios. Paean, on the other hand, is a somewhat baffling name: Paiawon, in an older form of the same name, was an independent divinity in Mycenaean Bronze Age Greece; after Homer, Paean is always used as an epithet of Apollo. Scholars have debated whether Homer regarded Paean as still an independent divinity or already as an aspect of Apollo. There is no decisive argument for either side, and perhaps Homer's formulaic language retains a state of affairs that is out of date with contemporary religious reality.

To placate an irate god, however, is not that easy; one cannot just flick a switch. A god's anger has to be calmed by ritual signs of submission and repentance; humans need to offer more than prayer: restitution and elaborate ritual honors are necessary as well. This explains the lavish ritual the Greeks performed in the sanctuary of Chryse. A hecatomb is an impressive and costly sacrifice, even if the figure of one hundred animals should not always be taken literally: repentance can always be measured by the value of the gift. On a purely human level, one should not forget that in Greek ritual the priest gets a good part of each animal, not only the tongue (which is highly valued as a choice cut), but also a thigh and the hide, and the sale of meat and hides adds additional income to the priest. Chryses must have profited nicely from a hecatomb, as did his god. Then followed the dancing and singing which lasted the larger part of the day: this was not so much entertainment of the human participants but a very specific form of honor for the god: a hymn is as much a "beautiful and marvelous thing" (in Greek, an *agalma*) as any work of art made from marble or bronze and dedicated as a gift to the god. In fact, Hellenistic cities inscribed hymns, sometimes with musical notation, and put them up in Apollo's sanctuary. This was not meant as an exercise in literature, but as a way to record and therefore to make last the voice and the music of the hymn: as long as the stone stood in the sanctuary, the beauty of music and words resonated and perpetuated the ephemeral musical performance.

The performance itself is a combination of dance and song, executed by a chorus of young men, *koûroi Akhaiôn*, as Homer explicitly says. The combination of song and dance, the *molpé* in Greek, is widespread in Archaic Greek choral performance; young male performers, *molpoí*, however, are especially connected with Apollo, and at least in Archaic Miletus, they seem to play an important political role; we shall come back to them. The hymn they are singing is the paean, the form of hymn that is bound almost exclusively to Apollo: only his son Asclepios will, much later, receive paeans as well. Its name has to do with the refrain of the hymn, *io Paian* which is to be understood as a ritual shout addressed to the god, "yahoo Paian." Thus, at least in the later paeans Paian is just another name of Apollo, especially but not exclusively as a healer. In the *Iliad*, the Greek *kouroi* sing their paean at the moment when they wish to obtain healing from Apollo. One would think that this would presuppose the identification of Apollo with Paion, the Homeric divine healer: if so, Homer certainly does not say it.

The narration is based on a precise model of how illness originates. Illness results from the anger of a god, and the anger results from a human transgression; the transgression must be rectified and the god must be placated and propitiated. Humans treat the god not so very differently from an angry but powerful ruler or chief; divine anger and human reaction are modeled on human experience. This model – one is tempted to call it anthropomorphic, "following human forms" – explains both epidemics and individual illness; it all depends on who is committing the transgression. Many myths, especially myths that explained cults in Greek cities (so-called etiological myths), used the model of collective transgression. To give one example: when the Athenians refused to honor Dionysus when his priests came first to their city, the god caused an epidemic sexual disease ("he struck the genitals of the men, and the disease was incurable," says a scholiast on Aristophanes, *Acharnians* 243); an oracle ordered them to honor the god, and they introduced his festival in which the ritual display of models of male genitals, *phalloi*, played a central part. This model of transgression, punishment, and rectification had a long history. When, in fourteenth-century BCE Anatolia, an epidemic decimated the Hittite kingdom, king Mursilis II pleaded with his gods: "I have now confessed my sin before the Storm-god: it is true, we have done it;" but he also asked for mercy: "I kneel down to you and cry out: 'Have mercy!'; . . . Let the plague be removed from the land of Hatti." Almost two thousand years later, Anatolian people struck by illness still confessed their transgressions and put up costly inscriptions, often illustrating what happened with a relief. Many of these inscriptions have survived, such as the following from the second century CE: "To Zeus Sabazios and Meter Hipta, Diokles son of Trophimos. After I caught some doves of the gods, I was punished in my eyes; I now have confessed the power of the god." In our case, the rectification concerned not the god as much as his human equivalent, the priest Chryses. Correcting Agamemnon's mistake, the Greeks fully recognized Chryses' sacred status as a priest and met his demand, the restitution of his daughter: this is why the shrewd politician Odysseus chose the god's altar as the place of restitution. Propitiating rituals, however, always concern the divinity: Apollo received a hecatomb and a day of paeans and dancing. If another god had caused the disease, another rite would have been used: the paean, at least here, is not necessarily a healing hymn but Apollo's specific ritual poetry.

But the story also uses a second paradigm of causation; we could call it ritualistic. While Odysseus and his delegation celebrated the god in his sanctuary in Chryse, the Greek army underwent a purification rite and performed a sacrifice on its own, another hecatomb of oxen and goats: thus, they too closed the period of disease and plague by rituals. The paradigm used here is one of pollution and purification. Again, the plague was the result of Apollo's wrath because Agamemnon had insulted Apollo's priest: a rash human act disturbed the concord and peace between humans and gods. Concord and peace had to be reestablished, and ritual purification achieved this aim. Purification is not so much a physical cleaning after an infectious disease, as we might be tempted to think, but a ritual act in order to restore harmony between the human and the divine world. Still, the term purification is more than a metaphor:

dirt, as we know, causes an existing order to be disrupted – any substance that is perceived to disrupt an established order can be understood as dirt. Clay on a potter's wheel in my study is part of how I perceive my well-ordered world; the same clay transferred from my shoes to the Persian rug in the living room is dirt because the order of the living room is such that there is no room for clay on the carpet. The disorder, the dirt, has to be removed, and order has to be restored. Homer does not explain how the Greek army did this; the only detail he gives is that they threw the *lymata*, the refuse, into the sea (*Il.* 1.314). In a real cleaning, the refuse is simply the dirt. A ritual cleaning is a symbolic act that uses images of cleaning to achieve its aim; here, "refuse" comes to mean a substance used to absorb the symbolic dirt – it is as if the sponge used for cleaning the carpet would not just be washed out but thrown away with its entire content of dirt. The sacrifice that ends the ritual – oxen and goats, sacrificed to Apollo on the beach – marks the moment when humans once again communicate with the god they had angered. The meal that usually ends a sacrifice demonstrates the newly established harmony where humans and gods find their peace once again in the community of the table. Homer narrates how the *knise*, the smoke from the sacrifice that feeds the gods, ascended to the sky: the communication is restored.

FESTIVALS AND SANCTUARIES OF APOLLO

Neither sanctuaries nor festivals are prominent in the Homeric epics (nor, for that matter, in Hesiod; although Hesiod's *Works and Days* mention some festivals in their calendrical section). It is all the more significant that several sanctuaries of Apollo are mentioned in Homer, and that one of the few festivals for a named divine recipient that Homer describes is Apollo's.

The festival was celebrated in Ithaca, on the very day when Odysseus, up to now in his disguise as a beggar at Penelope's court, revealed his identity and took his revenge on the suitors. The narrator introduces it rather off-handedly. The suitors assembled in Odysseus' hall, sacrificed "large sheep and meaty goats, fat hogs and a cow from the herd" (*Od.* 20.250f.) and had wine mixed to prepare for yet another sumptuous meal. Outside, in the city, a parallel action took place: heralds drove a hecatomb through the city, out to the sacred grove of Apollo "Far-shooter" where Ithaca's citizens assembled (*Od.* 20. 276–278). The city festival lasted the entire day, and the citizens were unaware of the drama that slowly unfolded in the palace with the shooting contest that would finally decide on Penelope's future husband. None of the suitors was able to string Odysseus' powerful bow that served as the weapon for the contest. After most had tried and failed, the chief villain Antinous grew tired of it and proposed to defer the contest to the next morning. The people of Ithaca were celebrating a festival of Apollo, and the suitors too should fill the rest of the day with eating and drinking, not with a boring sporting event: next morning would be early enough to continue, after a sacrifice to Apollo (*Od.* 21.258–268).

But of course this was not what happened. The archer Apollo dominated the day, in a way the suitors had not expected – always too self-assured for their own good, they claimed that "Apollo and the other gods will be friendly to us" (*Od.* 21.356f.). Odysseus, still in the guise of a beggar, is given the bow, strings it easily and shoots the arrow through all twelve axe-heads set up as a target. He prays to Apollo to bring him fame (*Od.* 22.7), reveals his identity, and turns the weapon against the suitors, the first arrow killing brash Antinous. Already the *Iliad* had taught more than once that a successful archer should first pray to Apollo; we know that Odysseus would not miss – and, although she did not yet know the beggar's true identity, Penelope also thought it possible that Apollo might bring him fame through the bow (*Od.* 21.338).

It is apt that Odysseus' fateful archery should take place on the day the city of Ithaca performed a festival of Apollo "Far-shooter," the patron of archery and master of silent killing; the butchery in the palace goes unnoticed outside. There might be more to it, however. Twice, Odysseus the beggar foretells that Odysseus the king will be back "on this very *lykábas*" (*Od.* 14.160–162, 19.305–307); and although linguists are still debating what this Greek word could mean, its most likely translation is "new moon day." The new moon day is the first day in the regular, lunar calendar of all Greek cities, and like the waxing quarter moon, the seventh day, it is sacred to Apollo who sometimes in called Noumenios, "He of the New Moon" (*Works and Days* 770). And perhaps this was no ordinary new moon day, but, as has been argued, the first day in the calendrical year: the king's return would coincide with the beginning of the new year, when the order of the cosmos is restored. But even if that goes too far – the thought is as suggestive as it is difficult to prove –, the return of the king on the first day of the month, in the sign and during the festival of Apollo, adds an additional depth to the story Homer tells. Festivals are not just occasions for merriment, as the suitors assume: they give order and meaning to the world.

The festival in Ithaca takes place in a grove, presumably outside the city. When Homer mentions a sanctuary, it usually has a correspondence in reality, provided, of course, it lies inside the geography of the Greek world. In the world to where Odysseus was blown by the storms, there are sanctuaries as well, such as the Posideion at the harbor of the island Scherie (*Od.* 6.266) or the sacred grove of Athena on the same island where Odysseus awaits the return of Nausicaa (*Od.* 6.291f., 321); in many respects, fairy tale Scherie mirrors an ideal Greek state. At present, however, no archaeological evidence can confirm that Apollo's sacred grove on Ithaca reflects topographical and cult realities of the island. The other sanctuary on Ithaca that Homer mentions, the sacred cave of the nymphs where Odysseus hid his treasures upon his nocturnal arrival (*Od.* 13.103f., 347f.), has been explored and described long ago. Or rather, Heinrich Schliemann, the German merchant and hobby-archaeologist who found Troy, described an impressive grotto in Ithaca with traces of ancient cult that he identified with the place where Odysseus hid his treasures. He trusted Homer more than the geographer Strabo did, two thousand years earlier: "The poet," Strabo wrote, "doesn't give a clear account of Cephallenia, Ithaca and the other neighboring places; commentators and historians therefore vastly disagree with each other" (*Geography* 10.2.10). Whatever the reality behind the narration, a sanctuary of Apollo as the place of assembly for the male citizens of a community makes intrinsic sense, especially if the festival time is the New Year. That a ritual detail in poetry makes religious and social sense is, of course, no proof of its factual truth.

Troy is a more complex case of Homer's *imaginaire* than the island of the Phaeacians. There must be some topographical reality behind his narration, otherwise Schliemann would not have succeeded in finding the city with the sole help of the *Iliad*. The citadel of Troy, the Pergamos, contained another sanctuary of Apollo, as we saw, this time with a temple where Leto and Artemis were curing Aeneas. We should not expect to ever find traces of such a temple any more than of the temple of Athena, at least in Bronze Age Troy; the *Iliad*, as a German scholar insisted, is no history text book. Iron Age Troy, the city that was established in the eighth century BCE under the name of Ilion, had a temple of Athena on its acropolis, but how this sanctuary relates to Homer's narration is not quite clear. Is it earlier and independent from it? Does the narrator, an Eastern Greek familiar with the region, describe a known reality, including the odd seated image of the goddess on whose knees the priestess Theano deposited votive gifts? Or – the most extreme possibility – was the sanctuary built because Homer's narrative was so compelling? Whatever the relationship, there is no indication of a corresponding sanctuary of Apollo. What matters with Homer's Troy and its city cults is not any correspondence with the small settlement that colonizing Greeks had established in the early Iron Age among the impressive ruins of the

Bronze Age town; what matters is the role that the two main divine antagonists, Athena and Apollo, play in the unfolding tragedy of the Trojans. Many Greek cities in Homer's time had a sanctuary of Athena on their acropolis, such as the small harbor town of Emporio on the island of Chios, the impressive city of Gortyn on Crete, or the city of Athens; far fewer, however, had a temple of Apollo in their citadel.

Things look differently for Apollo of Chryse whose altar witnessed the restitution of Chryseis, the daughter of the local priest, and whose temple Chryses had roofed several times, as he claims in his first prayer (*Il.* 1.39). Thus, the sanctuary is more than the simple grove we hear of in Ithaca: besides the altar that could be enough to define a sanctuary, it had a (presumably wooden) temple with a thatched roof, and it had a priest of some standing and power. The Homeric epic does not mention many priests; besides Chryses, there is Theano, the priestess of Athena in Troy (*Il.* 6. 299), and there is Maron, the priest of Apollo in Thracian Ismaros who is living "in the sacred grove rich with trees," and who gave Odysseus the wine that would be instrumental to his escape from the Cyclops Polyphemus (*Od.* 9.200f.); Maron, after all, is said to be the grandson of Dionysus (Hesiod, *Fragment* 238), and wine is indispensable for any Greek sacrifice. Theano, the wife of a leading Trojan nobleman, Antenor, is a typical city priestess, a member of the local aristocracy whom the citizens elected to her office; the office needs as much social consensus and dignity as special knowledge. Seen in the light of later Greek civic religion, Theano represents the type of priestess or priest that will be common all over the Greek world. The same seems to be true of two priests of the city of Troy, Dares the priest of Hephaestus (*Il.* 5.9f.) and Laogonos priest of Idaean Zeus (*Il.* 16.604): they belong to the city's nobility, and their sons fight and die in the battle against the Greek invaders. The two priests of Apollo seem to be of a different ilk altogether – more imposing, closer to their god, and entirely devoted to him. Maron, grandson of a god, is living in the sacred grove, a professional dedicated to his service; Chryses has served his god long enough to have thatched the roof of his temple several times. When Chryses appears for the first time, Homer calls him *aretêr*, the "specialist for powerful words," namely prayer and curse; his prayer to Apollo immediately turns into a curse for the Greeks. This is an unusual word; the common Greek term is *hiereús*, a word that designates the specialist for "working the sacred," as *chalkeús*, the "blacksmith," is a specialist in "working bronze" (*chalkós*). Apollo, the god of oracles, is a god of the powerful utterance, and a god whose oracular cult relies on specialized priests that devote their life to the service of the god, as we shall see presently.

In his prayer, Chryses addresses his god as Smintheus and as lord not only of Chryse, but of Killa and Tenedos as well. Tenedos is the small island off the coast of Troy, and Killa must be a town nearby for which Strabo had looked in vain; it must have been abandoned well before his time. The ancient and learned commentators of Homer refer the curious reader to Apollo Killaios, "He of Killa." His sanctuary was on the island of Lesbos: Pelops, the hero after whom the Peloponnesus is named, founded it in honor of one Killos, his charioteer, who died a sudden death when passing through the island – one of those sudden deaths of young men for whom Apollo was thought to be responsible. But Homer presumably cannot mean this sanctuary; Lesbos is further south, and Chryses seems more locally minded than that.

The sanctuary of Apollo Smintheus in Chryse, at any rate, was well known in antiquity, and is still visible. It lies somewhat inland, off the western coast of the Troas, about 25 miles south of Troy. Early travelers from the mid-eighteenth century on, who had memorized their *Iliad* (or brought the book along with them), found and described it. Some even excavated impressive column drums and some inscriptions which attest to local games sponsored by one local grandee named Paulos, in the epoch of the Roman emperors: Homer's fame had helped to give some glamor to an otherwise small and rather backwater place. Current excavations have not yet found anything spectacular beyond the fact that Greek settlers founded the sanctuary at a spot sacred already in the Bronze Age. Places could retain memories of sacrality over a long time, even without physical continuity of cult: there is no need to assume that Homer's Apollo Smintheus was a Bronze Age divinity.

But what sort of divinity was this god? Unlike many epithets, the name Smintheus does not immediately speak to us: "The name of Smintheus is a perplexity for the ethnographer, and suggests an interesting problem for anthropology" (L.R. Farnell, *The Cults of the Greek States*, vol. IV 164). And it seems that the Greeks too had their problem with the term. But the need for an explanation must have arisen early, especially with an author such as Homer whose text was so important for the education and self-definition of the Greeks: already the rhapsodes who, in Archaic and Classical Greece, recited their Homer from memory, were asked questions about the meaning of strange words in their text. They had to have answers; they were, after all, public personalities. The epithet Smintheus, as the learned commentators tell us, would derive from the word for mouse in the local dialect. These locals, some then go on to tell, were immigrants from Crete where the mouse was still called *sminthos*. And they told two stories that had to explain what the somewhat repulsive but innocent rodent had to do with one of the most exalted gods of Greece; neither story holds water. According to the first,

Cretans were emigrating towards the Black Sea, guided by an oracle that told them to found a sanctuary and a city where the "Earth-born ones" (*gêgeneis*) would attack them; they must have sailed away not without trepidation, since "earth-born" was a standard circumlocution for the giants whose mother was Gaia "Earth." While they spent the night on the shore of what was to become Chryse, mice ate all the leather of their weaponry. Thus attacked and defeated by rather unexpected "earth-born" creatures, they understood the oracle, founded city and sanctuary and, Apollo being an important Cretan god, dedicated it to Apollo Smintheus (Strabo, *Geography* 13.604, after Callinus of Ephesus). The second story tells of the anger of Apollo towards one of his local priests; the angry god sent mice on his land that laid it practically waste. A friend of the priest placated the god and made him shoot the mice; the grateful priest instituted the cult of "Mouse Apollo" (Scholiast on Homer, *Il.* 1.39, after Polemo of Ilion). Both stories are told by people with some local knowledge: Polemo of Ilion was living around 100 BCE and came from the city that succeeded Troy, and Callinus of Ephesos was a poet who lived around 650 BCE in one of the major cities further south on the coast of Western Asia Minor. The sanctuary, and Homer's story, must have been famous already in Callinus' time, and Ephesos was close enough for him to have visited it. Both stories, however, are inventions in order to explain the cult, and they hinge on the idea that *sminthos* means mouse; we have no way to check whether this was true. I suspect that the Cretans called the rodent *sminthos* but not the inhabitants of the Troad who spoke a very different dialect; this would account for the narrative need to bring in Cretan settlers. Smintheus thus would be a word that neither the ancient worshippers of the god nor Homer's audience would have easily understood. Since there are several cults of Apollo in the region, and words with the sequence -*inth*- belong to an older, non-Greek language, most likely the epithet preserves the name of an indigenous divinity supplanted by Apollo.

Whatever the accuracy of the etymology, the Greeks firmly believed that it had to do with mice; another local author tells us that there were sacred mice in the sanctuary. And when the locals wanted to enhance the image of the sanctuary, they turned to one of the most famous sculptors of their epoch (the fourth century BCE), Scopas of Paros. Scopas made for them not a new image of Apollo (that must have proved too costly), but at least a beautiful marble mouse that was placed beneath the foot of an existing cult image of the god (Strabo, *Geography* 13.604); local coins of the Imperial epoch show the god with the mouse. Apollo thus was understood as a god who kept away mice; this at least is what one of the two stories implies, and it goes together with a few other instances where the mighty god averts lowly pests.

To modern minds, made wiser by the experience of devastating plagues in early modern Europe that were spread by rodents (rats rather than mice, however), the Mouse-Apollo who sent the plague to the Greeks and killed mules, dogs, and men was irresistible: Homer must have known how rodents spread plagues, and the Greeks must have turned to him when ravaged by pests or plague. There is, however, no other indication that the Greeks were aware of the connection; no city that ever was hit by an epidemic turned to Apollo Smintheus – some cities called upon the oracular Apollo of Delphi or Clarus, and the Romans instituted a cult of Apollo Medicus, "Physician," which seems much more sensible. To connect Apollo, mice, and plague is the result of our wishful thinking, and maybe of our surprise at seeing Apollo connected with simple mice. The surprise is modern, as is the insight into how plagues spread.

Besides these local shrines that play a role in the action of the two poems, there were the two major Greek shrines of Apollo, on Delus and in Delphi: both are mentioned by the narrators of *Iliad* and *Odyssey*. The island sanctuary of Delus is present in a small vignette only: Odysseus, always the charmer, compares the slender Nausicaa to the beautiful palm tree he once saw on Delus next to the altar of Apollo (*Od.* 6.162). Delphi is somewhat more visible, not the least because its stone temple impressed the contemporaries who were used to wooden buildings: twice Homer mentions the "threshold of stone" of Phoebus Apollo in "rocky Delphoi," once together with the treasures kept inside (*Il.* 9.404f.), the second time when Agamemnon "stepped over the stone threshold to obtain an oracle" (*Od.* 8.80). Apollo's main oracle was already well established at the very moment the Greek world becomes visible to us through Homer's verses, and it already had made an impact all over the Greek world.

THE HOMERIC HYMN TO APOLLO

Apollo's cults in Delus and Delphi are the central theme of a somewhat later text, the *Homeric Hymn to Apollo*. The Hymn is part of a larger collection of Greek hexametrical hymns that neatly falls into two distinctive groups: it contains five long hymns belonging to the Archaic and early Classical Ages, and twenty-eight short hymns, many of which are much younger. At some point in time, they all were ascribed to Homer, because they are all composed in hexameters, and at least the language of the longer hymns is more or less consistent with the language of *Iliad* and *Odyssey*. Furthermore, they were seen as being part of the project that Herodotus described as "Homer and Hesiod gave the Greeks their gods": they contributed to an image of the Greek gods that was understandable and accepted all over Greece, so they had to be by Homer.

The *Hymn to Apollo* is the third in the collection, and it is the only one in which its author presents himself: he is "a blind man, who lives on rocky Chios" (173). The Athenian historian Thucydides (around 400 BCE) read this as a self-portrait of Homer (*Histories* 3.104), while a more recent ancient commentator disagrees and gives as the author a certain "Kynaithos of Chios who was the first to recite Homer's verses in Syracuse in the 68th Olympiad" (according to a commentator on Pindar, *Nemean Odes* 2.1), that is in 504–501 BCE, somewhat too late for the Hymn, which most scholars date earlier in the same century. But this is only one of two perplexities surrounding this text. The other is its structure: it neatly falls into two parts – a Delian and a Delphic one –, so neatly, in fact, that most scholars are convinced that it had been composed from two originally independent hymns to Apollo, or that the second part was a later continuation of the first; the two parts respond to each other in an often surprising way. All major hymns are intimately connected with a specific local cult about which the text talks and in which the Hymn originally must have been performed – the *Hymn to Demeter* with the mysteries of Eleusis, the *Hymn to Aphrodite* with a local family in the Troad, the *Hymn to Hermes* with athletic games for Hermes in the Peloponnesus. Most scholars think that the Delian part was connected with Apollo's cult on the island of Delus, the Delphic part with Delphi, or maybe with the cult of a local Apollo Delius and Pythius respectively; such cults were widespread. The combination of the two parts could have been caused by its performance at a joint festival of Apollo Delius and Pythius, such as the tyrant of Samos, Polycrates, performed in 522 BCE to celebrate the preponderance among the Aegean island states Samos had gained under his rule. Recently, however, an interpreter has found a tripartite structure in the Hymn: after an introduction (1–50), the text progresses from Apollo's birth on Delus (51–126) to Apollo's first appearance among the Olympians that also contains the self-portrait of the singer (127–182) to the extensive foundation story of his main oracular sancuary, Delphi (183–544). This would cast some doubts on the Polycrates theory, without making it entirely impossible: the Hymn is still organized around the two poles of Delus and Delphi.

Whatever the answers to these questions of authorship and origin, they only marginally affect the stories the text tells us; as to the date, a cautious assessment would put it somewhere in the sixth century. The Hymn is the most detailed literary document on the god, his mythology, and his two major cult places, and it is impressive and beautiful, both in the mythical narrative and the many parts that praise the god in a direct invocation. It begins with a powerful evocation of the divine archer at the moment when he enters Olympus, where the other gods are leisurely assembled. His sudden arrival spreads fear even among his peers: "They jump up, as soon as he arrives, all of them from their seats, when he tends his radiant bow": this happened, the poet thinks, not once, but this is the way the god arrives always – his entry into the *Iliad*, full of wrath, "like the dark night," is more than a coincidence. Only his mother Leto, sitting next to Zeus, stays calm, takes away her son's bow and quiver and hangs them on a golden peg next to Zeus' throne, and his father offers him a welcome drink in a golden cup. His archery, deadly and unexpected for mortals, is frightening even to the gods. At the same time, he is so visibly Zeus' favorite son that his mother even eclipses Zeus' legitimate wife, Hera goddess of rightful weddings, at least for the duration of the family picture. The poet's following invocation focuses on Leto, "blessed, since you gave birth to two radiant children, to Lord Apollo and to Artemis Archeress, to her in Ortygia, to him on Delus" (14–16) (figure 1). Later in the text, we will hear that Apollo reveals to humans the will of his father: none knows it better than Zeus' favorite son.

The invocation prepares the way for the first long mythical narration: it is Apollo's birth on Delus that the poet is going to narrate. Once he has announced this topic, he is again carried away. In a long geographical catalogue, he describes the sphere of Apollo's influence: "You reign over all humans," from Crete and Athens to the Aegean islands and the cities of Ionia; Eastern Greece is the world. Unexpectedly, however, the catalogue turns into a list of places where Leto, pregnant with her son, tried to stay and give birth but was turned away. The island of Delus alone is easily convinced: as Leto insists, it is a barren and rocky island that has no other way of gaining fame. Delus agrees, but is cautious: "They say that Apollo will be all too violent, and a mighty power among gods and mortal humans" (67f.); will he not be disappointed with such an unattractive birth place and sink the island with one kick of his foot? Leto promises under oath that it is here that "for all time the fragrant altar of Phoebus will stand, and his sanctuary" (87f.) – no word, however, of the oracular shrine that Delus had demanded as well, for good reasons. Despite all the Apolline glamour, Delus does not contain an oracle of the god. But it will also contain, well beyond what Leto promises, a sanctuary of Artemis and a temple of Leto which is still famous today for the alley of white marble lions that leads up to it. These shrines might just be somewhat later than the Hymn.

Even on Delus, however, the birth takes time. Jealous Hera prevented

Figure 1 Apollo and Artemis among the Olympian gods, with Poseidon to the left of Apollo. Part of the Parthenon Frieze, ca. 440 BCE. Acropolis Museum, Athens. Copyright Photo Verdeau/Art Resource, NY.

Eileithyia, the birth goddess, from tending to her rival; only after nine days of painful labor, Eileithyia finally arrived at Leto's side. Firmly embracing a palm tree, Leto gives birth, and "the goddesses around her are shouting loudly," as do the human companions of a human mother. And like any human baby, the new-born god is washed and swaddled. But as soon as he is fed with nectar and ambrosia, he sheds the restraining baby linen and calls for the attributes of his divine power: "To me belong the lyre and the curved bow, and I will reveal the unchangeable will of Zeus to the humans" (131f.). Music and archery – the beneficent and the deadly use of the same strings – are his own, and prophecy as well, because he is so close to his father. And off he goes, to see the world.

The poet, however, spends little time with the world at large. His glance quickly returns to Delus and to the main festival on the island, "where the Ionians in their long dress assemble with their children and their worthy wives. They are organizing games and honor you with boxing, dancing and singing" (149f.). Again, we focus on the Eastern Greeks: Apollo, although lord of all humans, is a major divinity especially among the Ionians, those Greeks that inhabit the middle region of the Aegean islands and the adjacent Anatolian west coast, between the cities of

Phocaea to the north and Miletus, Priene, and Myous to the south. In their annual festival on Delus, they celebrate, confirm, and renew the union of their city-states, all especially rich and proud in the sixth-century BCE; Chios, from where the blind singer of the Hymn comes, is one of them. The topics of the contest have a long Apolline history. Dancing and singing, *molpé*, were already dear to Apollo when the young men of the Acheans performed their paean in the sanctuary of Chryse, and the god himself is a master musician: whenever the gods celebrate a banquet on Olympus, his music and the song of the Muses entertains them, as not only the *Iliad* tells us (*Il.* 1.601–604); this very hymn describes such a divine banquet, adding that in Olympus the lovely Graces and the handsome youngsters Ares and Hermes are dancing as well (193–201). Boxing, the only combat sport the Ionians cultivate on Delus, is another of Apollo's prerogatives: as Achilles announces, the god will reward "steadfastness" in the boxing contest during the funeral games for Patroclus (*Il.* 23.660). In Greek culture, boxing, like dancing, is very much a young men's sport: it is the sport in which the "boys of Zeus," the Dioscuri excel, and is already depicted as a boys' sport in a Minoan fresco from the island of Thera (Santorini).

From Delus and, in a wide sweep into Anatolia, through Lycia, "lovely Maeonia and Miletos, beautiful city on the sea" (179), the poet has his god move towards Delphi or, as he says, "rocky Pytho" (183); the god is dressed in the long musician's cloak and plays his lyre. Delphi was a center of music; its musical contests were famous at an early time.

After a new invocation to the god, the poet sets out to tell the second myth, Apollo's quest for an oracular shrine. He follows his god who leaves Olympus (correctly situated in North-eastern Greece), walks first south to Euboea, then turns east, to the site of the later city of Thebes, "where there were no streets, nor roads through the plain rich in grain, nothing but forest" (228): we are dealing with primeval times, without agriculture or roads, although the route the poet describes follows a major road of historical times. Apollo sometimes pauses to check out a place, and sometimes the poet pauses to add a lengthy description; but always the god, unsatisfied, moves on, until he reaches Telphusa, a lovely spring in a quiet spot. He immediately likes the spot, intends to build "a temple and a grove rich with trees," and starts to lay its foundations. The divine spring, however, is dismayed at the idea of becoming a major cult site of Apollo, and thinks of a ruse. She alerts him to the many horses and mules that would daily pass and drink of her abundant water, and – even worse – of the distraction the many chariots with their fast horses would cause to the visitors of the planned sanctuary. He would be better off by going up to the lonely mountains, to Krisa "under the ridge of

Parnassus." As a shrewd psychologist, she correctly realized that Apollo was looking for a quiet place. The god moves on to the place Telphusa recommended, "Krisa below the snowy heights of Parnassus, a hillside open towards the south; a steep rocks rises over it, and below there is a deep valley" (283–285); the description is suggestive even to the modern reader. And swiftly he again lays the foundations of a temple; human architects, Trophonios and Agamedes, add the stone threshold, and "countless races of humans built the temple with well connected stones, a marvel forever." The poet is deeply impressed by the architectural achievement of what must have been one of the earliest stone temples in Greece. We lack information about how it looked; in 548 BCE the temple was destroyed by fire, and the site underwent a radical change. Historians of architecture, however, still admire a rain water drain that goes back at least to the seventh century BCE; its engineering quality speaks extremely well for the temple that went with it.

The Hymn depicts Apollo as a pioneer; he brings the civilizing force of architecture and cult into the mountain wilderness. Other accounts disagree and give both Apollo and his temple a prehistory. Apollo's predecessor as an oracular divinity was Themis, who in her turn had followed Gaia "Earth" (Aeschylus, *Eumenides* 2f.). The stone temple built by Trophonios and Agamedes was preceded by, first, a laurel hut, then a round temple made from bees' wax and feathers and brought by Apollo from the Hyperboreans who dwell in the far north, and finally by a temple of bronze built by the gods (Pindar, *Paean* 8; Pausanias, *Guide of Greece* 10.5–13). I shall return to this intriguing prehistory – it will suffice here to underline that the poet of the Hymn chose not to tell any such story. His god is too powerful to have had predecessors, and the stone temple he knows is too marvelous to follow more miraculous structures that would diminish its achievement and splendor.

The oracle, however, could not begin to work immediately; Apollo was distracted and threatened. Telphusa was more devious than the young god could ever have suspected; she sent him into great danger. Delphi was not deserted: a monster was living next to the spring that we know as Castalia, a huge female snake. Easily and swiftly, the archer god killed her: the poet is not interested in a fight whose outcome is clear to him and his audience, but in the snake's story that follows in a long digression. Her main claim to mythical fame is the fact that she served as a nurse to the monster Typhon. Hera had borne him when Zeus had, from his head, given birth to Athena; the slighted wife decided to take her revenge on her husband. After all, he not only cheated on her regularly but he now even violated her monopoly of giving birth to their children.

This is not just a mythical embellishment to show off the poet's abilities. Typhon was, after all, to become a major threat for Zeus' kingship, and Hesiod describes in long and graphic detail the cosmic battle that followed Typhon's bid for power (*Theogony* 820–867). In a later version of the same myth, Zeus even is caught and immobilized by his terrible enemy, and Hermes has to rescue him (Apollodorus, *Library* 1.6.3). Apollo's victory is comparatively elegant, as befits the god. Myths of dragon fights are always situated at the turning point from a chaotic primeval era to the orderly time of the present. The Oriental mother of all dragon fights, the young god Marduk's fight against the primeval goddess Tiamat in Babylonian mythology, was situated in a time before the creation of earth and sky; it was recited in Babylon during the annual New Year's festival. Apollo's foundation of his oracle follows the same pattern: it is a mythical feat that has cosmic dimensions, marking the beginning of the world as we know it. No wonder that neither Apollo nor his Delphic temple could have predecessors, and that Thebes, next to Troy the most powerful and marvelous city in the Greek mythical tradition, did not yet exist; the only human city we hear of belongs to the lawless Phlegyans (278).

After shooting the snake, Apollo leaves her body unburied, to rot in the heat of the sun. This is not only a fitting punishment for a lawless monster but provides the etymology of Pytho, Delphi's epic name: the Greek root *púth*- means "to rot" and is connected with our adjective "putrid." Then he takes his revenge on the insidious spring, covering her basin with a mighty rock and erecting his own altar nearby. From that day on, Telphusa was a spring whose water welled, rather unimpressively, from beneath a big rock.

But the sanctuary is still not finished. Apollo needs servants to perform the sacrifices and proclaim the oracles. Looking out over the sea, he spots a Cretan ship on its way to the Peloponnese; in the shape of a dolphin, he pulls the surprised merchants into Krisa, Delphi's harbor below at the Corinthian gulf, and orders them to follow him on the steep path up to Delphi after having built an altar to Apollo Delphinios, "He of the Dolphin," on the shore. The merchants are not exactly happy to be turned into sacred personnel, and when they see the desolate mountain wilderness around the temple, they revolt: "Lord, how will we survive? Please explain this to us: this lovely place has neither fields nor harbors" (528f.). Apollo, amused and annoyed at the same time, has an easy answer. "Each of you, with a knife in his right hand, will forever slaughter sheep; they will be ready in huge numbers, since the mortals will offer them to me" (535f.). Delphi's temple economy needs neither maritime business ventures nor the toil of farming; whoever approaches the god for an oracle first has to sacrifice a sheep, and priests, as we know, get their share of meat and hide. The god is not only a fast marksman and excellent architect but also a clever religious entrepreneur; there is a reason why he chose merchants as his priests in Delphi. It was Christ, not Apollo, who drove the money-changers out of the temple.

Delus and Delphi are Apollo's main sanctuaries in the Greek world, and in the Hymn, they are almost as old as the god. Both are rather unlikely places for major sanctuaries, as the poet of the Hymn is well aware: neither a tiny island, not much more than a rock in the sea, nor the small terrace at the side of a towering mountain seem made for the bustling crowds a major sanctuary attracts; a site in a large city or at least in a plain with easy access – such as Zeus' sanctuary at Olympia, or the site of the spring Telphusa at the intersection of two major roads – would have been more obvious choices. Apollo has his city temples, such as the temple in Troy, but he has also the sacred groves well away from a city, on a mountain top or in the forests.

SUMMARY

Apollo in Homer thus has many facets, and many faces. He is the protector of the city of Troy whose walls he helped to build, as he built his temple in Delphi. He is the protector of young men whose hair he receives at their transition from boyhood to adolescence, but he is also a swift and silent killer of males. His weapon is the bow, and his craft is archery; but he is also a boxer and an accomplished musician whose instrument is the lyre, and whose preferred song is the paean which is accompanied by dancing. His sanctuaries are often outside human settlements, and they often have the appearance of a sacred grove, with an altar but no temple; on the other hand one of the first and most impressive stone temples in Greece was his. And finally, he is the patron of divination: he is Zeus' favorite son, as Athene is Zeus' favorite daughter, and as such he has access to Zeus' will and is willing to mediate this access to humans.

To anyone who has a methodical and tidy brain, this mass of details must appear bewildering and confusing. Earlier historians of Greek religion, committed to a model of evolution, tried to arrange the data in a complex model of development from one or two basic functions, but they could not agree on details. Such models are now widely discredited, and we shall have to find out whether there is some underlying order.

APOLLO THE MUSICIAN

THE BOW AND THE LYRE

Immediately after his birth, while still on Delus among the goddesses who helped him into life, Apollo defined his spheres of influence: "Let the lyre and curving bow be possessions to call my own, and for humans let me proclaim the unerring counsel of Zeus" (*Homeric Hymn to Apollo*, 131f.). Music – or rather, to a Greek, *mousikē*, the combination of instrumental music, song, and dance –, archery and divination are the fields in which the singer of the Hymn sees Apollo's power at work. We touched upon archery in the first chapter, we will treat divination in the third: in this chapter, I shall look at the lyre, while being aware that it is tricky to segment the complex world of Apollo. The Hymn itself treats all three together. The foundation of Apollo's main oracle at Delphi – or rather, in the Hymn's perspective, his first, foremost and almost unique oracular shrine – is its second main topic, together with his birth. But the bow and the lyre are nearly as prominent. Twice, the singer presents his audience with the image of Apollo entering Olympus, and both times he insists upon the strong impression Apollo made on his fellow Olympians. In the opening scene of the Hymn, Apollo joins the assembly of the Olympian gods, his bow ready: the gods, alarmed and frightened, "all leap up from their seats," but Leto serenely "shuts the quiver and takes the bow from his strong shoulders, to hang it from a peg of gold against his father's column." This is a timeless scene of Apollo's epiphany, told to impress the audience with the power of the god who is both addressee and theme of the Hymn, and it prepares for the triumph of the young god who will easily shoot and kill the monstrous snake that lives in the mountains of Delphi. This first appearance in the Hymn contrasts sharply with the second Olympic scene, the young god's first arrival on Olympus shortly after his birth on Delus. As soon as he enters the assembly, "the minds of the immortals turn to lyre and song" (188), and the Muses sing a hymn about gods and men. "The fair-tressed Graces and joyful Seasons, with Harmony, Youth, and Aphrodite the daughter of Zeus, hold hands by the wrist and dance" (192–194), and Artemis, Ares, and Hermes join them. "But Phoibos Apollo plays on the lyre, stepping fine and high" (200). No other two scenes could be so different: alarm and fear contrast with a joyfulness that turns even blood-thirsty Ares into a young dancer. Joyfulness and dread belong both to this god, and are intimately connected. Apollo is the god of sudden death no less than of transports of musical joy.

MOUSIKĒ AND ARCHAIC GREEK SOCIETY

The splendid scene of song and dance on Olympus combines what we can divide into two separate events: the dance of young women and men, and the performance of a song by a chorus of nine young women. Both are guided by Apollo's lyre. His musical performance ties them together: it is this combination of a sung text, instrumental music and group dancing that the Greeks call *mousikē* and that some contemporary scholars term "song-dance."

In Archaic Greece, as in many other traditional socities, this complex of singing, dancing, and playing of an instrument is more than just entertainment. Its near ubiquity in early Greece is visible in the images of life in Homeric Greece with which Hephaestus, the divine blacksmith, adorned the new shield he was making for Achilles (*Il.* 18.483–608). The god and the narrator begin with two opposing cities, a happy and an unhappy one. While the unhappy city is attacked by a hostile army, two things characterize the happy city, justice and festivity. On its agora, the citizens take part in a murder trial, and justice is done; and "there were weddings and celebrations," with bridal processions and wedding songs, "young dancers whirled around, and among them flutes and lyres gave voice." Somewhat later, the poet has the god picture a vineyard with beautiful ripe grapes that young men and women are harvesting: "in their midst, a boy played the lyre, sweetly and full of desire, and he sings the beautiful harvest song (*línos*) with his clear-sounding voice; and they all together beat the rhythm and followed him, singing, shouting and jumping with their feet." And finally, there is a place for dancing (*khóros*), "such as Daedalus built in Cnossus for Ariadne with her beautiful locks." Young men and women are dancing, holding each others' hand, the girls with wreaths, the boys with golden swords; their dance is intricate and precise, and "a large crowd stood around the dance place, full of joy, and among them two jesters were leading the song-dance (*molpḗ*) and whirled round in their midst."

The happy city is filled with entertainment. In the last scene, there is an audience, and there are two professional entertainers, but it is also a scene that represents a performance without a context, dwelling at length on the intricate dance movements: it is a virtuoso piece of narration. Still, there might be more than sheer entertainment and virtuosity. The young men and women are unmarried but ready for marriage, and their dance demonstrates their readiness and desirability for marriage. In the men's case, the dance also signals their readiness for citizenship: they know how to collaborate as a group, and they carry the free citizen's weapon. The harvest scene combines serious work – the harvesting of the grapes – with dancing and singing: the young people working in the vineyard do their work as a dancing chorus, lead by a young lyre player. Song and dance express the joy of a successful year and the anticipation of new wine, but they also help with the work. Common song and rhythmical movement transform the individual workers into a homogeneous group, unify and speed up their toil, and help them to forget fatigue. Harvest songs such as the Greek *línos* are known from many cultures. In Greek myth, their personification, Linus, is the son of Apollo and a Muse. The good city also is ruled by justice and lawful social reproduction: Themis, the goddess of divine Rightfulness, is among the divinities invoked in the wedding ritual. There is the wedding song, *hyménaios*, whose personifaction, the god Hymenaios, is either the son of a Muse, of Apollo or, somewhat more surprising, of Dionysus: this latter genealogy gives mythological expression to his somewhat ribald character. Song and dance contribute to the festivity of the event, but they also carry a social message: the not yet married but nubile young men present themselves as a homogeneous and collaborative group and demonstrate their bodily fitness.

All this indicates the high social relevance of the scene of Olympian *mousikē* in the *Hymn to Apollo*: the gods' actions mirror human concerns. The Olympian dancers are divine embodiments of what Archaic Greek society expected dance to be. It is a prerogative of youth (Zeus, Hera, or Poseidon remain seated spectators), presents harmony and beauty, and evokes erotic feelings among spectators and participants. The dance floor is the space where the nubile young women and men display their bodily charm and prowess, and where matches are made, by the bystanding parents as often as by the participating young people. The singers represent poetic performance in Archaic Greece: the Muses, daughters of Zeus and Memory (Mnemosyne), put to words what is vital in the group's self-definition – among the Olympians, it is the opposition between the immortal gods and the weak and dependent mortals, the very opposition that fuels the performance of the Hymn.

In the same way as the god's entry, frightening and splendid in his weapons, foreshadows his triumph over the Delphic snake, his musical performance on Olympus corresponds to the description of the festival of all the Ionians on Delus. Here, the very singer of the Hymn ("a blind man from Chios," 175) performs his art; the Delian Maidens praise Apollo, Leto, and Artemis and "remember and sing a hymn of the men and women of old, and charm the tribes of humans." The Delian festival with its games, the *Delia* founded by Theseus, is the event that, in Archaic Greece, defines the Ionians and shapes their cohesion and identity. Under the protection of Apollo, his mother, and his sister, "Ionians trailing their robes" gather once a year "with children and wives," sacrifice and perform "boxing, dancing, and song." This gathering was the splendor of the Delian sanctuary. In the sixth century BCE, when the Hymn was composed, the sanctuary had three temples, a very old one of Artemis, a very recent one of Apollo, and the magnificent sanctuary of Leto, set somewhat apart and adorned by a row of white marble lions along its access road, following the model of Egyptian procession roads. Apollo's main monument was not the temple but the altar, the famous *Keratôn* or "Altar of Horns," said to be built by Apollo himself. It was constructed by the left horns of innumerable goats sacrificed to the god, and thus proclaimed by its very form the zeal of the human worshippers, as did the huge Altar of Ashes in the sanctuary of Zeus in Olympia. It was the focus of a dance peculiar to Delus, the *geranos* or "crane dance" that persisted throughout antiquity. According to Delian mythology, Theseus performed it for the first time when he returned with the Athenian youths saved from the labyrinth of king Minos, and its complex movements were said to mirror the way through the labyrinth.

The same complex of *mousikē* characterized performance at Delphi; its games, the *Pythia*, were to Delphi what the *Delia* were to Delus. Originally held every eighth year, the games consisted only in the performance of a hymn, Apollo's paean; the prize was a laurel wreath, comparable to the Delian prize of a palm wreath; athletics, already part of the Delian games at the time of the Hymn, were absent. Early in the Archaic Age, the games were reorganized; they were now held every fourth year, the musical contests were multiplied, and athletics were added after the model of the Olympian Games, with whose importance the Pythian Games competed. The musical performances consisted of cithara-playing, flute-playing, and singing to the cithara. This last discipline, *kitharôidia*, was deemed the most outstanding contest of the games since it combined musical and poetical invention: throughout the ancient world, Apollo himself was often represented as a *kitharôidos*, a singer to his cithara, in the long dress typical of such performers.

LYRE AND FLUTE

Despite the addition of flute-playing to the Pythian Games, the flute did not belong to the world of Apollo; his instrument was the lyre. The *Hymn to Hermes* tells the story of how this came to be: on his first day out, baby Hermes stumbled over a tortoise, killed it, and turned its shell into the body of the first string instrument. On the same trip, he stole Apollo's sacred cows and slaughtered one of them, thus inventing the sacrifice. Hermes is the Greek form of a wide-spread mythical figure, the trickster; as in most mythologies, the trickster is also the inventor of culture, which in Archaic Greece means music and sacrifice that characterize communal festivities. When his older brother Apollo found him out, he was so impressed with the first citharedic performance Hermes gave that he eagerly accepted the lyre as a compensation for his sacrificed cow. When he asked for the lyre, Apollo stressed the effect of the new music: "Truly: joy, love and sweet sleep can be gained all together," and he is eager to introduce it to the world.

In this same passage, Apollo compares flute and lyre. He characterizes himself as a helper of the Muses "who love dancing and the sweet ways of song, the flowering melodies and the call of the flutes that awakens desire" (451f.). Thus, *mousikē* already existed before Hermes' invention, and it was in the care of Apollo and the Muses, but its only instrument was the flute. The lyre, however, easily outdoes all this: "Nothing among the skillful feats at the banquets of the young has impressed my soul so deeply" (454). From now on, the lyre will be Apollo's instrument. The flute was tolerated; after all, it formed part of the Pythian Games, and both lyre and flute were used to accompany sacrifices; but in the system of values ascribed to different instruments, the lyre ranks higher, well above the flute.

Mythology expressed this hierarchy of musical instruments in stories that talked about inventors and performers, and in the course of the late sixth and early fifth centuries BCE, this hierarchy of instruments became more rigid, as the myths make clear. Whereas the lyre had Hermes as its inventor and Apollo as its performer, the flute, although invented by Athena, was rejected by her and became the instrument of Marsyas. Marsyas was either a Silen or a Satyr, and he was not Greek but Phrygian. As Silen or Satyr, he was connected with Dionysus, and he was only partly human, more on the side of nature than culture; Silens and Satyrs were represented with horse tails and animal ears. As a Phrygian, he was non-Greek and had close ties with the Great Goddess Cybele for whose ecstatic cult he was said to have invented songs. The opposition that is visible here – lyre versus flute, culture versus nature,

Apollo versus Dionysus and Cybele – turns into a violent conflict in another story that is known since the fifth century BCE. When Marsyas challenged Apollo to a musical contest, Apollo easily won and flayed Marsyas alive, to punish him for his arrogance (figure 2). The lyre ranked so high above the flute that even to challenge the hierarchy became a crime.

One reason for the opposition between these instruments lies in the way their different players were forced to perform by the very nature of their instruments. A citharedic performer sang a text that he accompanied by his lyre: the music was subordinated to the words. Flute-playing cannot be accompanied by words, at least not by the same person; the instrument alone has to tell the story. Saccadas of Argus, a flute virtuoso who won the first prize in the Pythia in three consecutive contests (in the years 586, 582 and 578 BCE), was famous for his musical compositions that evoked mythical events (what we would call program music). His instrumental pieces were able to narrate the sack of Troy, or the fight of Apollo with the dragon in five movements. Understanding the story necessitated close attention to the music, whereas the citharedic story called close attention to the verbal text.

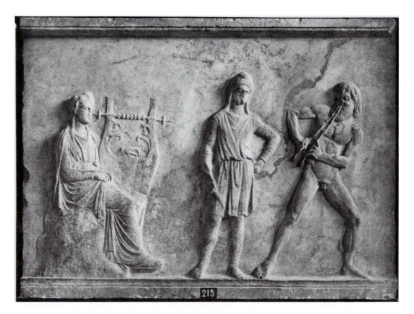

Figure 2 Apollo and Marsyas in contest. Relief, late fourth century BCE. Athens, Greek National Museum. Copyright Alinari/Art Resource, NY.

The hardening of the antithesis between lyre and flute, which is visible in the myths of Marsyas, is a result of developments in fifth-century culture and education; both instruments had always performed in the Pythian Games. In education, the lyre was the aristocratic instrument that every cultured aristocrat should be able to play. In fifth-century Athens, aristocratic values decreased, and boys turned to the much easier flute: the story of how Heracles killed Linus, his lyre teacher, may reflect this change. The late fifth century also developed a new musical style which traditionalists such as Plato regarded as dissolute and dissolving the firm borderlines between the genres: its disorderly nature was thought to be as dangerous for the community as rock music was judged in its early years. The exponent of this new style was Timotheus (ca. 450–360 BCE), a citharede who was highly acclaimed as a performer of dithyrambs. Dithyrambs are connected with Dionysus, not with Apollo: although Timotheus still played the lyre, we sense a tension between the music of Apollo and of Dionysus. This will occupy as much later, when we will explore the prehistory of Friedrich Nietzsche's Apollo.

APOLLO LEADER OF THE MUSES

The scene of Olympic *mousikē* in the *Hymn to Apollo* is not isolated in Archaic Greek literature, which confirms the importance of "song-dance" in Archaic Greek society. From Homer to Pindar (early fifth century BCE), poetry depicts Apollo playing on Olympus together with the Muses, and the occasion is always a festival. In the first book of the *Iliad*, the singer describes a banquet of the gods where the food is accompanied by "the beautiful lyre which Apollo had, and the Muses who were singing, answering with beautiful voice" (1.604f.). At least two centuries later, at the very beginning of the classical age, the poet Pindar narrates the wedding of Peleus and Thetis: "With willing mind, the most beautiful chorus of the Muses was singing on Mount Pelion, and in their midst Apollo was leading manifold melodies, playing the seven-tongued lyre with his golden plectre" (*Nemean Odes* 5.23–25). Throughout Archaic Greek poetry, the banquets and festivals of the gods are accompanied by the music of Apollo and the chorus of the nine Muses.

This reflects social practice all over Archaic Greece. The song and dance of a chorus that was led by a musician who played the lyre accompanied the all-male banquets of the aristocracy as well as the religious gatherings of groups of all kinds. At the beginning of the first *Pythian Ode* (performed in 470 BCE), the poet Pindar addresses the lyre (*phórminx*) and puts its music into the context of a festival: "Golden lyre, common treasure of Apollo and the violet-haired Muses: to you the dancers' footstep listens as it begins the splendid celebration, and the singers heed your signs whenever you elicit from the trembling strings the chorus-leading preludes." But the effects of the music go well beyond creating a festive atmosphere. The tunes of the lyre quench Zeus' weapon, the fiery thunderbolt, and they pour sleep over the eyes of his eagle. Mighty Ares, slumbering, forgets his weapons, "and its power charms also the gods' minds through the art of Leto's son and of the deep-breasted Muses." Pindar easily outdoes the scene of Apollo's entry to Olympus in the Hymn.

An admiring scholar called this Pindaric passage "perhaps the greatest praise of music ever written," and it certainly resonates through later literature. This resonance was firmly rooted in the realities of Greek festival life, and went well beyond the performance of dance and citharedic song. Major festivals not only displayed musical and choral performances, they put a temporary halt to the nearly permanent inter-city warfare that charactized most of Greek history before Alexander the Great. It was not just the great panhellenic festivals such as the Olympia, the Athenian Mysteria, or the Pythia which were protected by a temporary sacred truce; local festivals could also enjoy the benefits of temporary peace. The quenching of Zeus' thunderbolt and Ares' sleep in Pindar, or Ares dancing with abandon in the *Hymn to Apollo* reflect the Greek understanding of what a festival was, and the truces surrrounding them were more than just a practical matter that allowed the embassies and visitors to passage to and from the sanctuary. Practicality was part of the motivation, but underlying it is the ideological reading of the festival as a space carved out from the grim reality of Greek life. To give just one example of a more local festival that combined a sacred truce with musical performances as its main content, I turn to the Spartan Hyacinthia, the festival of Apollo in Amyclae.

The festival was held in the sanctuary of Amyclae four miles outside of Sparta. The sanctuary dated back to late Mycenaean times, before the Spartans arrived in the valley of the Eurotas, and was famous already in the archaic period; down through the ages, it preserved a strange and highly archaic image of Apollo, "very old and fashioned without much art," as Pausanias has it (3.19.2), similar to a tall bronze column in shape, with a helmet on its head and a lance and a bow in its hands. This warlike image stood on an altar-shaped base said to contain the grave of Apollo's boy lover Hyacinthus whom he killed by accident with a stray throw of his discus. The festival lasted three days and attracted large crowds. Its first day was dedicated to Hyacinthus who received a sacrifice through a bronze door in his altar; observers noted the manifold signs of grief for his boy lover – no wreaths were worn, no bread or cakes brought to the sanctuary, no paean was sung; "everybody dines very orderly and then goes home again." The second day was Apollo's, an occasion for the main sacrifice to the god and for large and lavish meals for the Spartans, their guests, and their slaves. On this day, athletic and musical performances were held, as the local historian Polycrates tells us.

> Boys in long, ungirded cloaks play the lyre; singing to the accompaniment of a flute, they strike all seven strings with their plectrum and hymn the god in anapaestic metre and in a high pitch . . .; numerous choruses of young men enter the theatre and sing traditional songs, and dancers move between them in traditional figures that are accompanied by flute and song.

Other young men performed riding exercises, while girls held contests, and a new cloak was presented to Apollo: his column-like image must have been dressed in such a cloak during the rest of the year.

This description makes one think of a New Year's festival, and it was certainly one of Sparta's most lavish festival periods. The strange, dark atmosphere of the first day, with its reversals of festive behavior, enhances the festivity of the second day: here as elsewhere, a ritual dichotomy intended to mark the suspension of normality translates, in mythological terms, into the opposition between a brilliant god and a dead hero, killed through a mistake of the god, his lover. Musical performances by boys and young adolescents are at the center of Apollo's second day, and they combine the lyre, the flute, song, and dance: it looks as if the opposition between flute and lyre developed after the traditions of the Hyacinthia were fully established, as was the case with the musical contests of the Delphian Pythia. Our ancient witness emphasizes the lavishness and opulence of the festival. But the festival also hindered the Spartans from going to war: they regularly seemed to have refrained from military action not only during the festival, but well in advance of it. Apollo's festive charm rests on the realities of Greek festival life.

THE PAEAN

During the Hyacinthia, as during the Pythia in Delphi, the festival on Delus and many other festivals of Apollo, choruses of boys, adolescents, or men performed the paean. The *Hymn to Apollo* describes how Apollo himself introduced this song to Delphi. When he led the Cretans up from the shore where they had built an altar to him, sacrificed and held a banquet,

Lord Apollo, son of Zeus, went before them, with the lyre in his hand, playing marvel-ously and walking with beautiful and high steps; they followed him beating the time, the Cretans, up to Delphi, and were singing a paean (*iēpaiēona*) similar to the paean (*paiēones*) of the Cretans into whose hearts the divine Muse put sweet song.

(514–518)

In this account, the paean is a native Cretan song. The Hymn uses two terms for it that are closely related: the second term is the Homeric version of the later word *paiān* (*paiōn* in the dialect of Athens), the former reproduces the cultic shout that exists independently or as a refrain of the paean-song, *iē paiān*. This double terminology has irri-tated some scholars who were uncomfortable with ambiguities; and since in Homer the god Paiēōn is the court physician on Olympus, they understood *paiēones* to mean "healers." The Cretans would sing the song which they knew as the song of their own god-inspired healers. This is extremely intriguing and will occupy us later; the Cretan origin of the "song-dance" paean is what matters for the time being.

Over time, probably unhappy with the idea of the paean as a foreign import, the Delphians told a different story. When young Apollo was about to shoot the dangerous monster, local bystanders or his mother Leto were encouraging him, shouting either "shoot, Paean" (*híe, Paián*), addressing him by one of his cult titles, or "shoot, son, an arrow" (*híe, paî, ión*). The story must have been invented after the Hymn, and the word-play sounds like one of those etymologies fifth-century intel-lectuals were fond of. Still, the connection with the dragon story is sig-nificant. In Near Eastern and Indo-European mythology, the killing of the dragon is a founding event of cosmic dimensions. In Delphi, the shooting of the dragon is not only the founding event of Apollo's main oracle but of his song as well. This gives to both a cosmic importance: the Delphic sanctuary, after all, contained the "Navel of the Earth," the very centre of the cosmos; the paean is the song and dance that belongs to this center.

The juxtaposition of these two myths, however, points to an under-lying problem. In recent years, several scholars have worked on the genre paean, and they all came up with the same insight: paean is a rather fuzzy genre whose one reliable characteristic is the shout "*iè paiān*." This contradicts the Greeks themselves who had no problem defining the paean. The first definition appears in the beginning of Pindar's third *Dirge*: "There are paean-songs in due season belonging to the children of Leto with the golden distaff." The poet sees the paeans as the songs of Apollo and Artemis, and in what follows he opposes them to other songs, the dithyrambs of Dionysus, the wedding-songs of the god

Hymenaios, and the dirges that the Muse Melpomene sings for her dead sons. Pindar's voice is authoritative, and later grammarians used this passage to define the paean as the song of Apollo.

Real life is, as always, messier, whatever Pindar said, or meant. He might have simplified reality in order to achieve his goal, to give a forceful introduction to a dirge; his song moves from the celebrative and joyful paeans, dithyrambs, and wedding-songs to the dirge, in a complex move that opposes joy and grief and at the same time creates an atmosphere of glory that is part of the dirge for a dead aristocrat. When we look at what the ancients said about paeans, or at the extant songs themselves, we see a complex picture. First, we have to distinguish between paean as song and paean as shout; both can be described with the Greek verb *paionízein*, "to sing/shout *paean*." The spontaneous shout *iē paiān* expressed surprise or joy, very rarely dismay, and it was used by men only (most Greek exclamations were gendered). In a more ritualized context, it could be used during sacrifice. But this exclamation was closely related to the song, since it functioned as its refrain and gave the name to the genre. Paeans were sung in different circumstances: before battle or after victory, at the beginning of a symposium, or before any risky undertaking, such as setting sail or, in comic parody, going to court. Paeans were also sung during the wedding ceremony, yet another uncertain beginning. In all these situations, the refrain could be understood as the invocation of a helping divinity, Paean, even though this divinity had a different name, Zeus in the banquet or Hera in the wedding ceremony; Greeks often addressed their gods not with their overall names, but used epithets as addresses that expressed a specific aspect of their personality and function. But in the overwhelming majority of cases, the divine recipient addressed was either Apollo or, later, Apollo's son, the healer Asclepius. Even in a ritual context where another divinity seemed to be in the foreground, Apollo was not far away. A long and complex sacred law from the city of Miletus from about 450 BCE prescribes the activities of an all-male group of worshippers of Apollo Delphinios known as *molpoí*, "singer-dancers." An important ritual was their procession from Miletus to Didyma during which they sacrificed and performed: "The paean is performed first for Hecate in front of the city-gate, for Dynamis, then in the Meadow at the top for the Nymphs, then for Hermes in Kelados, for Phylios, around Keraites, at the statues of Chares." This traces the sacred topography of the processional road, from Miletus over a mountain pass to the statues that stood alongside the monumental entry into the Didymaean sanctuary, again, as in Delus, after an Egyptian model. The different sacred places along this road were more markers for the performance of the Molpoi than addressees of their song: they performed the paean because they were worshippers of Apollo.

The paean can thus be understood as a ritual performance that addressed a divinity in a situation of danger and uncertainty; one of Apollo's functions was to be "Averter of Evil," Alexikakos. It fits that, according to a Spartan tradition, a certain Thaletas of Gortyn halted a plague in Sparta; he is well known as the singer of paeans. To a Greek, it goes nearly without saying that the same song that asked for help can be performed again to thank the god when he has responded favorably: this explains the paean after victory, or the paean which the Greeks performed to Apollo Smintheus after the plague. At the same time, the paean was also viewed as a controlled and celebratory song, opposed to the wild and even subversive Dionysiac dithyramb. The performance of a paean during a wedding and during the Eleusinian Mysteries and the Athenian Panathenaia might be a result of this festive and celebratory character. However, it should be kept in mind that Mysteries rites and Panathenaia are also auspicious new beginnings, of the Athenian year at the Panathenaia, and of an entirely new relationship towards the goddesses of wealth and of the afterlife, Demeter and Persephone, in the case of the Mysteries. A similar richness of meaning accounts for paeans that, in Hellenistic times, were performed for kings and generals: on the one side, these powerful men were seen as real sources of salvation and help (or evil and destruction, if they were antagonized); on the other hand, it was only fit that rituals in their honor should be stately and festive.

Thus, the genre paean has no firm and clear-cut boundaries, but there is a firm core that has to do with salvation, and with Apollo or Asclepius. It is only from the sanctuaries of these two gods that we have inscriptions preserving entire texts of paeans, recorded on stone (sometimes even with musical notation) in order to keep the memory of the performance alive. There were developments after the Archaic Age: the paean was extended to Asclepius who, during the fifth and fourth centuries BCE, became a much more powerful healer than Apollo, and to the kings and generals who were more immediate saviors or threats than any Olympian god could ever be. But even then, the tie with Apollo was often present. When the small city of Erythrai in Northern Ionia introduced the cult of Asclepius in about 375 BCE, the city assembly passed regulations for the cult of the new god: it bound it firmly together with the already established cult of Apollo. In the new city festival, both received a sacrifice, and the text stipulated that "first one has to perform the following paean at the altar of Apollo," after which it gives the text of a paean to Apollo, then another paean for Asclepius. About ninety years

later, in 281 BCE, the assembly decided to add a third recipient of a
paean to the same text: King Seleucus whom the Ionian cities greeted
as new overlord and liberator from a much harsher regime. Apollo, his
son Asclepius, and the divine king are all lined up together as saviors of
the city.

DIVINE POETS AND INSPIRED MEN

We have seen that Apollo was regarded not only as the divine musician,
but also as the father of mythical figures that were personifications of
certain types of songs: the harvest-song, Linus, or the wedding song,
Hymenaeus. In his third *Dirge*, Pindar lists them not as sons of Apollo,
but of the Muse Calliope who was singing dirges for them, since they
died young:

> One song sang *ailinon* for the long-haired Linus; another sang of Hymenaeus, whom
> the last hymn took away when at night his skin was first touched in marriage; and
> another sang of Ialemus, whose strength was fettered by a flesh-rending disease.

Linus, the story goes, was killed as a young man by the hunting dogs of
his grandfather; Hymenaeus died young while singing the wedding song
at the wedding of Dionysus and Ariadne. Ialemus is yet another son of
Apollo: his song is the dirge (*iálemos*) that was sung the first time after
his untimely death. The early death of so many musical heroes is somewhat disconcerting, although, as has been pointed out long ago, most
heroes die an untimely death. One wonders whether this has to do with
the predominance of child or adolescent choruses in Greece.

To this list, Pindar adds a fourth hero: "The son of Oeagrus, . . .
Orpheus of the golden lyre." Orpheus too was a son of the Muse Calliope;
and whereas Pindar here gives him the Thracian king Oeagrus as a
father, in another passage he claims that "from Apollo came the father of
songs, the widely praised lyre player Orpheus" (*Pythian Ode* 4.176).
Mythological consistency is less important than the immediate aim of
the song: while the context of the former passage is lost, this second
passage is a list of the Argonauts, "the voyage of the demi-gods" and
Pindar stresses the nobility of the participants, many of them sons of
gods, and their heroic undertaking enhances the glory of the victor
whose praise Pindar sings, an aristocrat from Cyrene.

Orpheus is much more complex than his three (half-)brothers Ialemus, Hymenaus, and Linus with whom he shares only his untimely
death. The story is well known (although fully narrated comparatively

late, by the Roman poets Virgil and Ovid). When his bride died of a snake bite on their wedding day, Orpheus decided to fetch her back from the Underworld. His song easily gained him access and enchanted even Hades and Persephone; they gave him back his wife under the condition that he would not look back while walking in front of her up to the world of the living. But of course, Orpheus turned back, driven by his love and the uncertainty whether she would be following him. Having failed to honor this condition and returning alone, he fled to the wilderness of Thrace and was killed there, either by the incensed wives of the Thracians whom he brought under his musical spell, or by the menads, the followers of Dionysus whom he spurned, being a follower of Apollo. Throughout Greek tradition, Orpheus is the arch-poet, the originator of Greek poetry, the citharede who received his art, and perhaps his lyre, from Apollo and whose powerful songs enchanted the powers of the underworld, the animals and even rocks and trees in the wilderness of Thrace; a rare image shows his head singing on in Apollo's presence, dictating a text to an attentive youth, perhaps his son Musaeus (figure 3). As an Argonaut, he easily outsang the Sirens who killed themselves out of shame for being beaten. Art shades into magic, and song (*ōdē*) was closely related to spell (*epōdē*) in Greek thought; the Romans even lumped both together as *carmina*. Orpheus was also credited with spells that had miraculous healing powers. No wonder that the geographer Strabo derided him as "a wizard because of his music and divination, and because he peddled initiations into mystery cults." The cults in

Figure 3 Apollo supervising Orpheus' head that gives oracles. Attic red-figure cup in Naples, ca. 430 BCE. Reproduced after Minervini, *Bulletino Napoletano*, serie nuova 6, p. 33, tav. iv.

question were the mysteries of Dionysus with which Orpheus became connected in the late sixth century BCE: the cult promised a privileged life after death through private initiations, and who would be better suited to give guidance through the Underworld than the singer who himself had gone down and returned alive, albeit without his beloved wife? Thus, the son of Apollo was turned into a prophet of Dionysus whose very followers were responsible for his death. Among his poems, a "Descent to the Underworld" was known already in the fifth century BCE. But the same poet was also credited with providing information about the origin of the world and the gods: several theogonical poems were composed under his name. In Orpheus, musical poetry (*musikē*) is again more than entertainment: it has not only the power to enchant gods, humans, and nature, but to heal, and its words convey information about worlds otherwise unknown to humans, both in time and in place.

Other legendary poets were also connected with Apollo. Olen, a native of Lycia in Southwestern Anatolia, was said to have written the traditional hymns that were sung on Delus in the fifth century BCE; others even thought that he was Apollo's first prophet in Delphi. Lycia is closely connected with Apollo: his mother Leto possessed the major sanctuary of the region, the Letoon in Xanthus, and Apollo himself had an epithet, Lycius (*lúkeios*), that ancient and modern authors alike understood to mean "Lycian." Another son was Philammon, poet and lyre player who instituted girls' choruses in Delphi and was among the first victors. He became the father of the poets and singers Thamyris and Eumolpus, both Thracians like Orpheus; Thamyris challenged the Muses and lost contest and life, Eumolpus moved to Eleusis and founded the clan from whom, until the end of antiquity, the Athenians selected the high-priest of the Eleusinian mysteries: the resonances with other Apolline themes are obvious. Then there was Abaris, a Hyperborean and priest of Apollo who regularly spent his winters in the north; he came to Greece led by Apollo's arrow, and some claimed that he could fly on it. He foretold epidemics, and in Sparta he performed sacrifices that kept them away for good. Classical Greece knew him as a writer of oracles and spells; later, there were epical poems under his name, including *Purifications* and *Apollo's Coming to the Hyperboreans*, as well as a prose theogony. One Aristeas of Proconessus, an island in the strait northeast of Istanbul, left better traces: already in the early sixth century BCE, Greeks read his poem *Arimaspeia* in which he narrated how, possessed by Apollo and accompanied by his servant in the form of a raven, he traveled far north and heard about the fabulous people up there, the Arimaspi who fought with the griffins, and the Hyperboreans, "The People Beyond the North Wind." A local legend, preserved in Herodotus (4.15), tells how he died but was seen later in other places, while his body had disappeared. The same historian also narrates how Aristeas appeared in Metapontum in Southern Italy and asked the Metapontians to build an altar to Apollo, since they were the only Italians to whom Apollo had manifested himself, "and he, Aristeas, had accompanied him in the form of a raven," Apollo's sacred animal. The altar, an image of Aristeas and the laurel bushes next to them were still visible on the agora of Metapontum in Herodotus' time.

PYTHAGORAS AND SHAMANISM

Yet another sage had ties to Southern Italy where he founded his school, and he is relevant here as well: Pythagoras, son of Mnesiarchus, who settled in a city close to Metapontum, Croton, after he left Samus after the Persian invasion of 547/6 BCE. He was a sage (rather than a philosopher) who combined in his person ritual practices, religious teaching, and philosophical speculation, as did Empedocles of Acragas, priest, healer, wizard, and philosopher two generations later. Pythagoras was regarded by his followers as the reincarnation of Hyperborean Apollo; legend has it that he proved the truth of this assertion by showing his golden thigh one day, and that he met the Hyperborean Abaris, took away his arrow and made him his follower. Like Orpheus, he went to the Underworld and was regarded by his followers as being dead; after a year, he came back and, in order to prove his story, was able to tell of everything that had happened in between. His followers, the Pythagoreans, were deeply concerned with music, both as a model for the cosmic relevance of numeric harmony and as a means of purifying and healing the soul: speculation and ritual, musical practice and mathematical theory, opposites in our way of thinking, were closely intertwined in this world.

For a while, scholars used to call all these figures shamans. But the term has gone out of fashion, for several reasons. First, "shaman" is a term that originally belonged to a very small and clearly defined area among the Tungus in Northern Siberia: these societies believed that a specialist could communicate with the powers that govern the world and distribute or withhold health or a successful hunt. He did so in an ecstatic journey to these powers with the help of spirits that he had acquired during his initiation. Mainly through the work of the historian of religion Mircea Eliade, this narrow definition of a shaman has been broadened to encompass all religious specialists that combine ecstasy and healing; the underlying notion is that shamanism is a phenomenon that was shared at one time by most human societies. This assumption and its underlying evolutionary concept are highly problematic; it works only at the price of emptying the term of much of its specificity. As for Archaic Greece, a less general concept had been used to justify the term: at some point in the early Iron Age, it was argued, when commercial and colonial expansion had opened up the northern shore of the Black Sea, the Greeks came into contact with Eurasian shamanistic cultures, and thus stories and even historical figures based on shamanism entered Greece. The constant association of these figures with the Hyperboreans and Hyperborean Apollo seemed to confirm this: the Hyperboreans were the people "Beyond the North." The problems with this theory are historical and methodological. Although the historical dates seem to fit more or less – Olbia at the mouth of the Dniestr was founded in about 600 BCE, both Aristeas and Abaris appear in the sixth century –, we do not know whether the cultures with which they came into contact (the Scythians of Southern Russia) knew shamanism in the same form as the Tungus in Siberia: the distance between the northern shore of the Black Sea and Siberia is considerable, and contacts are unclear at best. But even if this could be proved, it is obvious that none of these figures shared the pivotal social role of a Tungus shaman, not even Pythagoras; he was the founder of a religious sect and leader of a political movement. Early Greece had no shamans. If one insists on the term, one could claim that Abaris, Aristeas, and Pythagoras (and, for that matter, Empedocles) were somewhat influenced by Northern Eurasian shamanism; but the probability of such an influence is low indeed.

What, then, were these men, and why were they connected with Apollo? The first question is somewhat easier to answer than the second. Whether they were legendary or historical (but even then heavily overlaid by legend), they are examples of archaic wise men who posessessed special knowledge of rituals, divination, and healing and who had gained this knowledge through ecstatic experience. In the cases of Abaris and Aristeas, the colonial push northwards anchored the stories in an imaginary north whose depiction was based on travelers' tales about the wonderlands north of the Black Sea. Aristeas' *Arimaspeia* responded to a demand for stories about those far-away lands. Proconessus, Aristeas' home city, was a Milesian colony, as was Olbia, and the Milesians were at the forefront of the colonizing movement. Pythagoras, on the other hand, was the historical founder of a secret society in Southern Italy that was politically highly successful and which combined an esoteric religion centered perhaps on the mysteries of a Great Goddess with philosophical speculation on arithmetic, music, cosmology, and healing. Contemporaries perceived him as being close enough to figures like

Abaris that they narrated legends which linked the two even more closely.

One reason why Apollo was brought into the stories of such men was his close ties with ecstatic experience. As we shall see in the next chapter, he was, from early on, connected with ecstatic divination, be it institutional as in Delphi or freelancing as with Cassandra and the Sybil. At the same time, he was also the god of music and healing: at least outside the Homeric epics whose distaste of ecstasy is well known, Apollo looks like the divine template for these healers, poets, and miracle workers. The ecstatic side of his character found narrative expression in stories that associated him with travel and arrival from abroad. In this respect, he is similar to Dionysus whom one could characterize as "the arriving god." Dionysus was thought to arrive from the East; in the prologue of his *Bacchants*, Euripides gives a geographical list of his travels that reach as far as Persia, Bactria, and Arabia. After Alexander's conquests, India was added to the list: the Greeks associated the type of subversion that came with the ecstatic cult of Dionysus with the ambivalent delights and temptations of Eastern civilizations. Apollo was made of sterner stuff, and the tougher but not less marvelous lands of the Far North proved a more adequate expression of his character. The association with the Hyperboreans does not end with Abaris and Aristeas. In Delphi, the oracle ceased during the winter, Apollo stepped back, and Dionysus took over: Apollo, it was said, had travelled to his Hyperboreans. On Delus, the sanctuary contained the grave of two pairs of Hyperborean girls, Arge and Opis, and Laodice and Hyperoche, who had died there: the former pair had come "with the gods themselves," the latter brought a tribute to the island when Leto was about to give birth (Herodotus 4.34); their cult was living testimony of Apollo's tie with the Far North.

APOLLO *CITHAROEDUS*

This chapter dealt mainly with Archaic Greece. In this epoch, the musical-literary-ritual phenomena connected with Apollo had a surprising unity which began to dissolve during the classical period. Pindar of Thebes, the last "song-dance" poet, and Empedocles of Acragas, the last sage who combined ritual wisdom, medicine, magic, and philosophy, are rough contemporaries; both were living outside Athens which was slowly moving to the center of the cultural stage. During the following centuries, when literature turned from orality and performance to literacy and reading (or at least reciting), Apollo the Musician changed into a narrower god of poets and poetry, both in Hellenistic Greece and in the Roman renewal of Hellenistic poetry after the mid-first century BCE. Republican Rome preserved an earlier state of affairs since her poets belonged to the guild of scribes who were under the tutelage of that arch-intellectual, Minerva. The proem of Callimachus' *Aetia* (ca. 250 BCE), perhaps the most seminal text for several centuries to come, introduces Apollo as stern teacher of the young poet:

> When I first put the writing tablets onto my knees, Apollo Lycius said to me: "Sheep, singer, have to be fat, but the Muse, dear man, should be lank. I command you not to walk the streets where cars are racing, . . . but on paths not trodden by anyone, even if they are narrow."

The god himself thus authenticates a new literary program, and his voice will reverberate through late Republican and Augustan Latin literature.

SUMMARY

With this, literature and cult seem to separate for good; the unity of song, dance, and musical performance, *mousikē*, has fallen apart. In Archaic and Classical Greek society, this unity was placed under Apollo's protection, and it played a vital social role; we shall see that this role was even more central to Greek politics in the Archaic Age than we might imagine. At the same time, literature and cult were already in some tension in the Homeric poems, insofar as Homer's poems do not provide us with descriptions of contemporary institutions. They are reticent on large areas of religion such as the women's cult of Demeter, or the ecstatic cults of Dionysus; the Homeric gods are as artificial and synthetic as is the Homeric language which corresponds to no dialect ever spoken in Greece. It is time, after two chapters on literature, to deal with the cult of Apollo: this will be the topic the next three chapters.

ORACULAR APOLLO

As soon as he is born, Apollo stakes out the areas of his responsibility – "the lyre, and the curving bow," and "to proclaim the unerring counsel of Zeus" (*Hymn to Apollo* 131f.), that is *mousikē*, shooting, and divination. We talked about the former two in the preceding chapters; this chapter is devoted to the third item. Divination – rituals to acquire "the foresight and knowledge of the future," in Cicero's somewhat narrow definition (*On Divination* 1.1) – played no great role in the Homeric world. Certainly, there were the seers: Calchas who accompanied the army in the *Iliad*, Tiresias whose ghost Odysseus consulted in the Underworld, and the Trojan Helenus who claimed to "hear the voice of the timeless gods" (*Il.* 7.53). And there were two main oracles, that of Zeus in Dodona "where thy prophets live, the Selloi, bare foot and sleeping on bare earth" (*Il.* 16.234), and Apollo's oracle in Delphi where Agamemnon asked for advice about the outcome of the expedition to Troy (*Od.* 8.80). But neither Homeric poem seems aware of the important and often decisive role oracles played in the ancient world, from the Archaic Age of the Greeks to the end of pagan antiquity.

Divination was as much concerned with the present as with the future: most of the time, it was a present crisis more often than a future undertaking that led people to use divination. Like the members of most societies around the globe, Greeks or Romans could choose between several different ways of seeking divine advice about their problems. On the one hand, there were long-established institutions that offered divinatory services through ritual means; most of them belonged to Apollo. In some cases, the client would directly meet with the divinity, usually in a dream. After specific rituals that prepared him for contact with the divine, he would spend a night in the sanctuary, in what was often called the "sleeping room," *enkoimeterion*; if the need arose, temple-priests would help to interpret the dream in the morning. This method, called "incubation" after the Latin for "to sleep in," *incubare*, was widely practiced in the healing sanctuaries of Apollo's son Asclepius, and it survived in Christian times when local saints began to replace the pagan healing divinities. Contact also could be indirect and rely on a medium who connected the human petitioner with the divinity, such as the famous Pythia in Delphi. Such a human medium was thought to have access to the god's mind because she or he was possessed by the divinity. Spirit-possession as a way of communication with the supernatural world is an almost global phenomenon, although the specific forms and explanations vary from culture to culture. Sometimes, however, the communication relied solely on a set of oracular texts, inscribed on lots or on a chart; the petitioner drew a lot or threw one or several dice in order to determine which answer would be his. Sometimes, a human medium was added to this, such as the boy who, in the oracle of Fortuna Primigenia in Roman Praeneste, modern Palestrina, drew the lot for the petitioner. Children were thought to have an easier access to the divinity, and they also acted as medium in many private oracular cults in antiquity.

Besides these institutional oracles, there were the "free-lancers." Professional seers inspected the entrails, especially the livers, of sacrificial animals, interpreted the flight of birds, or knew how to perform divination with a bowl of water or a mirror or by yet another of the many methods of private divination we hear about in antiquity. Oracle-sellers (*chresmologoi*) sold answers from bookish collections of texts that had been uttered, as they claimed, by famous inspired prophets, such as the Sibyl. Interpreters of dreams counseled people whose dreams seemed to predict some future event, and astrologers, in growing number through the centuries, offered the services of their discipline that was riding on the tenuous borderline between science and religion. Sometimes, these free-lancers were quite respectable: they served as seers with the commanders of regular armies or of mercenary groups, or advised kings and emperors. Often enough, however, they were on the margins of society, foreigners traveling from city to city, selling their services to whoever was willing to pay for them, and complementing these divinatory services with other useful rituals, such as initiations into mystery cults that promised a better life after death, or spells that put one's enemy out of action, attracted a desired person, or helped one's favorite charioteer win the race.

In cognitive terms, divination exploits the human need to make sense of as many data as possible that are constantly fed into our brains. This ability to make better sense of the world than our animal competitors gave humans the cutting evolutionary edge. Recently, scholars have begun to explain religion in the same terms. To put it somewhat simplistically: to understand otherwise inexplicable (and therefore disturbing and frightening) data with which the human brain must deal, we assume that superhuman agents intervene in our lives. These divine agents act and react just like we do, but they are stronger, wiser, and better than we are. This theory explains why what to our modern rationality are random phenomena were understood as signs in ancient divination – mostly opaque signs that needed further interpretation but that certainly were not random. The shape of a sheep's liver, the flight of birds, a chance uttering overheard in a critical situation, the constellation of certain planets at a given time, or the working of the brain during sleep were all taken as signs with which a divine agent announced future events or answered anxious questions in a crisis. When divination did not focus on random natural events, it created them in a ritual process. Throwing dice, drawing lots (helped by naive children or irrational animals), falling into a trance, viewing the chance patterns made by oil on a surface of water were randomizing devices that opened up a crack in the rational causality of daily life; through it the hand or voice of a superhuman being signalled an answer to the more or less pressing question a human might put before it.

APOLLO'S DIVINATION

Nothing of this was necessarily connected with Apollo; he was not the only oracular divinity in the ancient world. If one assumed that gods knew more than humans, then any divinity could reveal the future; the same was true for heroic seers, and perhaps even for all dead ancestors. Zeus was not only consulted in Dodona but also in his sanctuary at Olympia and, in the guise of the Egyptian god Ammon, in his oasis sanctuary of Siwa in Northeastern Egypt. Ammon became famous among the Greeks when he greeted the visiting Alexander as his own son – hence the ram's horns on coins of Alexander, the ram being sacred to Ammon. Hermes presided over oracles that were guided by chance, such as those relying on dice or a chance utterance by an unrelated passer-by. The Boeotian god or hero Trophonios received visitors under the earth; they arrived after a harrowing Underworld journey. The hero Calchas sent prophetic dreams to whoever slept on the hide of a sacrificial ram in his Southern Italian cave sanctuary.

But these cases pale in number, quality, and impact before the role Apollo played in divination. The god himself was well aware of it. When, in the *Homeric Hymn to Hermes*, the new-born trickster Hermes tries to blackmail his older brother into granting him the gift of divination,

Apollo flatly refuses: "It is divinely decreed that neither you yourself nor another immortal may learn it. Only the mind of Zeus knows the future, and I in pledge have agreed and sworn a mighty oath that I alone of the immortal gods shall know the shrewd-minded counsel of Zeus" (v. 533–538). Prophecy is Apollo's, and Apollo's alone. This became more and more pronounced over the course of time. In the second or third century CE, someone asked Apollon in Didyma why so many oracles in the past were inspired either by sacred springs or by vapors rising from the earth but had now disappeared. The god himself answered:

> Wide Earth herself took some oracles back into her underground bosom; others were destroyed by long-lasting Time. By now, there are left under Helios who sends light to the humans only the divine water in the valley of Didyma, and the one of Pytho under the high peaks of Parnassus, and the spring in Clarus, a narrow opening for a prophesying voice.
>
> (Porphyry, *Fragment* 322 F.)

Only the three major Apolline oracular shrines, Didyma, Delphi and Clarus, remained functional, out of a much larger number in the past.

But already long before this date, almost all Greek oracular sites that had an international reputation belonged to Apollo, with the sole exceptions of Zeus' oracles in Dodona and, later, Siwa in Egypt. And there was a host of minor oracular shrines of Apollo throughout the Greek world, sometimes known to us only through the text of an ancient author or the chance-find of an inscription. A single inscription provides the evidence that the sanctuary of Apollo in the beautiful sacred grove at Gryneion in the Troas functioned as an oracle in late Hellenistic times, and a single text tells us of an Apolline oracle in Hierakome ("Sacred Village") in the Maeander valley: "There is a venerable sanctuary of Apollo and an oracle; the prophets are said to give responses in poetry of some elegance" (Livy 38.43, in an aside when describing a military expedition in the region). Minor oracular deities, such as the Boeotian god Ptoios, were identified with Apollo, as were indigenous Anatolian deities that had oracular cults. Even the dream healer Asclepius often operated in the shadow of his father Apollo: in several sanctuaries throughout the ancient world, Asclepius' cult was later added to an old cult of Apollo.

This dominant role is not easy to explain. After all, it is not Apollo whose plans and designs make the world function, but Zeus. The Greeks could rationalize this by saying that Apollo had access to Zeus' thoughts and plans as his favorite son, as does an oracle in Herodotus (7.141), or Apollo himself when he explains to his little brother Hermes why Hermes could not take over his brother's divinatory powers. But some

Greeks at least were not so sure that Apollo simply proclaimed Zeus' counsel. One Hegesipolis first consulted the oracle of Zeus at Olympia, and then went to Delphi and asked Apollo "whether the son was of the same opinion as the father." Aristotle, who tells the story (*Rhetorics* 2.23 p. 1398 b 34), is silent about Apollo's reaction. In the late nineteenth and early twentieth centuries, historians explained Apollo's role as an oracular god from his role as god of music and poetry, and constructed an impressive tribal past for it. "The god of Delphi, in fact, possesses all the attributes of the medicine-man, song, divination, healing, the unseen darts which strike down his opponents, and even the wand of laurel," as one scholar phrased it. Nowadays, medicine-men or, as they were called in more recent times, shamans, have lost some of their lustre as an explanatory paradigm in Greek religion (as we saw in the last chapter). Rather, most oracular shrines were situated outside the city and the outlying farmland in what the Greeks called *eschátiē*: it was in the wilderness, outside the space of civilized human activity, where humans were most likely to meet a god. One area of Apollo's activity is this wilderness, as it is his twin sister's, Artemis, whom scholars have called "Mistress of (wild) animals," *Pótnia therôn*, and "Lady of the Wilderness." Here, Apollo hunted game and chased nymphs such as Daphne, the daughter of a river-god who escaped his wooing by being changed into the laurel (*daphnē*), Apollo's sacred tree. Here too, he presided over the training of the young city warriors, the ephebes. Many myths talk about the isolation of Apollo's oracular shrines. The Cretans whom Apollo abducted to Delphi to become his priests were dismayed and shocked by the loneliness of the barren mountain he had moved them to. The foundation legend of the Didymaean sanctuary tells how Apollo seduced young Branchus "in the sacred wood" near Miletus (Callimachus, *Fragment* 229): Branchus was rewarded with the gift of prophecy and the "sacred staff of the god," and he became the ancestor of the Branchidae, the clan from which Didymaean prophets came in the Archaic Age. The Asklepieion of Epidauros was founded at the spot in the woods where the future healing hero was born, at the bottom of a hill on whose top Apollo had a lonely peak sanctuary.

THE HISTORY OF THE THREE MAJOR ORACLES OF APOLLO

Divination was a serious matter, from the peasant asking for advice about whether he should take up sheep-farming to the king consulting the god about matters of state. According to a story told by Herodotus (1.46–53), Croesus, the rich and powerful ruler of Lydia in Asia Minor in the sixth century BCE, went about the process with more than customary care – after all, he was planning an attack on the Persian Empire, the greatest power of his time. Thus, he first tested the most prominent oracles, those of Apollo in Delphi, Didyma, and little-known in Abae in Phocis, of Zeus in Dodona, and the Egyptian Zeus Ammon in his oasis in the Libyan desert, of Trophonios in Boetian Lebadeia, and of the seer hero Amphiaraus in Oropus in the borderland between Attica and Boeotia. He asked them all to tell him what he was planning at that very moment – but only the Pythia in Delphi and Amphiaraus in Oropus answered correctly: the king intended to cook a turtle and some lamb in an iron pot with an iron lid. Elated by this success, he sent immense sacrifices and gifts to Delphi, and he asked the god the second, vital question: should he attack the Persian king? The god gave the famously ambiguous answer: "When Croesus goes beyond the Halys, he will destroy a large empire" – his own, as it turned out, and not the Persians', as Croesus had assumed.

Fame and decline of Delphi

Even though Herodotus saw Croesus' fabulous dedications in Delphi, the story might be an invention, but it highlights the fame of Delphi in the Archaic Age. The antiquity of the Delphic sanctuary was already being debated in antiquity. Myth made Apollo its third or fourth oracular god, after Earth (Gaia), Themis, and perhaps Phoibē (whoever she may be): this may date the foundation of the oracle before the reign of Zeus who was the lover of Themis. Such a mythical date does not reflect any actual history. There are no traces of a Bronze Age antecedent for the Iron Age sanctuary: Delphi must have been founded in the early Iron Age, at some time between 900 and 700 BCE. But it soon made a deep impact on the Greek world, as already Homer shows, and was regarded as the major Greek oracle sanctuary of the Archaic and Classical Ages. Its early architectural splendor impressed the Greeks. Homer's audience must have admired the stone temple (the "stone threshold") of Delphi, an unusual sight anywhere in Geometric Greece, and even more so high up in these lonely mountains, far away from civilization: no wonder Greeks sometimes thought that Apollo was his own architect and builder. During the Archaic Age, this lone stone temple developed into the bustling sacred complex that we still can see today, even in its ruined state. A wide and curving road lead through a forest of statues and past dazzling buildings (the marble treasuries which the most powerful Greek cities vied with each other to build) up to the impressive temple on its terrace, with a monumental altar in front (figure 4). And if one looked at the landscape while walking up towards the temple, one could see the mountain peaks of Parnassus towering above the sanctuary; one could see the deep valley and the far sea below, with a narrow, steep and winding road that lead up from a small harbor. These vistas brought home once again what Apollo's civilizing force could achieve in the wilderness that was early Greece, as soon as one was outside its small cities. All this splendor resulted from Delphi's central role in Archaic Greek political and religious life. The Delphic god approved of most colonial ventures around the Mediterranean. He sanctioned laws such as the Spartan constitution, the so-called "Rethra," or the complex regulations of ritual purity for the colony Cyrene that we still possess; he legitimated changes in the constitution, such as the democratic revolution which Cleisthenes imposed upon Athens. He advised the Greeks on matters small and large, on how to be saved from the Persians as well as who should be honored with public dining in the city hall. And his advice was central to the denouement of many mythical narratives, not the least those put on the Athenian stage, such as the story of the Theban king Oedipus or of the Athenian king Aegeus and his wish for a son. So it does not surprise

Figure 4 Temple of Apollo in Delphi. View from the west. Copyright Alinari/Art Resource, NY.

that many grateful cities, kings, and aristocrats sent splendid gifts to Delphi and instituted sacrifices or festivals to Apollo Pythios at home; these gifts displayed the generosity and wealth of their donors to the international crowd that frequented the sanctuary. The Pythian Games, Delphi's athletic and musical contest, were among the four most prestigious contests in Archaic and Classical Greece, almost on a par with the Olympic Games. And even though the oracle was suspected to side with the Persians when they attacked Greece in 490 and again in 480 BCE, after the Persian Wars this was conveniently forgotten; Delphi's glory and credibility were quickly restored. In Hellenistic times, the oracle advised the senate of Rome, as it had advised the king of Lydia centuries earlier. Its fame was so great throughout the Mediterranean that even pirates heeded it: when the Romans sent a golden mixing bowl to Delphi, to thank the god for helping them conquer Veji in 395 BCE, pirates from the island of Lipari intercepted the ship but let it go when they learned about the addressee of the cargo (Livy 5.28). A lasting moment of glory came in 278 BCE, when a snowstorm or, as pious legends had it, the god himself drove away a marauding army of Gauls who had pushed south from the Balkans and were attracted by the gold hoarded in the sanctuary. The Delphians seized this as an occasion for self-propaganda, instituted a new festival and new games, the Soteria, "Salvation Day," and sent out invitations to all Greek cities to participate.

The decline of Delphi began in 88 BCE. The Greeks let King Mithridates of Pontus, a minor local ruler in the southeastern corner of the Black Sea, seduce them into a misguided revolt against the oppressive rule of Rome; in Ephesus alone, a resentful mob killed 80,000 Italians. Rome's bloody and destructive revenge led to sharp economic decline throughout Greece and Asia Minor.

> When traveling back from Asia Minor, I sailed past Aegina towards Megara, (a friend of Cicero wrote in 45 BCE) and I began to look around. Aegina was behind me, Megara in front of me, to the right was the Piraeus, to the left Corinth: all these places were once flourishing, but now you see only ruins lying in the fields.
>
> (Servius Sulpicius, in Cicero, *Letters to his Friends* 4.5.4).

This decline affected Delphi, as it affected other oracles all over the Greek world that, after all, lived off the fees ("gifts") of their grateful clients. A century later still, Plutarch of Chaeroneia (about 46–120 CE), a philosopher, historian, and a Delphic priest, felt compelled to write a dialogue on *The Decline of Oracles* in which he pondered the reason for the loss of influence and prestige Delphi and many other oracles suffered. In Plutarch's time, however, Greece was on the rise again, not the least thanks to Nero's love for everything Greek. Half a century later, the new economic and cultural splendor was consolidated by hellenophile emperors, such as Trajan and Hadrian. This brought some glamor back to Delphi. The sanctuary survived, albeit in a diminished form, until a fire, perhaps intentional, destroyed the temple in the Christian fourth century. Restorations under the short-lived pagan revival of the emperor Julian (360–362 CE) had no long-term effect. In 385 CE, the Christian emperor Theodosius prohibited the practice of divination under penalty of death. At the time, Delphi had already ceased to give oracles.

Clarus and Didyma

During the Imperial epoch, two other oracular shrines of Apollo eclipsed Delphi's fame by far. Both were situated in Western Asia Minor, in the old colonial region that the Greeks knew as Ionia and that the Romans had organized as the province of Asia; it contained several impressive and old cities, from Smyrna and Ephesus in the north to Miletus in the south. One was the shrine in Clarus outside of the city of Colophon not far from Smyrna, the other the sanctuary of Didyma in the territory of Miletus. Both sanctuaries date back well into the Archaic Age; at that time, however, Didyma was much more important and visible than the rather small shrine at Clarus.

Clarus is mentioned already in the *Homeric Hymn to Apollo*. Its oracle, although not far from Lydia, did not attract the attention of Croesus, unlike the oracle of Didyma; it must have been too small, as was another oracular shrine of Apollo, at Gryneum, not much further north. The Clarian sanctuary lies in a small valley between Colophon and its harbour city Notium, and was surrounded by a sacred grove, as were the shrines of Didyma and Gryneum and many other temples of Apollo and his son Asclepius. The excavated temple remains belong to early Hellenistic times. But its greatest fame came later, when it had grown into an important international sanctuary, thanks to the sponsorship of Roman generals and emperors. Recent excavations have brought to light the main altar of the temple with provisions for the sacrifice of a hecatomb, one hundred cows or bulls: a lavish offering to the helpful god. During the second and third centuries CE Clarian Apollo was consulted by embassies from small and large cities in Western, Central and Southern Anatolia and as far north as the Hellespont, and he was so famous as to appear in some magical texts in far-off Egypt. The fame of Clarus survived into Christian times, despite the end of the cult imposed by the new religion: in some of its oracles, Christian writers argued, Apollo had spoken out in favor of monotheism. When asked "What is God?," he had answered in a long hexametrical text which begins thus: "Born from itself, teacherless, motherless, unshakable, not giving in to one name, but having many, living in fire: this is god, and we, his messengers (*ángeloi*) are a tiny bit of God." The text impressed a Christian thinker enough to cite it, centuries later, in a Christian collection of pagan arguments for monotheism.

Unlike Clarus, Didyma was consulted by Croesus in the middle of the sixth century BCE. Its history goes back even further than that. Pausanias claimed that the site preceded the settlement of the Ionians, and the myth names it as the place where Zeus had seduced Leto, the mother of Apollo and Artemis. Historical reality is less fantastic. The archaeological record of the sanctuary goes back to the eighth century BCE; the first preserved oracular inscription dates to shortly before 600 BCE. At that time, the sanctuary stood alone in its sacred grove, about ten miles south of Miletus to which it belonged politically. Milesians could reach it by sea: the sanctuary had its own small harbor. If they preferred, they could walk: a long and splendid sacred road connected the city with its outlying sanctuary; processions regularly used it. The last part of this road, before it entered the sanctuary, was built as an alley of magnificent statuary, after the example of monumental entrances into Egyptian temples; Milesian merchants had been doing business in Egypt and must have been deeply impressed by its splendor. Today, most of the statues are in the British Museum: an impressive monumental lion, statues of local dignitaries, princes, and aristocrats, but especially oracular priests, solemnly sitting on their thrones. The priests must have belonged to the clan of the Branchidae whose members were running the sanctuary in the Archaic Age: the major priest, the *prophétés* or prophet, had to come from this family. Their mythical ancestor Branchus was Apollo's boy lover and, as in other cases, the god rewarded the boy with the gift of prophecy (Conon, *FGrHist* 26.33).

After Croesus' misguided decision to attack the Persian king, bringing about his own downfall, the Persians conquered and ruled Asia Minor. We lack information about the fate of Clarus; again, as when Croesus disregarded it, it must have not been significant enough to attract attention. The noble Branchidae however, we are told, surrendered eagerly and handed over their treasure to the Persians. This did not prevent the destruction of their sanctuary, together with the city of Miletus, as a brutal reaction to the revolt of Ionia against the Persians in 494 BCE. When the Greeks liberated Ionia after the battle of Salamis in 479, the Branchidae went into exile to Persia, together with their treasures and the cult statue. Xerxes gave them a city; a century and a half later,

Alexander destroyed it, and his successor Seleucus brought the statue back to Didyma. During most of this time, the sanctuary must have stayed silent, although annual processions from Miletus to Didyma resumed immediately after the liberation from the Persians. The oracle itself sprang back into life for Alexander, proclaimed his divine descendance, and foretold his victory over the Persians. Seleucus in turn not only returned the cult image, he also initiated the rebuilding of the temple on a much grander scale: this is the temple whose imposing ruins still stand today. The sanctuary rapidly grew rich and survived the vicissitudes of late Hellenistic history surprisingly well, pirate raids included. But its most prosperous phase came, as with Clarus, under the philhellenic emperors of the second century CE. The emperor Trajan not only paid for the reconstruction of the sacred way from Miletus to Didyma, he even accepted the office of honorary prophet, as did his successor Hadrian and, much later, the emperor Julian whom the Christians called "the Apostate." Together with the entire Mediterranean world, the sanctuary suffered from the economic and military crisis in the third century, and even more from the hostility of the Christians. A Christian author gleefully preserves the oracle with which Apollo answered the emperor Diocletian when he consulted the god about how to treat the Christians: Apollo was plainly hostile to Christianity (Lactantius, *De mortibus persecutorum* 11). The end, however, was inevitable, and the edict of Theodosius that outlawed divination sealed the fate of this sanctuary as well. To mark the Christian victory, the innermost sanctum of the temple, the very place where the prophetess had sat and relayed the god's messages, was converted into a church.

METHODS OF DIVINATION

There were many methods of divination, in ancient Greece as elsewhere; this is not the place to list them all. One method, however, seemed to be the most widespread, and the most noble in the eyes of the Greeks: ecstatic divination, or, as Socrates calls it, madness (*manía*). "The best things," Plato has him say,

> arrive with us through madness when the gods give it as their gift. The prophetess in Delphi and the priestesses in Dodona have worked many gods for the Greeks, both for private men and for states, when they were in a state of madness, while they did little or nothing when they were in a sober mind. And if I would also talk about the Sibyl and all the others, I would unduly draw out my discourse.

> (Plato, *Phaedrus* 244 ab)

And in order to underline his point, he resorts to etymology: does not the Greek term for the science of divination, *téchnē mantikē*, derive from the term for science of madness, *téchnē manikē*? This etymology is whimsical and playful, but it makes its point: "mad" divination is the main Greek way to gain access to divine foreknowledge. The Delphian Pythia, the prophet in Clarus, the prophetess (and, perhaps, before the interruption worked by the Persians, the male prophet) in Didyma as well as the Sibyl or Cassandra uttered their prophecies in an abnormal state of mind, beyond sober rationality. They were, to the Greeks, *éntheoi*, "having a god inside," or *kátochoi*, "held down," being controlled by a superhuman agent.

It is not easy to translate what this meant to the Greeks into our own cultural perceptions. Historians of religion usually called all this possession, even spirit-possession, and psychologists made a case that the ability to enter such a state may be common to all humans. Even if this is true, it has also become clear that every culture has its own set of phenomena that manifest themselves in such an altered state of consciousness, and its own way of thinking about them. Modern anthropologists and historians of religion prefer the term (spirit-) possession to any other, thus following the lead given by the Greek term *kátochos*; the term, however, seems to have a somewhat negative Christian bias. The Gospels as well as many saints' Lives tell stories about demons possessing a human being and driving it into all sorts of antics. The saint or Christ himself has to restore serene normalcy by driving out the demon: autonomy of the mind seemed preferable to superhuman control of it. But there is also, at least in early Christianity, a positive view of such experiences, presumably carried over from the Jewish prophets. Paul is aware that God, or rather his Spirit, can grant "the gift of prophecy" or "the gift of tongues of various kinds" (1 Corinthians 12:7–10), and he is not averse to this, since it may show "that truely God is in you" (1 Corinthians 14:25). After all, he had such an experience himself when he "was caught up into paradise and heard words so secret that human lips may not repeat them" (2 Corinthians 12:4). However, once Christianity developed a strong hierarchy with the aim of controling religious teaching and spiritual life, Church authorities realised that it was easier to control minds that were not able and even proud to receive their own divine revelation. Thus, already in the third century CE the Montanist Christians, a group that practiced individual prophecy, were outlawed as heretics.

Paul's description of the church of Corinth makes another point. The altered state of consciousness of his congregation could take many forms, among them prophecy and glossolalia (speaking in tongues), but also healing, miracle-working, or interpreting the words of those who were speaking in tongues. Modern assessments of these types of ritual behavior – as frenzy, ecstasy, chaos, or loss of control – are unable to do justice to such a variety of forms. In order to keep away from such notions, I prefer to use the term "inspired divination," in the case of Paul or the Montanists as well as for Apollo's prophets and prophetesses.

THE PROPHETS OF APOLLO

The Pythia

The medium in Delphi was usually called the Pythia, reflecting simply that she was a part of the religious establishment at Pytho, Delphi's other name. When the Pythia becomes visible through our texts, she is a mature woman: in the opening scene of Aeschylus' tragedy *The Eumenides*, she describes herself as old (v. 36), and vase paintings of this scene show her with white hair. A much later account explains her age as the result of a reform: originally, the Pythia could be a young woman and a virgin, but when a Thessalian raped a young and very attractive Pythia, the Delphians decided that, in order to avoid further incidents of this sort, no Pythia should begin her office before the age of fifty. But even being an old woman she should wear a maiden's dress in memory of the former state of affairs (Diodorus of Sicily, 16.26). The dress was more than just a symbol: during her time in office, the Pythia was always supposed to live chastely; but since she was not elected before a mature age, she could not be expected to have lived a celibate life during the many preceding years. And virginity was never a condition for election: in some inscriptions, proud Delphians claimed the Pythia as their grandmother. However, a virginal life *was* expected from her colleague, the prophetess in Didyma; here, nothing is said about an age limit, and it seems reasonable to assume that the Didymean prophetess was elected as a young girl into a life of permanent celibacy.

Behind all this is a specific view of inspiration and sexuality. Christian authors could be quite crude about it, for obvious reasons: Apolline inspiration competed with their own inspired religion, and they did not like it.

> They say that this woman, the Pythia, sits on the tripod of Apollon and spreads her legs; a nefarious vapor enters her body through her genitals and fills the woman with madness (*mania*): she loosens her hair, falls into a frenzy, has foam around her mouth and utters words in a state of madness.
>
> (John Chrysostom, *Homily in 1 Corinthian 29, 260 BC* [after 350 CE])

This is a polemical parody of a divinatory session in Delphi which did not just influence all later Christian authors; modern accounts of the frenzied Pythia leave out the sex but keep the foam. But as with every successful parody, there is a factual basis to it, although heavily distorted. Apollo, as we saw already with Branchus, distributed prophetic gifts as rewards for sexual gratification. Furthermore, in some descriptions of possession, there was a sexual undertone: it was unmistakable when Virgil described the possession of the Cumaean Sibyl by Apollo (*Aeneid* 6.77–80), and Herodotus told how the ecstatic priestess of Apollo in the Lycian city of Patara slept with the god in the sanctuary (1.157). Similar ideas are found in other cultures as well. This explains why the Pythia, Apollo's prophetess, had to be a virgin, no human's lover: the god is a jealous lover, as many of his myths make clear, and he would not bestow the gift of prophecy upon someone else's beloved. If this condition was impossible to meet, as with many Pythias, it could at least be created by ritual: there is no need to think that a Pythia was always a young girl.

We do not know how a Pythia was selected. Presumably, she had to show a disposition for mediumship, but no sources tell us whether or how this was tested. In Imperial times, some Pythias came from leading families in Delphi, just as the Didymaean prophetesses of that period came from the leading local families of Miletus: a disposition for mediumship might be hereditary and bring prestige. On the other hand, Plutarch the Delphian priest is aware that the woman who was serving as Pythia in his time "grew up in the house of poor farmers and brought no poetical skill or any other faculty and experience with her: . . . inexperienced, uninformed in almost everything and a virgin in her soul, she is together with her god" (*On the Oracles of the Pythia* 22. 405 CD). And as with every other Pythia, she was prevented from gaining more experience during her entire period of office. She lived in her own house, somewhere inside the sanctuary, and was carefully isolated from contact with any foreigner. This may have been intended to keep her from being unduly influenced by any client's interests.

Most of the time, a Pythia's life must have been fairly monotonous, if not outright boring. Originally, our sources assert, the god only spoke once a year, on his birthday – the seventh day of the spring month Bysios. Later he deigned to answer once every month, or more frequently when special guests came. But even then, the Pythia might in the end remain silent. Whoever sought the god's advice first had to pay a fee and then had to offer a sacrifice, usually a goat – had not Apollo promised abundant sacrificial meat to the shocked Cretans whom he had abducted as his first priests? His imposing marble altar, a gift from the island state of Chios, is still visible next to the temple doors. Before being killed, the sacrificial animal was drenched in water: if it did not very vigorously and audibly shake the water off, the god was not ready for consultation. This developed from regular Greek sacrificial practice; there, the animal was sprinkled with water to make it nod its head as if consenting to the sacrifice. The Delphic practice exaggerated the traditional rite: there was more at stake than the simple consent of the victim, the god must also be willing to communicate intimately with the Pythia. We know of one case when the priests forced the Pythia to prophesy despite the goat's bad omen: she lost her mind and died a few days later. However, if the sacrificial animal signaled the god's agreement, the Pythia entered the most holy room (*ádyton*), took her place on the tripod, Apollo's sacred symbol, and waited for the answer from the god. To prepare herself, she bathed with water from one of the sacred springs, Castalia, and fumigated flour on a small altar in the sanctuary. The adyton was in the innermost part of the temple, though all archaeological traces have been destroyed by the construction of a church. Archaeologists have discerned the traces of a barrier (or a thin wall) that separated the first third of the temple's interior from this innermost part. While some personnel – a priest, a prophet (if he is not the same as the priest), the "Sacred Men" – accompanied the Pythia into the adyton, the client waited in this ante-room from which he could at least hear, if not see the Pythia.

The details of how the Pythia communicated with her god are still highly debated. A French scholar remarked pertinently: "The last Pythia took this knowledge with her into her grave." Two issues are crucial: did she prophesy in ecstatic frenzy (as John Chrysostom graphically depicted), and was she possessed by the god? Opinions have diverged widely over time. Ancient accounts are few and contradictory, and the crucial area of the temple is lost beyond restoration. Lack of evidence has never prevented scholars from attempting answers, however. For a long time, it seemed accepted knowledge that the Pythia prophesied in an incoherent ecstasy, caused by gaseous emanations arising from the soil; the priests then turned her babblings into proper hexameters, and inserted their own political reading. More recently, scholars have objected to the crude materialism and simplistic Machiavellianism of this picture. Although some ancient sources mention specialists who were versifying the Pythia's utterances should they be in prose, this does not mean that the Pythia talked gibberish, or that the priests needed such an instrument of political manipulation. Thus, scholars preferred to understand her as a spirit medium comparable to modern examples such as the famous Madame Blavatsky, with the god entering into her and using her vocal organs as if they were his own. Others again, still thinking of ecstatic frenzy, followed a lead in a Byzantine author that she was chewing laurel; well before drug-induced trance became fashionable after 1968, these scholars assumed that the leaves contained a hallucinogenic substance which brought about her ecstasy. Other late sources tell that she was drinking water from a sacred spring that flowed in the adyton; this was recently combined with reports of possible hallucinogenic vapors into the hypothesis that this water contained traces of a psychotropic substance.

Over time, most of these ideas have been disproved. Chemical analysis showed that laurel does not contain any hallucinogenic substance, and archaeologists who valiantly tried to chew it ended up with nothing more spectacular than green teeth. Archaeological excavations showed no trace whatsoever of a spring in the adyton; a small spring, the Cassotis, was flowing at some distance uphill from the temple, but its water never entered it. More fundamentally, it has been shown that the Pythia did not speak in frenzied ecstasy, with loosened hair and foam around her mouth, or in tongues as Paul's Corinthians. Ancient accounts about the actual session insist on the serenity and clear language of the Pythia, and vase-paintings always show a composed female prophetess sitting on the tripod, be it the Pythia or her mythical predecessor, the goddess Themis; vase painters were able to depict ecstasy, as the many menads on Greek vases show. Only one pagan text talks about her frenzy, but this was the result of her being forced to enter the adyton against her own and the god's will; this was the incident that killed her. Plutarch contradicts the idea that the god spoke through her vocal organs; he insists that one heard only the Pythia's voice: "Neither the sound nor the inflection nor the vocabulary nor the metrics are the god's, but the woman's; he grants only the inspiration and kindles a light in her soul towards the future; such is her *enthousiasmós*" (*On the Oracles of the Pythia* 7.397 CD). And his contemporary Dio Chrysostom, a famous orator from Prusa in Western Anatolia, pointed out that Apollo would speak "neither Dorian nor Attic" nor any other human language, but that it was the medium's language one was hearing: the Pythia basically was a translator of Apollo's thoughts, and if already translations from one human language into another are always defective, even more so the translation from god to human: "That is why oracles are often unclear and deceive humans" (*Oration* 10.23). Thus, far from being frenzied and talking in tongues, the Pythia as a translator is as much *traduttore* as *traditore*, in the famous Italian saying.

All this does not mean that the Pythia, when prophesying, was in an ordinary state of mind: she could quietly and lucidly answer the questions of her clients, and nevertheless be in that altered state of consciousness that her own culture associated with being inspired. After all, everybody agreed that she prophesied in a state of *mania*, madness, and that she was *kátochos*, controlled by Apollo. In the *Eumenides*, Aeschylus has her talk on her own function: "I tell the future wherever the god leads me" (*Eumenides* 33). He is in control, not she: "The god makes use of the Pythia in order to be heard by us" (Plutarch, *On the Oracles of the Pythia* 21.404 D).

Control, however, is ambivalent. It can come from outside, as with a puppet on a string, or from within, with the god slipping into a human body. Both views are found in antiquity. "It is utterly simplistic and childish," says one of the interlocutors in Plutarch's *On the Obsolescence of Oracles*, "to believe that the god himself would slip into the body of the prophetess (as in the case of the bellytalkers who . . . are now called *Pythones*) and that he would speak using their mouths and vocal chords as his instruments" (9. 414 DE). This protest has a theological basis. The divine world is essentially different from the human – how could a god slip into a human body? But the vehemence of the criticism shows that the very idea existed, and that Apollo could be understood as a body-snatcher, in Delphi and elsewhere. Why else would the bellytalkers (Greek *engastrímythoi*, "having words in their bellies") be called *Pythones*, with a word that is again connected with Delphi's other name, Pytho? But Plutarch's friend, as other ancient observers, opted for the other solution: the god controlled the Pythia from outside.

Despite the many voices that insist on the Pythia's serenity, the view that Delphic prophecy implied some sort of violent trance is not entirely unheard of in antiquity. It existed in the Christian parody; and the parody was based on pre-Christian stories. There are two competing myths about the origin of the Delphic oracle. One is the story told in the *Homeric Hymn to Apollo*, where the god himself founded his oracle after having killed a dragon, and where he called the place Pytho, "Stinkton," after the stench of the dragon's rotting body. The other is the account of how Delphi's divinatory properties were discovered; here, these properties pre-exist the foundation of Apollo's sanctuary. The story is attested long after the Hymn: it is repeated in several sources with only minor variations, from Diodorus of Sicily in the first century BCE onwards; parts of it are alluded to as early as Aeschylus' *Eumenides*. In this story, a herd of goats was instrumental in discovering the source of the oracle. In very early times, these goats were grazing around a chasm in the ground which channelled subterranean gas to the surface. This was the spot where the adyton of the sactuary would be located. Goats that happened to breathe the gas pranced about strangely and made unusual sounds, a sort of goatish glossolalia. When this happened repeatedly, one curious goatherd inspected the spot, inhaled a whiff of the gas himself, and promptly began the same sort of outlandish behavior. The travel writer Pausanias even credits him with fully formed Apolline oracles. Whatever it was, news of the occurrence attracted a crowd who, in turn, shared the same ecstatic experience. The early Delphians founded an oracular shrine on the spot and dedicated it to Gaia, the goddess of what there is in the earth. Later, the oracle was taken over by Themis, goddess of divine justice, and finally by Apollo, its present-day owner. The story explains the role of the goat as the main sacrificial animal. Goats were as susceptible as humans to the phenomenon, and thus came to play a major role in the oracular ritual. It also defines the state of consciousness in which humans gave oracles as ecstatic (*enthousiasmós*, in Plutarch's words); it attributes this to the force of a subterranean gas that was fed into the adyton; and it sketches a divine history of the oracle: from an oracle of Gaia, it developed into an oracle of Apollo.

Thus, there is a double tension already inherent in the ancient accounts of Delphi and its prophecies. First, as to the Pythia being controlled by the god: Some understood this as the result of possession, with the god entering the Pythia's body, others contradicted this view on theological grounds. Secondly, as to this control expressing itself as an altered state of the Pythia's consciousness. In the foundation myth, this took the form of ecstatic behavior and even some sort of glossolalia, whereas in the reality of the oracle's daily practice, the Pythia spoke in her own voice, either in hexameters or in a prose that experts then versified. This double tension has to be explained. For practical reasons, any divinatory system tries to keep the line of communication between the divine source of information and the human client as short as possible. The shortest distance possible would be the immediate revelation of a god to a human, but this happens very rarely in any religion. Given the essential gap between god and human, some distance is unavoidable, and in the cultic reality of Delphic divination, it is the Pythia – a human being who has a special relationship with the god – who bridges the divide. The myths, however, extrapolate from this to indicate a much larger distance between humans and gods. Possession by a god means the loss of a vital and central part of one's humanity – loss of control, memory, and identity. Both views, the mythic and the cultic, are necessary for the function of the oracle where two such incompatible worlds, god and humans, come together, and they supplement each other. Modern scholars created a monolithic theory out of what in reality had only been complementary views.

This leaves us with the mysterious gas, the source of inspiration and ecstatic behavior both in the foundation stories and Christian polemics. Its existence and role had been challenged already by Plutarch; the Church Fathers took it as a given, since such a materialistic view helped them to unmask the oracle as substance abuse. In the first century BCE, the geographer Strabo described the adyton as

> a cave, very deep but not very wide at the top, out of which an inspirational gas (*pneuma enthousiastikón*) was rising and over which a high tripod was set; the Pythia ascended it, received the gas, and prophesied in prose and in metre.
>
> (9.3.5)

Other sources concur and make the gas a standard feature, and one might even be tempted to derive the name Pytho with its easy etymology ("Stinkton") from a very specific and not very agreeable smell in the region. The French excavations of the temple that started in the late nineteenth century found only solid rock, with no visible chasm or cave out of which a gas could rise. This seemed to be the end of the story: archaeology, once again, had exploded the ancient myths.

The reality, however, seems to be more complex. Among Apollo's oracles, Delphi is the only site where we hear of a gas as the source of the medium's ecstasy. Under another oracular temple of Apollo, in Hierapolis in Phrygia, a late philosopher claimed to have found a cave in which toxic gases collected; excavations have confirmed it. But no ancient source connects this with ecstatic prophecy; inscriptions attest only to a lot oracle in this sanctuary. Moreover, no one ever came up with a convincing explanation as to why so many ancient sources mention vapors rising from a chasm in the adyton to induce the Pythia's trance: why not assume that they, after all, knew more than we do? And it seems that antiquity may have been finally vindicated. A few years ago, the Greek government ordered a geological survey of the wider region of Delphi, for reasons that had nothing to do with archaeology: the government needed a site for an underground waste deposit that would be safe from earthquakes. The geologists found two fault lines that cut through the mountains behind Delphi; they cross each other exactly under the adyton of the sanctuary. The original French excavation reports in their turn had mentioned tiny fissures in the rock, but they were dismissed as insignificant: conditioned by the ancient sources, the archaeologists were looking for the chasm or cave mentioned in the texts, not for minuscule cracks, although even those could have released subterranean gas. More interestingly still, the faults lead down to geological layers that carry petroleum and from which gas might emanate. Chemists surmise that these fumes might be related to the kind of gas used as an anaesthetic in nineteenth-century dentistry. Rising through the fissures, it would have appeared above ground; the smell may have led to the installation of the oracle. And if it collected in the closed space of the adyton, its presence would have been even more strongly felt.

But there are still problems with such an explanation. Already Plutarch had insisted that only the Pythia was affected by trance, never her attendants in the adyton or any other person in the temple. Yet would not the vapors be dispersed through the entire interior of the temple (*On the Obsolescence of Oracles* 46)? Plutarch used this observation as an argument against any presence of vapors; the Platonist could not agree with a material explanation. But it might simply show that, whatever substance it was, it was not strong enough to induce trance; it simply smelled. And there is no urgent need to explain the trance in purely material terms. Trance, like any altered state of mind, can be induced by mental processes alone; it is a conditioned reflex, set off by any sensory trigger to which a susceptible person has been conditioned. In the case of Delphi, the Pythia had been well prepared for her encounter with the god through a series or ritual acts, from a preliminary bath to sitting on the tripod; the smell of the gas might function as the final trigger. In our present state of knowledge, this is not much more than a hypothesis that may explain some of the idiosyncrasies of the Delphic oracle. Future archaeological research is needed in the adyton to verify the presence of fissures and, if possible, to trace the source of the gas, if there was gas.

Clarus and Didyma

> There are those who give oracles having drunk water, such as the priest of Clarian Apollo in Colophon; others are sitting over openings in the ground, such as the women who give oracles in Delphi; others again are breathing inspiration from water, such as the prophetesses in Didyma.

With these words, the Neoplatonic philosopher Porphyry (243–*ca.* 305 CE) characterized the inspirational methods in the three major oracle shrines of Apollo (Iamblichus, *On the Mysteries of Egypt* 3.11, p.123.14). Like Plato, he emphasized divine inspiration as a divinatory method, whatever the exact method of achieving it: the Neoplatonists were convinced that ecstasy was the only route to knowledge of the supreme god.

Clarus

Clarus and Didyma have the use of water in common. Both sanctuaries are built around a sacred spring; both are well excavated: this supplements the meager literary record. In the Clarian sanctuary, the spring flowed in an underground chamber, at the very end of a somewhat labyrinthine subterranean floor under the temple; this spring chamber was directly under the image in the temple cella (figure 5). From its front hall (*pronaos*), two symmetrical flights of stairs led into a narrow hallway that opened into a large chamber with benches on two sides. From here a passage led into the small spring chamber. When asked to prophesy, the priest descended into this chamber, drank from the spring, entered into inspired contact with his god and answered in verses; like the Pythia, he was "a man without great knowledge of letters and poetry." According to the historian Tacitus, who gives us this description (*Annals* 2.54), he did not even know the question: "It was enough to hear the number and the names of the visitors." It was the visit of the prince Germanicus in 18 CE which prompted Tacitus to this description; "we are told," Tacitus concluded his account, "that he predicted an early death to Germanicus,

Figure 5 Sanctuary of Apollo in Clarus, late fourth century BCE. View of the underground chamber from the west. Copyright Vanni/Art Resource, NY.

although in an ambiguous way, as oracles are wont to do." This description, the only substantial one we have of a visit to Clarus, is vivid and detailed; perhaps Tacitus was drawing on the memoirs of Germanicus' wife Agrippina who traveled with her husband.

Germanicus, the descendant of Augustus, and a visitor of distinction, could presumably descend into the underground chamber; but he had to wait on the benches in the larger room. From here, he would have heard the murmur of the spring and the verses spoken by the inspired priest. Not everybody, however, was allowed to come so close: in order to "go down" (*embateuein*), one had to undergo an initiation, a presumably costly privilege offered only to the select few. Throughout Greece, initiations were a ritual means of entering into close and often personal contact with a divinity. At the same time, the ritual imposed utter secrecy on the experience of such an encounter: this must have been true for Clarus as well. Ordinary clients waited upstairs, in the pronaos of the temple, for an attendant priest to bring them the oracle's answer, written down and sealed.

At least when a city sent an ambassador to Clarus, as cities did with all oracles (nor had Croesus traveled to the shrine, but he sent an emissary), he was not supposed to learn the god's answer before his return. Once he was back in his city, he would report to the assembly; only then, he would break the seal and read the text. His voice served as a substitute for the god's, as it does in this oracle for the city of Pergamum:

> To you, descendants of Telephos – you are living in your lands, more honored by king Zeus than most others, and the children of thundering Zeus, his gray-eyed daughter Athena who withstands all wars, Dionysus who makes forget pain and makes grow life, Asclepius the healer of evil disease; among you, the Kabiroi, sons of Ouranos, were the first to see new-born Zeus, when he left his mother's womb on your acropolis – to you, I will tell with unlying voice a medicine in order to escape a terrible plague. . . .
>
> (Merkelbach and Stauber, *Epigraphica Anatolica* 27, 1996, 6 no. 2.1–11)

The text is too long to be cited in full, but its style is clear: it is a complex poetical composition in which the god addresses the city directly. He evokes its mythic history and its major myths and cults: the city as the birthplace of Zeus, founded by Zeus' son Telephus, and protected by Zeus and Athena, whose sanctuaries were on the acropolis, and by Asclepius, whose healing sanctuary at this period, the mid-second century CE, was one of the major sanctuaries of the region. The god, it seems, was well adapted to an age that had a mania for mythic history, and preferred a poetic style that privileged almost baroque complexity over unadorned simplicity.

Didyma

Whereas the priest in Clarus drank the water from the spring in the sanctuary, the prophetess at Didyma had a less direct contact with the sacred water. After Seleucus had brought back Apollo's statue from Persia, the Milesians replaced the earlier temple with an unusual and monumental building that centered on a sacred spring. From the outside, the building looked like an ordinary temple, albeit a very large and roofless one. A flight of steps led to the impressive pronaos with two rows of giant columns in front of the main entrance. This monumental entrance did not lead into a cella, as in any other temple: its double doors opened over a threshold that was almost as high as a man. No human could step over it; it led into another realm. On the other side of the threshold, a flight of stairs descended into the main space, a monumental roofless enclosure that took the place of the usual cella. Its high walls surrounded a large open area containing a small temple that sheltered the sacred spring. At the beginning of a prophetic session, the prophetess either dipped her foot into the spring water or wetted the hem of her sacred dress with it: this was enough to send her into a trance. Like the Pythia, she uttered her oracle while sitting on a special seat; our only source calls it "axle" (*axôn*), whatever that means (Iamblichus, *On the Mysteries* of Egypt 3.11, p.127.6). She had prepared herself for this task by bathing and fasting, methods commonly used to purify oneself for an encounter with a god. Visitors to the oracle, one imagines, were waiting in the vast pronaos: after a preliminary sacrifice to Apollo, they had already handed over their request to a temple attendant. Then, once the prophetess had uttered her oracle, a priest walked up to the door and repeated the text to its addressee, or perhaps handed it down in written form. We know some of these oracles from inscriptions that were dedicated in Miletus, or in the sanctuary at Didyma itself. Other oracles are transmitted in literary sources, not least the Neoplatonist and Christian authors who were interested in the theology contained in Apollo's answers. Didymaean oracles of the second century CE are couched in verses just as grandiose as those from Clarus: Apollo had adapted to the style of the epoch in Didyma just as he had in Clarus.

We have no information from either place about the characteristics of the sacred water that inspired the prophets. Was it ordinary spring water, or did it contain a hallucinogenic substance such as some scholars have suspected in Delphi? Iamblichus rejects the claim that "a divine spirit (*pneûma*) passed through the water" of Clarus, whatever that meant (*On the Mysteries of Egypt* 3.11, p. 124.17). The learned Pliny insisted that the Clarian water, while it inspired the priest, also shortened his life, but he did not explain why this was so (*Natural History* 2.232). One could suspect that the water was enriched with minerals: the wider region is rich in mineral sources – the hot springs of modern Pamukkale are not that far away, and closer still are other hot springs, the bath of Agamemnon where the king of Mycenae was cured of an ailment during the Trojan War; it still functions as a spa that cures rheumatism. However, the water that nowadays fills the Clarian temple basement is ordinary groundwater that is seeping in from the local river. The Didymaean source provided the locals with water in times of crisis, and none of them began to prophesy. And no mineral water has ever been known that would induce ecstasy: again, we are probably dealing with a conditioned reflex of the medium who was carefully prepared for the task.

Other Apolline oracles are also said to have made use of water or, in one case, of the blood of a sacrificial victim; animal blood is even less likely to contain hallucinogens than is mineral water. More importantly, the use of liquids as a trigger for inspirational divination is wide-spread in Apolline divination; Delphi with its chasm and its vapor is the one exception. But Delphi had sacred springs too. There was the small spring a few yards above the temple, the Cassotian Spring or Cassotis, and the large and famous source outside the sanctuary, the Castalian Spring or Castalia; the Castalia provided the water for the Pythia's preliminary bath. It is at least conceivable that in late antiquity, when Delphi paled before the fame of Clarus and Didyma, their rite, drinking sacred water, was introduced in Delphi as well. There are two authors from the second century CE, the satirist Lucian and the travel writer Pausanias, who affirm that the Pythia drank water from a sacred spring. Lucian combines water drinking with chewing laurel, and Pausanias claims that the Cassotis went underground and surfaced again in the adyton. This, however, is not accurate, for as we saw earlier, the latter is disproved by the excavations and and the former by experiment. And there is no earlier evidence for Delphic water-drinking: either Delphi adopted the practice of the more successful shrines, or the information we have is simply wrong.

OTHER PROPHETS: CASSANDRA, HELENUS, THE SIBYL

Apollo's role as patron of divination did not manifest itself only in specific oracular shrines. At least in mythology, many seers also were closely connected with him.

Cassandra

Mythical Troy had two seers, both children of king Priam: the twins Helenus and Cassandra. When their parents visited the shrine of Apollo Thymbraeus not far from Troy, they left the twins behind in the sanctuary. Coming back next morning, they found them asleep, and two snakes were licking their ears and eyes: this is why Helenus could hear the voice of the gods, as the *Iliad* has it (7.53), and why Cassandra had prophetic visions. But unlike Helenus, Cassandra was a highly problematic seer. The most beautiful among Priam's daughters, not only was she raped by the lesser Ajax in Athena's sanctuary, she attracted the attention of Apollo himself. The god promised her the gift of prophecy as a reward for her love; but as soon as he had bestowed his skills on her, she refused to surrender, and he took cruel revenge: while he could not remove his gift, he could see to it that nobody would believe her prophecies. Divination can be a problem to the prophet. In his *Agamemnon*, Aeschylus has Casssandra utter a last ecstatic prophecy in Argus immediately before her death in front of a chorus of Argive citizens. She invokes Apollo who "has ruined me utterly for the second time" (v. 1082), and foretells not only her own murder at the hands of Clytaemnestra, but also that of Agamemnon who had brought her home as part of the booty. The chorus is amazed that she, although now a slave, still prophesies: "The divine remains in the mind, though it be enslaved" (v. 1084). But then they stubbornly refuse to understand her: "Of these prophecies I have no understanding" (v. 1105).

The Sibyl

Another mythical prophetess was the Sibyl, and like Cassandra, her prophecies were ecstatic: "The Sibyl sounds with raving mouth," according to Heraclitus (late sixth century BCE). She was thought be the daughter of a nymph and a human: the human father made her mortal, the divine mother long-lived (according to some, nine hundred years) and, perhaps, prone to ecstasy; a Greek way of describing that someone was in an altered state of consciousness was to say that he was "seized by a nymph," *nymphóleptos*. Over the centuries, several places in the ancient world claimed to have been the home of the Sibyl, from Babylon to Praeneste in Italy. Ancient scholars solved this problem by assuming a plurality of Sibyls: this is why, on the ceiling of the Sistine Chapel, Michelangelo could combine Biblical prophets with Sibyls as the representatives of pagan and Biblical prophecy. Many Sibyls were thought of as priestesses of Apollo – such is the case with the Sybil of Erythrae in Ionia, the Sibyl of Troy who was a priestess of Apollo Smintheus, or the most famous one, the Sibyl of Cumae in Italy. When, in Virgil's *Aeneid*, Aeneas visits her, he finds her in the vicinity of the temple of Apollo that was on the town's acropolis (*Aeneid* 6.9–10). Another Sibyl was connected with the sanctuary of Delphi. Not far from Apollo's temple, visitors were and are still shown a rock on whose top "the first Sibyl sat after her arrival from Helicon, where she had been reared by the Muses" (Plutarch, *On the Oracles of the Pythia* 9): like the Muses (and like the Pythia), the Sibyl spoke in hexameters. And like the Pythia and Cassandra, the Sibyl was a virgin, for the very same reason: it was Apollo who claimed exclusive control over her sexuality.

But unlike the Pythia whose oracles were spoken and reflected the knowledge of Apollo himself, the Sibyl prophesied alone. Unlike the Pythia, she could no longer be consulted in person: she was dead in historical times, despite her life-span of nine hundred years; instead, her oracles were collected in books. Rome was said to possess three of these. According to legend, an old woman – the Sibyl of Cumae, as it turned out – visited the Roman king Tarquinius Priscus and offered him nine books; they contained, as she claimed, the fates of Rome. Tarquinius refused to buy them; the Sibyl burned three of them and insisted on the same sum of money. The king refused once more, and the Sibyl burned the next three while still demanding the same price. Finally, perplexed and angered, the king gave in and bought the three remaining books. These offered guidance to the Roman senate in times of crisis: at such moments, the senate would order one of its standing committees, the "Committe on the Performance of Rituals" (*de sacris faciundis*), to consult the books and relate the oracle to the senate. The books were kept on the Capitol in the temple of Jupiter Optimus Maximus, the main god of the Roman state. When in 83 BCE the temple burned down, the books were destroyed with it. The senate set up a committee that was to collect samples of Sibylline oracles from all over the Mediterranean world and to find out which of the rival Sibyls was the "real" one. When the committee selected the verses of the Sibyl from Erythrae, the senate sent its members to the small Ionian city to buy all the available verses and to organize them into a new set of Sibylline books. Later, the emperor Augustus had the books transferred to his new temple of Apollo on the Palatine. It proved to be a wise decision, since the Capitoline temple burned down again during the civil war of 69 CE. Apollo proved a better guardian of the Sibyl's verses than Jupiter had been, and only the Christianization of Rome ended the consultation of these books.

At that time, the Sibyl herself had been adopted by the Christians.

Since she was speaking in her own name and not in Apollo's, any god could inspire her. In the struggle of Judaism against hellenization, the Sibyl turned into a prophetess inspired by the One God, who had already inspired his own prophets in their fight against over-powerful Jewish kings. After the rise of Christianity, the Sibyl again switched sides: her oracles began to "predict" the arrival of Christ, his miracles, and his Passion. The Emperor Constantine, impressed with these prophecies, issued "from the temple of foolish superstition" (*Oration to the Saints* 18–21); his contemporary, the Christian writer Lactantius, collected the parallels between the sayings of the Biblical prophets and of the Sibyl and showed that these oracles were not fictions, as some pagans asserted, but true prophecies (*Divine Institutions* 4.15). For this reason, almost the only Sibylline oracles preserved today are a set of eleven books of Jewish and Christian origin.

SUMMARY

Throughout antiquity, Apollo remained the central god of prophecy. His little brother Hermes became the patron of minor divinatory forms, such as lot and dice oracles, and in Dodona and Siwa in Egypt, humans could access Zeus directly to gain information. But it was Apollo's major shrines – Delphi, Didyma, Clarus – where Apollo informed humans through his inspired priests or priestesses; and there existed smaller sanctuaries that offered similar services. The methods for gaining inspiration – for entering the altered state of mind that opened a window to the god's mind – varied from oracle to oracle and depended on local conditions. The main principle, however, remained the same: a priest or priestess, selected for the task because of his or her special ability for mediumship, served as the channel of communication between the god and the human inquirer. Mythical figures such as Cassandra, Helenus, or the Sibyl followed the same pattern of inspiration. Oracles from Delphi, Clarus, and Didyma were inscribed on stone and collected in books by pagan and Christian authors, in the latter case to prove Christianity's claims even through the mouth of a pagan god. In a similar way, Apollo's inspired prophetess the Sibyl served not only pagans, but Jews and Christians as well, and Sibyls could be paired together with Old Testament prophets to represent the reality and truth of divine inspiration.

APOLLO, GOD OF HEALING

GODS AND EPIDEMICS

In the *Iliad*, Apollo sent the plague, but also healed it. Homer's narration inserts itself into a background of Near Eastern story-telling. Apollo used arrows to spread a disease, as did Erra, the Near Eastern god of war and disease. And like Erra, Apollo was incensed about human behavior. Erra was angry because mankind neglected his cults, Apollo because Agamemnon violated the honor of his priest; in both cases the epidemic ended only when the god's wrath had been calmed. Ending the plague, however, was more difficult than triggering its inception: whereas the prayer of his priest, Chryses, was sufficient to set Apollo against the Greeks, the reverse prayer of Chryses had to be supplemented by ample atonement. In order to placate the god, the Greeks offered him a hecatomb, danced, and sang the paean for an entire day.

Unlike Erra, however, Homeric Apollo is not necessarily a plague god and a divine healer. Attack and release are part of a specific action pattern that explained disaster through a story of divine anger and allowed human counter-action through the ritual of placating the god. Throughout antiquity, and well beyond the world of the Greeks and the Romans, both individual diseases and vast epidemics could be understood as having been sent by a god whose rights a human had violated. Countless myths follow the same basic narrative sequence of the Chryses story, and many ancient texts attest to it as a personal experience. It has four parts: (i) knowingly or unknowingly, humans anger a god; (ii) the divinity sends a disease; (iii) divination determines the divine agent and the reason for divine wrath; (iv) a ritual placates the divinity and restores health. In the late fifth century BCE, the unknown doctor who wrote the treatise *On Sacred Disease* recognized the same pattern behind the traditional cure of epilepsy, and he vehemently argued against it: for him, epilepsy, the "sacred disease," was not a punishment sent by a god that would need ritual cures. Plain medical art is enough. There was no need for a seer to diagnose from the patient's symptoms which of the gods was thought to be responsible for the attack:

> If the patient imitate a goat, if he roar, or suffer convulsions on the right side, they say that the Mother of Gods is to blame. If he utter a piercing and loud cry, they liken him to a horse and blame Poseidon. Should he pass some excrement (as often happens under the stress of an attack) the name of Enodia is invoked; if it be more frequent and thinner, like that of birds, it is Apollo Nomius. If he foam at the mouth and kick, Ares has the blame.

Nor is there any need for elaborate ritual means of healing, "purifications and incantations," a special dress, and a special diet; the patient would be better off consulting his doctor than his seer or purification priest.

In the realities of ancient life, this chain of action and reaction, of divine intervention, human illness, and human ritual, did not have to be continous and unbroken; it is a construction to make a severe illness understandable and to find human action against it. Outside the intellectual needs of theologians, doctors, and poets, the explanation of a specific disease is less relevant than the protection which a superhuman being can give against the random attacks of maladies that have been the lot of humans since time immemorial. For countless centuries, afflicted humans turned towards powerful ancestors, gods, or saints, depending on their belief system. "Being at a loss, and having no treatment which would help, they concealed and sheltered themselves behind the divine and called the illness sacred, in order that their utter ignorance might not be manifest." This analysis, through which the learned Greek doctor tries to discredit the priests, might be called sneering and unjust, but it is not entirely wrong. Helplessness in the face of omnipresent disease has made humans turn towards the gods much more often than has the effectiveness of supernatural cures. Even in our epoch of industrialized medicine, religious healers and saints – Christian, Muslim, Hindu – still command an impressive following, and numerous pilgrims assemble at the shrine of the Virgin in Lourdes or walk for days to the temple of the Hindu and Muslim saint Ramdev in the Thar Desert in Northwestern India. Whereas in theory any divine agent should be able to help, in practice some are vastly more successful than others, in the past not otherwise than today.

Among the Olympians of Greek and Roman religion, Apollo was the most successful healer, and he might be more closely connected with illness already in *Iliad* 1 than the story is willing to concede. The paean that the Greeks address to him was generally used in healing songs, and Apollo the Doctor was worshipped in many places in Eastern Greece, from where Homer was said to come. Apollo shared this function with a local hero from Thessaly or Messene, his son Asclepius, who in the course of time eclipsed his father's reputation as a healer and appropriated his father's sacred song, the paean. The paean's name itself is connected with Paeon, the name of the gods' private physician in Homeric epic and one of Apollo's epithets in later Greece, where it is usually spelled Paean (*Paián*).

APOLLO (AND) PAEON/PAEAN

In the Homeric epics, Paeon (or rather, in Homer's spelling, *Paiēôn*) appears only rarely. In the *Odyssey*, the Egyptians are called "kinsmen of Paeon" because everybody in that fabulous country excelled at medecine and pharmacology (4.232): whoever Paeon was, he was a healer who knew his herbs and drugs. In the fifth book of the *Iliad*, the narrator describes how the mighty hero Diomedes, guided by Athena, fought and wounded even the gods: Ares himself was injured and rushed up to Olympus to show Zeus his "immortal blood," in a rather puerile act of hurt pride. Zeus did not seem to care overmuch, but at least "he ordered Paeon to heal him" (5. 899). Paeon promptly applied a salve that brought immediate relief. He had done the same for Hades, a generation before, when the Lord of the Dead received an arrow in his shoulder from Zeus' son Heracles (*Il.* 5. 401).

At a first glance, it looks as if, to the epic singers, Paeon was an independent god of healing. But there is a problem with this. Outside these Homeric passages, Paean is only once attested as an independent healer, and again in epic poetry. In a fragment of an obscure poem ascribed to Hesiod, Apollo, and Paean are clearly treated as two divinities: "If neither Phoebus Apollo [this singer says] does save us from death, nor Paean who knows remedies for everything" (Hesiod, Frg. 307). Everywhere else in ancient texts, the name Paean is a used as cultic epithet of Apollo that defines him as healer, in the same way as the paean is Apollo's song. It is thus possible that in the Homeric poems, too, the name Paeon really designated Apollo; Greeks and Romans could use epithets alone to stand in for a divine name, such as Delius for Apollo or Olympius for Zeus. When, in 73 BCE, Cicero accused Verres, the governor of Sicily, to have stolen "a marvellous and venerable statue of Paean" from a sanctuary of Asclepius, he meant an image of Apollo the Healer; the epithet alone was sufficient, and the context was clear. In

Homer's case, scholars have argued that he was reluctant to use epithets like this; a decision either way is not easy. It may well be that already the Homeric singers were uncertain about Paeon's identity; if pressed, different singers might have given different answers. It is interesting to note that a later scholar in Egyptian Alexandria, as puzzled as we but more radically minded, replaced Paean with Apollo in order to "clean up" the *Odyssey* passage.

Singers would have been uncertain with good reason. The name Paie-ôn had been handed down in their oral tradition from late Bronze Age Greece. Among the many divine names preserved in the texts of the Mycenaean Greeks, written in the so-called Linear B script, there is one Paiawon who received offerings, together with other divinities, Athena, Enyalius, and Poseidon. Paiawon is one of the Greek Bronze Age gods and goddesses whose cult disappeared after the collapse of the Mycenaean world; he left a trace only in the oral tradition that becomes visible to us through epic. If we can rely on the singers' memory (and there is no reason that we should not), Paiawon was a god of healing, a divinity with a formidable knowledge of herbs and drugs, the Mycenaean equivalent of the many healing divinities attested in the Bronze Age cultures of the Ancient Near East.

There is no evidence for Apollo from the Mycenaean period, and it seems safe to assume that he was not present in the pantheon of the Bronze Age Greeks (see Chapter 6). He must have arrived later replacing Paeon, whose name then became Apollo's epithet, expressing this fusion of divine personalities. In Iron Age Greece, Apollo Paean is present in several cities through all, from fifth-century Athens to Hellenistic Sicily and Lydia in the Imperial Age. There is no telling at which epoch Apollo was identified with the Mycenaean god, but it must have happened early, perhaps well before the age of Homer. After all, Apollo is worshipped as well as a healer in the *Iliad*, albeit not of gods, as Paean is, but of men: when the hero Glaucus is wounded, he calls upon Apollo, and the god tends him and stills the pain (*Il.* 17.528). And it may be more than just a consequence of Apollo's partisanship for the Trojans that he saves Aeneas from the battle and carries him to his temple where Leto and Artemis tend the wound he received from a sharp stone thrown at him by Diomedes (*Il.* 5.445).

This opens up a parenthesis on how we envision the fusion of different deities as a historical phenomenon. There is some guidance from later, better documented times for such a process, which was often the identification of a native local god with the imported god of immigrants or conquerors. Gods exist only as far as they are believed in, and belief usually manifests itself in cult, in prayers, sacrifices, processions, thank-offerings for their help. Thus, in order for a divinity to exist, there must be worshippers, a group that regularly performs a cult. "No man is an island": communication among groups leads to exchanges about one's own gods. Both groups may then see that these gods are very close in function and even appearance. From here, it is only a small step to the insight that each group is actually worshipping the same divinities, only under different names. This happened in early Bronze Age Mesopotamia, when the Sumerian-speakers who were living in the south of the vast plain of Euphrates and Tigris realized that many of their gods were the same as those adored by their northern neighbors, whose language was Akkadian. The Sumerian Enki, the trickster god, was understood as being the same as the Akkadian Ea; myths were borrowed and exchanged, and in the course of time, local scholars drew up entire lists of such linguistic equivalents, dictionaries of divine names. Another variation on the same process is visible when Greek merchants, mercenaries and travelers arrived in Egypt some time before 600 BCE. They tried to make sense of the complex pantheons of the Egyptian cities, and they did so by identifying Egyptian gods with their own. The result is visible in Herodotus' splendid account of Egyptian religion in the second book of his *Histories*: Isis was the same as Demeter, or Osiris as Dionysus. The Greeks, unlike the more scribally minded Akkadians, did not draw up lists; but when they finally conquered Egypt several centuries later, they fused the personalities in cult as well. The god whom the natives worshipped under the name of Amun was worshipped by the Greeks as Zeus, and since they were used to differentiating many single forms of Zeus by epithets, they hellenized the Egyptian name, turned it into an epithet and called the Egyptian god Zeus Ammon. The basis for such identifications was sometimes flimsy and impressionistic, which was certainly the case with this example: Amun was the supreme god of the Egyptian pantheon, and that was enough for the Greeks to call him Zeus, notwithstanding his ram's head.

Projected back to the undocumented transition period from the Bronze Age to the Iron Age, this means that a group of people who worshipped a god called Apollo met Mycenaeans who worshipped a healing god Paiawon, and since their Apollo was, among other things, a healer, they identified the two. Over time, it was the cult of Apollo that spread all over Greece, while Paiawon slowly disappeared, for uncertain reasons: perhaps the people who brought Apollo and who must have been non-Mycenaeans became dominant, or Apollo was perceived as such a powerful and helpful god that the descendants of the Mycenaeans took him over und subordinated their own Paiawon to him. Whatever the process, we only see its result: many local cults of Apollo with the epithet

Paean, and a dim memory of a god Paiawon in the traditional oral stories of the early Greek singers.

OTHER FORMS OF HEALING APOLLO

Overall, epithets that attest Apollo's healing power are not very common; we gain the impression that, after the Archaic period, the healer Apollo became somewhat less important. The inhabitants of Lindus, on the island of Rhodes, had their Plague Apollo, Apollo Loimios: he must have helped them during an epidemic. But there are two epithets that are widely attested: Iatros "Doctor" and Oulios. "The Milesians and the Delians call Apollo *Oulios*, which means 'Provider of Health' and a sort of Paean, since the word *oulein* means 'to be healthy' ": thus the geographer Strabo (14.1.6). When he adds: "Apollo, that is, is a healer," he may have been pointing out an aspect of the god that to his readers was no more self-evident, or he may have been simply stating the obvious. There are a few other cities whose inhabitants worshipped Apollo Oulios, and there was at least one association of doctors that did the same.

This association was at home in the South Italian city of Velia, and it has been found by archaeologists in the splendid excavations of this city, halfway between Naples and Reggio di Calabria. Velia was a Greek city, inserted into a native settlement whose name it adopted and hellenized: the Greeks called it Elea. Elea was founded by settlers from Phocaea, a small city not far north of Miletus; the Phocaeans were intrepid and enterprising sailors who, for a while, dominated the Western Mediterranean. Elea grew fast and turned into a beautiful and large city, as its ruins still show, with a spectacular tunnel under its acropolis hill that connected the old town with a more recent quarter. But its main claim to fame was not its beauty nor its richness, but its learning: it was the home-town of the philosopher Parmenides (early fifth century) and the philosophical school founded by him. Parmenides' revolutionary and intricate thinking about Being and Non-being deeply influenced Plato, and through Plato the entire Western philosophical tradition. But Parmenides left more tangible traces than this in his city.

When a visitor of early Imperial Velia entered the city from its harbor, a stately building on his right, immediately after the gate, would have aroused his curiosity. If he yielded to his impulse, he would have walked up a wide flight of stairs and entered a large court, surrounded on three sides by arcades; in its center stood an altar. A door to his right led him into a hall and, through it, into a large garden that again was surrounded by arcades. Both in the entrance court and the garden, he would have seen many portrait statues, most of them unmistakably Roman: their inscriptions showed them to be doctors and former presidents of the religious club housed in this complex: like any other decent club, this one too demonstrated its proud past through a picture gallery of its former presidents. Three statues, however, stood out among the busts of all the Roman notables: a statue of Asclepius (what we would expect in a doctors' club), a statue of Apollo, singing and with the lyre in his hand, and the portrait head of a bearded Greek philosopher: "Parmenides," as the inscription said, "son of Pyres, Ouliades, nature philosopher." "Nature philosopher" (*phusikós*) is the common Greek term for what we now call Presocratics, and Ouliades means literally "clansman of Oulios." Here, it cannot be anything but an honorary title: Parmenides was understood as the first member of this club that derived its legitimation from Apollo, and whose members in Roman Velia must have been mostly (or solely) doctors; we can assume that the altar in the court was dedicated to Apollo Oulios. It is, nevertheless, somewhat intriguing that this Apollo was represented as a musician. It might be nothing more than a coincidence: the statue is a copy of a famous classical Apollo, and the club bought and displayed it because of its fame. But it might just be that they attributed a special significance to a musical Apollo: at least among the Pythagoreans, music was regarded as a cure for psychic troubles. Pythagoras saw himself as a follower of Apollo, and his most prominent Sicilian follower, Empedocles, was both a *phusikós* and a physician.

The other epithet of Apollo as a healer is Iatros, "Doctor." Apollon Iatros was worshipped all over Ionia and the Black Sea colonies which the Ionians, especially the Milesians, founded between the seventh and the fifth century. He certainly was central in Miletus' most prominent and most northern colony, Olbia on the Crimea, at the mouth of the river Dniepr, the Greek Borysthenes. When Milesian settlers founded Olbia in about 600 BCE, they took their native cults with them, as Greek settlers usually did; this suggests that Apollon Iatros (or *Iētrós* in the local dialect) must have had a cult in Miletus itself, although we lack direct evidence. In Olbia, Apollon Ietros gained remarkably in importance, as did other forms of Apollo. The city's oldest sanctuary belonged to Apollon Ietros, Apollo Delphinios (another important Milesian god) had a temple next to the agora, and an Apolline oracle, presumably from Didyma, prophesied the future of the city in steps of seven, Apollo's sacred number: seven years, seventy years, seven hundred years. Settling so far north in a climate that is much harsher than the climate of Turkey's west coast, the settlers must have felt an acute need for divine protection of their health: this explains the rise of Apollo "Doctor." The same is true for other Milesian settlements along the Black Sea coast. The were built next to the often swampy mouths of the great inland rivers, such as Tyras at the inlet of the river Dniestr or Istrus in the wide delta of the Danube. Swamps bred disease, in antiquity no less than today.

But health was only one of the concerns of Apollon Iatros, as it was with most other healing divinities. The desire for children, especially male children, was another, and the perception of divine assistance with this problem was often expressed by the choice of the child's name. Greek personal names were easily understood by any native speaker. They were usually composed from two Greek words, one often the name of a god: Apollo-doros is the boy "whom Apollo has given." All over the Greek world, we find boys and men whose name contained the word Iatros, such as Iatrokles, "the Fame of Iatros," or Iatrodoros, "Gift of Iatros." The names indicate that the parents, or at least the mother, had prayed to a divine healer for a healthy son, and the wish was fulfilled. It need not have been Apollon Iatros: there were many places where Iatros did not refer to Apollo but to a Heros Iatros, a "Hero Doctor," as in Athens. In the cities of Ionia and their colonies, however, where this group of personal names is especially common, we can safely assume that parents wanted to thank Apollo "the Doctor" for his assistance.

FROM GREECE TO ITALY

In a world infested with hostile bacteria and often enough plagued by hunger and drought, the need for health is universal; a god whom people believe to be an efficient healer will gain widespread cult. Apollo the Physician made a career for himself not only in the cities of Greece and in the Greek colonies around the Black Sea. As soon as he gained fame in the flourishing colonies of Southern Italy, his worship spread north, to the Romans and the Etruscans.

Ap(u)lu among the Etruscans

To the Etruscans, Apollo came early, and was primarily known as a character in Greek mythical narratives. As with almost everything else we know about the Etruscans, the evidence is archaeological. Engravings on bronze mirrors have survived to show us scenes from well-known Greek myths featuring Apollo. A beautiful life-size terracotta statue of the god was part of a group that represented his fight with Heracles for the Cerynthian hind and stood on the roof of a temple in the Etruscan city of

Figure 6 Apollo from the temple in Veii, late sixth century BCE. Museo Nazionale di Villa Giulia, Rome. Copyright Erich Lessing/Art Resource, NY.

Veii (figure 6). When the bronze mirrors have his name inscribed, he is called Apulu or, shortened, Aplu.

All this is mythology, not cult, and for a long time, scholars on Etruscan religion could find no indication for the cult of Apollo in their material; the fact that Etruscans dedicated votive gifts in Delphi did not prove a local cult back home. There is, however, one dedication to the god from Etruria itself. The bronze statuette of a sitting boy in the Museum of Fine Arts in Boston is dedicated to Aplu; although all archaeological context is lost, its style hints at a time and a place: it is thought to have been made in the third century BCE and dedicated in a sanctuary in Southern Etruria. Similar statuettes are known from many sanctuaries all over the Eastern Mediterranean, and they had usually been dedicated in the shrine of a healing divinity. A large number was found in the sanctuary of Eshmun, the Phoenician Asclepius, in Sidon, and others came from sanctuaries of Apollo on the island of Cyprus. Parents dedicated them to thank the god for saving their children from an illness, or for having given them the son they desperately longed for. The person who dedicated the Etruscan image to Apollo would have done it for the same reason.

The Etruscan Aplu has no epithet, and the dedication to him as a protector of children is the only certain information we have about his cult in Etruria. Since there is no archaeological context for the Boston statuette, it is unclear whether it should be understood as coming from an independent sanctuary of the god, or as a dedication in the sanctuary of another divinity; in another Etruscan sanctuary, Aplu is worshipped together with Ceres. Nor is there any certain way of knowing how the god came to the Etrurians. He may have come from Southern Italy where Apollo had many sanctuaries, or he may have come directly from Greece, as in another case. One Greek merchant from the island of Aegina dedicated a large stone anchor in Graviscae, a harbor town of Etruscan Tarquinia, to Aeginetan Apollo; such dedications might have inspired an independent local cult. Or, finally, the god may have come from Rome where Apollo the Doctor, *Medicus*, had an important cult.

Roman Apollo Medicus

The Roman historian Livy tells how, in 433 BCE,

> a plague brought everything to a halt. They vowed a temple to Apollo for the health of the Roman people. After consulting the Sibylline books, the *duumviri* [the Senate Committee for Ritual Matters] performed many rituals in order to placate the wrath of the gods and to avert the plague from the people; nevertheless, in the city and on the countryside, many humans and many animals perished. And since the farmers suffered from the disease, the officials feared widespread hunger and sent to Etruria, to Cumae, and finally to Sicily for grain.
>
> (Livy 4.25.3–4)

Two years later the Romans dedicated a temple to Apollo (Livy 4.29.7): they must have attributed the end of the epidemic – although it was more a tailing-off than a dramatic conclusion – to the Greek healer and been thankful for it, despite its long duration and catastrophic impact.

They built the temple in a place where there was already an altar to the god, an *Apollinar* as the Romans called it, erected as early as 449 BCE for reasons unknown to us. In the temple, they added Apollo's mother and sister, Leto/Latona and Artemis/Diana – not surprisingly, given the very frequent Greek practice of worshipping the entire Apolline triad in Apollo's sanctuaries. The temple stood on a high podium, as all temples did in Rome, and it was located a short distance northwest of the Capitol, at the southeastern border of the Field of Mars. At that time, the sanctuary would have been more or less isolated in an open space. Later, other temples were built close by, and in 13 BCE, Augustus inaugurated a large stone theater immediately to the west which he named after his grandson Marcellus, whose early death had crushed his hopes of making him his heir and successor. The theater is still a landmark of contemporary Rome. Next to it, visitors can still see several columns of Apollo's temple, although not of the early Roman one. The construction of Augustus' theater impinged rather heavily on the old sanctuary, and the temple, already restored several times over the centuries, was replaced with a more modern one.

Before Augustus built his own temple to Apollo of Actium on the Palatine, the temple of Apollo Medicus was the only temple of Apollo in Rome. The Romans regarded the god basically as a healer. He received dedications as "bringer of health" (*salutaris*) and "provider of medicine" (*medicinalis*), and the Vestal Virgins addressed him in their routine prayers as *Apollo Medice, Apollo Paean* to the very end of paganism.

Two centuries after the consecration of the temple of Apollo Medicus, between 212 and 208 BCE, the Romans instituted games in his honor, *ludi Apollinares*. This was another period of acute crisis for Rome – not because of a plague this time, but because of a foreign invader: Rome was engaged in a desperate struggle against the Carthaginian army of Hannibal, but things were not going well for them. In fact, the Romans later regarded this war, the Second Punic War (218–201 BCE) as the longest and most dangerous of the many wars they had to fight. As often happened during the long agony of this struggle, oracles were consulted to help Rome hobble along after yet another set-back. Both the Sibylline books and the oracles of an ancient seer, Marcius, recommended that the Romans turn to Apollo and institute games in his honor. At first, these games were held annually but on varying dates, whenever the god's help was needed. But when yet another epidemic hit Rome in 208 BCE, the senate decided to perpetuate the games and gave them a firm date, July 13. This remained until the end of pagan Rome, and the games were always very popular.

Later Romans debated the reasons for the games of Apollo. Livy insisted that it was "not for the sake of health, but of victory." An etiological story seemed to confirm this: during the first performance of the games, we are told, an enemy (the story is rather vague about his identity) attacked the festive city. While the citizens were frantically trying to get hold of their weaponry (for one did not usually watch horse races and other spectacles in full armor), "a cloud of arrows was seen to fly against the enemy and drove him away and made it possible for the Romans to turn back to the games of the hospitable god again" (Macrobius, *Saturnalia* 1.17.25). Clearly the god did not like his games to be disturbed by hostile foreigners. The story must be an invention, and it could have been modeled on the story of how Apollo defended his Delphic sanctuary against the marauding Gauls in 278 BCE. But whatever its origins, it turned Apollo the Healer into Apollo the formidable Archer.

A HEALER AMONG BARBARIANS

In the course of the late second and first centuries BCE, the Romans expanded northwest, into what is now France. At first, they conquered the south and made it into their province, Gallia Transalpina; we still call it Provence, after the Roman word. This move secured the land passage from Italy to Spain after Rome's Spanish conquest. When, in 58 BCE, Julius Caesar became governor of Gallia, he systematically extended the power of Rome northwards, up to the Rhine. In doing so, he broke both Roman law and international customs with an undeclared preemptive war against the Celtic tribes of Gaul and a massacre that raised protest in the Roman senate. But Gaul became Roman for good, and with it the cults of Gaul.

In his *Report on the War in Gaul*, one of the most skilled pieces of propaganda ever written, Caesar talks about the religion of the people he conquered, and he gives a list of gods: "In second place [after Mercury], they worship Mars, Jupiter and Apollo, and they believe of them about the same what the other people do: Apollo averts disease . . ." (Caesar, *On the War in Gaul* 6.17.2). In this somewhat one-dimensional view, healing is Apollo's only function. Or rather, any male divinity in Gaul who would heal or avert disease would be called Apollo, whatever name the natives had given him. Tacitus had called this kind of reasoning *interpretatio Romana*, "the Roman way of explaining things." It was the same basic method used by all ancient cultures in dealing with their neighbors' gods, as we have already seen: they would look for one or a few salient traits a foreign god had in common with one of their own divinities, and that would settle the matter. Different divine names were just a matter of language; they could be translated from one language into another, as any other word. Roman conquerors, administrators, merchants, and settlers in Gaul (and elsewhere) would use the Latin name, and over time, the natives would follow suit.

Because of this linguistic habit, ancient sources are able to name several temples of Apollo in Gaul. The first sanctuary we hear of is in a Greek account *ca.* 300 BCE about an island off Gaul, either Britain or one of the Channel Islands: the local tradition had Apollo born here. Roman inscriptions confirm the ubiquity of Apollo all over Gaul, often in connection with one of the many thermal springs there (France, after all, is still the country of mineral water). Archaeological research showed how many Gallic sanctuaries of Apollo fused native traditions with new influences: they usually had the square shape typical of indigenous temples. Inscriptions often record a native name as well, treating it as an epithet, such as Apollo Belenus or Apollo Grannus, or, more typically Celtic, Apollo Toutiorix, Apollo "Leader of the Clan." Some cults gained popularity well beyond the border of the province. The emperor Caracalla, chronically ill, was visiting healing sanctuaries throughout his realm, but could find no remedy, "neither from Apollo Grannus nor from Asclepius or Sarapis" (Dio Cassius, *Histories* 77.15.5). Grannus, or Apollo Grannus, had his main sanctuary in Aquae Granni, a spa that eventually became the German Aachen, capital of Charlemagne's empire. By then, the cult had long disappeared: most of the healing sanctuaries of Apollo in Gaul were destroyed during the Christianization of the fourth century CE, though a few were taken over by a local saint.

APOLLO AVERTER OF EVIL

Perhaps the debate of the Roman theologians on why the games were founded was misguided, and there was no fundamental opposition between Apollo the Healer and Apollo the helper in battle. Bow and arrow, Apollo's constant attribute, are weapons of attack as well as weapons of protection: they kept away the enemy from the games, but sent the plague into the Greek camp before Troy, and they also killed the seven sons and seven daughters of Niobe, the proud queen of Thebes who had belittled Leto for giving birth to only one boy and one girl (figure 7). A copy of a famous group of Niobe and her dying children was among the artwork exhibited in Rome's temple of Apollo, as was a statue of Apollo the Archer: his deadly power was never forgotten.

A series of oracles from Clarus point to the same direction. During a period after the middle of the second century CE, five different cities in Western Asia Minor were suffering from an epidemic, and they sent an embassy to Clarus for help. In some cases, the disease must have been

Figure 7 The slaying of the Niobids. Attic red-figure krater by the Niobid Painter, *ca.* 460–450 BCE. Musée du Louvre, Paris. Copyright Alinari/Art Resource, NY.

the plague (whatever its exact medical definition was) that the armies of the emperor Lucius Verus caught during a campaign in Mesopotamia in 165 CE and brought back with them to the West, spreading the germs wherever they went, to places as far-flung as Britain. But since no oracle is clearly dated, more local outbreaks of disease cannot be excluded. In one answer, the god recognized an attack of sorcery and recommended a ritual that would destroy the sorcerer's hidden voodoo dolls. Such rituals were practiced in Bronze Age Mesopotamia, and one cannot but admire the deep ritual learning of the Clarian god, or of his priests. In all other answers, the god diagnosed the wrath of the gods as reason for the disease and prescribed complex rituals of purification and sacrifices to placate them. In three cases, he added a final recommendation in order to avert future epidemics: "At every gate, consecrate the sacred image of Clarian Apollo, equipped with his arrows that destroy disease, as if he would aim far at the disastrous plague." Apollo the archer not only sends the disease with his arrows. His weapon also keeps it away.

Disease, that is, is just another enemy, a sort of evil demon secretly trying to sneak in through an unguarded city gate; the guardian archer is as able to fend it off as he is able to drive away an attacking horde of foreign foes. Today, we differentiate between enemies and germs, or between war and disease, which Greeks and Romans would not necessarily have done: Apollo, the excellent sharp-shooter, kept both away. We understand Apollo the Physician as a specialization of a function the god had all over the ancient world, "Averter of Evil," *Alexikakos*. As such, he and his sister Artemis – an excellent and frightening archeress herself – were often invoked as "Guardians of the Gates," *Propýlaioi*, to keep out evil from the city, as did Hecate who, in many respects, is Artemis' close relative. And just as images of triple Hecate also guarded domestic dwellings, an image of Apollo protected the entrance of many Greek houses – this time not an anthropomorphic statue, but a column or pillar as the sign of Apollo who protected the doors, Apollo "He of the Street," *Agyieús*, as the Greeks called him.

When the plague is driven out, health is restored. Health, then, could be nothing else than the absence of disease. This has a philosophical ring to it: one can define the good simply as the absence of evil, as did the Epicureans. Others, demanding more of life, prefer to have real good follow the driving out of evil; to a Platonist, the idea of the good is the highest reality he can think of. The philosophical debate is far from idle; it mirrors attitudes to life that are reflected in religion as often as they are in philosophy.

Apollo, to stay with our god, can preside over both ways of looking at things, as the ritual cycle of the Thargelia teaches. The Thargelia is a festival common to all Ionians, and it gave its name to the month Thargelion, the second last month of the Ionian year; in the climate of the Aegean, the year did not end with the mild winter but with the summer heat that parched all vegetation. Festival and month thus go back at least before the moment sometime at the end of the Bronze Age or the very beginning of the Iron Age when the mainland Ionians settled across the Aegean on the west coast of Asia Minor and took with them the calendar of their lands of origin. The main day of the Thargelia was the seventh Thargelion which the Ionians regarded as Apollo's birthday. The same day was Plato's birthday, while the sixth was the birthday of Socrates and of Artemis; the Greeks regarded this as more than a coincidence. In Athens and the Ionian cities of Ephesus and Colophon, the sixth of Thargelion was also the day when the scapegoats (*pharmakoî*) were driven out: a ritual which fascinated scholars even in antiquity. The pharmakoi – two in Athens, one for each gender – were captives who were fed by the state. On sixth Thargelion, they were adorned with a necklace of figs, led through the city in a procession with the music of a flute, often beaten up and finally driven out of the town. Stories that tell how they were killed are extrapolations from the ritual that spell out its hidden meaning: the scapegoats were the embodiment of all that was evil in the town and so had to be destroyed. After this ritual purification of the sixth day, the seventh was the day of renewal and plenty. New corn cakes were baked and carried to Apollo's temple in another procession, together with a pot that contained a pulp cooked from the first, immature ears of corn and with twigs that were adorned with wool and hung with bread, fruit, and small containers of oil and honey; after the procession, these twigs were hung over the house-door. In Athens at least, new fire was brought in from the sacred hearth at Delphi and used to rekindle the public hearth in the council-house from which then the private households got their own new fire, as did the temples. New fire is the most powerful ritual symbol of renewal and belonged to many New Year's festivals in ancient Greece as well as to other moments of radical renewal: after the crisis of the Persian War, the Greek altars got new fire from the Delphic altar. In a ritual movement reminiscent of the Spartan Hyacinthia with its contrast of grief on the first day and exuberance on the second, the cycle of the Thargelia represents the renewal after the cleansing of the city from evil. Unlike the cases we talked about earlier, where happiness returned simply after the city was purged from disease, the ritual of the Thargelia did not simply purify the town but added new and tangible goods, from cakes and honey to new fire.

APOLLO AND ASCLEPIUS

In later Greece, Apollo the Healer was much less prominent than Apollo the patron of divination, or of music. From the fifth century BCE onwards, another healer, Asclepius, enhanced his own standing all over the ancient world. The *Iliad* mentions Asclepius as a healer taught by the centaur Chiron: the wise centaur bridged the gap between nature and culture and possessed, among other things, a deep knowledge of healing herbs.

Myths and sanctuaries of Asclepius

After Homer, Asclepius' story is narrated in three different local forms. The most common version is first heard in Pindar's third *Pythian Ode* (about 474 BCE). Here, Asclepius is Apollo's son by a local, Thessalian heroine, Coronis the daughter of Phlegyas, king of the mythical Phlegyans. Apollo fell in love with the beautiful princess; but when she was pregnant with his son, Coronis, "in the errors of her heart," gave in to the advances of a local prince, Ischys. Worse, "she waited not for the coming of the marriage feast." Apollo's sacred animal, the raven, informed the god of his lover's brazen infidelity (this was the common version; Pindar, the pious theologian, prefers to trust the power of the omniscient god: "He perceived it in his mind that knows all things"). Angry at the deception and infidelity, Apollo shot his human rival and sent his sister Artemis to kill Coronis. Some later writers add that Apollo also punished the unlucky messenger bird; before this affair, it had been white. Having killed his lover, Apollo still cared for his unborn son: he snatched the baby from his mother's pyre and gave him to Chiron to be raised. So it was from Chiron, and not from his father, that Asclepius learnt the art of healing.

In Archaic Greece, Asclepius is firmly connected with Thessaly, as are the Phlegyans, his mother's people. His sons Podalirius and Machaon are not only the physicians in the Greek army before Troy, they are commanders in their own right, with warriors from the Thessalian cities "Tricca, Ithome, and Oechalia." The location is not only a matter of mythology: Tricca had a sanctuary of Asclepius that the Greeks regarded as "the oldest and the most famous" (Strabo) – this then was where the sons of Asclepius came from. The cult of Apollo is closely connected with that of his son: before entering the innermost sanctuary of Asclepius in Tricca, one had to sacrifice to Apollo.

The second version of Asclepius' myth can be pieced together from the fragments we read in the *Catalogue of Women* (ascribed to Hesiod, but composed in the late sixth century BCE). Here, Asclepius is the son of Apollo and Arsinoe, the daughter of king Leucippus of Messene. This leads us to an entirely different region, the Southwestern Peloponnese, and connects the myth with another important sanctuary of Asclepius. For many centuries, Messene was subject to Spartan rule; after it regained political independence, the Messenians built a splendid temple to Asclepius. It stood on a square in the center of their town, with smaller sanctuaries under the arcades that surrounded the square. The myth precedes the sanctuary by more than two centuries, and there must have been an older cult in Messene about whose location we know nothing.

The two myths clearly disagree with each other; there is no way to combine the Thessalian and the Messenian origin of Asclepius. Given the early dates of both versions, we have no certain means of knowing where Asclepius came from. Messene and Tricca both compete, and Strabo's remark on the sanctuary of Tricca – that it was "the oldest and the most famous" – takes sides in this debate.

Technically, Asclepius is a hero, the son of a god and a mortal woman.

But some sons born from such a union became much more powerful than most other heroes and could be regarded as gods: Dionysus, the son of Zeus and the mortal princess Semele, was an Olympian god; Heracles, son of Zeus and the Theban queen Alcmene, was elevated into Olympus after his death. A similar fate awaited the hero Asclepius: thanks to his healing powers, he quickly came to be regarded as a divinity. Epidaurian texts narrating his miracle cures, for one, always call him "the god," and in late antiquity, he could even be called Zeus Asclepius.

When grown up, Asclepius became the best physician that ever existed. Carried away by his success, however, he forgot the limits that Zeus had set to mortal men: he tried to resuscitate the dead. Zeus killed him with his lightning, restoring the cosmic order which Asclepius threatened out of arrogance or out of greed; some at least say that he was seduced by money. No mortal can become immortal, if not by the decree of Zeus; to Greek story-tellers, the art of the physicians had the potential to break down these firm limitations of human existence.

During the late Archaic Age, Asclepius' cult began to spread. In the early sixth century BCE, it arrived in the lonely forests near the small Peloponnesian town of Epidaurus. Here, Apollo had a long-standing cult on a hill-top overlooking a beautiful valley. In the later Bronze Age, there had been a peak sanctuary on this hill; it is unclear whom the Mycenaeans worshipped there. The cult died out before the end of the Bronze Age, but the memory of the sanctuary must have lingered on. After an interruption of several centuries, the locals built an altar and then a small temple to a new god whom they addressed as Apollo Maleatas. The sanctuary of Asclepius was built in the valley below Apollo's shrine, and the two shrines and their owners belonged closely together: even many centuries later, when Asclepius' sprawling healing sanctuary had by far eclipsed his father's modest hill-top shrine, official documents still address Apollo Maleatas and Asclepius together. Local theologians rewrote the myth of Coronis; this is the third version of the Asclepius story. When secretly pregnant with Asclepius, she accompanied her father, who had business in the Peloponnesus. In Epidaurus, she furtively gave birth to a boy and exposed him in a lonely forest glen nearby. As happens always in such tales of exposure, the baby was miraculously saved – not by his divine father, however, but by helpful animals. A goat suckled him, the watch-dog of the herd guarded him, and finally the goat-herd followed his animals, found the boy and brought him up as his own. This explains not only why Asclepius' main sanctuary was far away from any major settlement, but also why Asclepius rejected goat sacrifices and why there were sacred dogs in his sanctuaries. There were also sacred snakes, and they were explained by another story. When he promised to resuscitate the dead son of king Minos, Glaucus, Asclepius retreated into the woods in order to think about a cure. A snake wound itself around his staff; angered at being disturbed, he killed it, but then observed another snake bringing an herb and reviving its dead companion. He used the same herb to cure Glaucus, adopted the snake as his sacred animal, and made the staff with the snake his symbol.

The Epidaurian sanctuary grew rapidly and spread its cult far and wide. Many tales were told about how patients, grateful for the god's assistance, introduced the cult of the healing hero into their home towns. In 421/420 BCE, Asclepius arrived in Athens; at about the same time, an inscription attests his worship in Etruria; the form of his name it used, *Aiskhlapios*, derives from the dialect of Epidaurus. The cult also spread to the island of Cos where it was connected with the famous medical school that claimed Hippocrates as its founder; in 366 BCE, the cult of Asclepius was added to the sanctuary of Apollo Cyparissius. The modest shrine in its cypress grove (hence Apollo's epithet) rapidly grew into a large religious healing complex; it that was so impressive that, in the third century BCE, the inhabitants of the Italian town of Fregellae adopted its architectural form for their own sanctuary of Asclepius. In the later fourth century BCE, "Archias, son of Aristaechmus, was healed in Epidaurus after spraining his ankle while hunting": this was the reason why he brought the god's cult to the city of Pergamum in Northwestern Asia Minor (Pausanias 2.26.8). In this sanctuary too, Apollo and his son were worshipped together; and it too became a major healing institution throughout antiquity. In 293 BCE, when Rome was ravaged by yet another epidemic, the Roman senate sent an embassy to Epidaurus to ask for an image of the god. Instead, a sacred snake slipped into the ship. The Romans sailed back to Italy; when traveling up the Tiber on the last leg of their voyage, the snake slid off the boat and settled on the Tiber island. In this way, the god indicated where he wanted his sanctuary to be. The healing tradition on the island survived pagan Rome: a twelfth-century well in the church that supplanted the sanctuary still claimed healing properties for its waters.

Rituals of Asclepius

Sanctuaries of Apollo the Healer were indistinguishable from those of other gods; they all had an altar, a temple, and a retaining wall as their main architectural elements. There were no special cures in these sanctuaries, prayers and sacrifices were enough to bring divine assistance. This was different with Asclepius. The main ritual in all his sanctuaries was incubation, a ritual that made the god appear in a dream; he would either advise the dreamer as to therapy, or actually heal him. At nightfall, the patients retired into a sleeping hall, after a sacrifice to the god and many other powers that were supposed to help them. Among them were Themis, "Divine Law," and Mnemosyne, "Memory": one should have a good and rightful dream, not a dream that deceived the dreamer; and one should not forget it when waking up. The next morning, the dream was explained by the priests who often translated the nightly vision into therapy. And since parts of this therapy could take place in the temple, the main sanctuaries of Asclepius turned into large complexes that were both sacred sanatoriums and community centers. They not only contained a temple and a room for the dreams, but also fountains, guest houses, meeting rooms, and even a theater for entertaining the patients and any other guest who chose to dwell close to the god for a while.

In this way, the son of Apollo emancipated himself from his father to become the main healing god of the ancient world in the Hellenistic and Imperial epochs. Divine healers in other religious cultures, such as the Phoenician Eshmun or the Egyptian Imouthes/Imhotep, were hellenized as Asclepius, not as Apollo; only Italy and Gaul remained devoted to Apollo the Physician. In a world where specialization had set in and where individuals were more and more looking for a very personal helper in their anxieties, the divine medical specialist Asclepius seemed to be much more attractive than his father, the all-rounder Apollo.

CONCEPTS OF HEALING

This difference between Apollo and Asclepius rests on two different conceptions of what illness is. These concepts are determined by different cosmologies. In one cosmology, disease is part of the larger world of evil that confronts and limits human freedom and happiness, and there is no essential difference between disease and other troubles that affect humanity and have the potential to destroy individuals or to wipe out entire cities; in the other cosmology, disease is entirely different from other evils and can be often treated as a bodily defect.

The first cosmology is Apollo's, and it is best articulated in a well-known myth in Hesiod's *Works and Days*. Before Epimetheus opened Pandora's box, the treacherous gift from Zeus, "the tribes of humans were living on earth without evil, without difficult labor, and without painful diseases that bring death to the men" (v. 90–92). This contrasts with the present state of human existence: "Full of evil is the earth, full is the sea; silently and on their own, diseases stalk humans by day and by night and bring evil to mortals" (v. 101–103). In this world, Apollo's role is twofold. On the one side, he is a powerful Averter of Evil, as is Heracles, the hero who fought in order to purify the earth from many monsters but was also regarded as a healer. Heracles was more successful with the Lernaean Hydra and the Nemean Lion than he was with Geras "Old Age," Thanatos "Death," and Hades, the King of the Dead whom he also attacked: not even the most powerful hero could remove the limits imposed upon human existence. All these evils are beyond human control, it needs superhuman power to ward them off; humans turn to the powerful gods and heroes with prayers, vows, and sacrifices. But the origin of evil and especially of disease is not always clear. Very often, divination must be used to find the source before any healing can begin, and healing might be contingent on human atonement for angering a god: the plague in the first book of the *Iliad* is a case in point. Divination is very much Apollo's province.

But not only divination calls for Apollo the healer. In this world, disease is understood as pollution, a disturbance in the cosmic order. Pollution calls for purification, and this too belongs to Apollo. While Odysseus was sailing down the coast on his embassy of atonement to Chryses and his Apollo Smintheus, Agamemnon gave order to purify the Greek army: "They performed the cleansing and threw the refuse into the sea" (*Il.* 1.314). The purification priests that the enlightened author of *On Sacred Disease* attacks continue this tradition, as do the priests whom, almost a century later, a bigot Athenian would consult and whom Menander's comedy mocks: "Get the women to wipe you round in a circle and fumigate you!" (Menander, *The Ghost* 54). In Archaic Greece, however, these things were much more serious and beyond any questioning. Its practioners were seers and as such under Apollo's tutelage, and Apollo himself combines these gifts of prophecy and purification. When the Delphic prophetess in Aeschylus' *Eumenides* sees the terrible goddesses besieging Orestes in Apollo's temple, she gains her confidence by reminding herself of Apollo's power: "He is a seer-healer (*iatromantis*), an expounder of ominous signs and a purifier of houses" (v. 62f.). The mythical seer or, in an early characterization, *iatromantis* Melampus cured the daughters of Proetus or the women of Argos whom Hera had driven mad and blighted with a skin disease; he had received his art from Apollo himself. His grand-son was Amphiaraus, another seer "whom Apollo loved dearly" (*Od.* 15.245); Amphiaraus' sanctuary at Oropus specialized in healing. When the women of Sparta collectively became mad, Apollo sent the seer Bacis to cure them. The wandering Abaris, a shadowy figure of Archaic Greece, was a priest of Hyperborean Apollo who was said to able to fly on Apollo's arrow; he taught both Athenians and Spartans sacrifices to avert a plague, and charms and oracles were attributed to him. Thaletas the Spartan was a musician and composer of paeans, but he also cured an epidemic that ravaged Sparta, presumably with his paeans. Branchus, the founder of the oracle of Didyma, healed the Milesians from an epidemic by sprinkling them with laurel twigs and singing a hymn with strange, non-Greek words. The nexus between Apollo, divination, and ritual healing is constant, and serious.

Scholars disagree whether Apollo himself could act as a specialized purifier. The Greeks at Troy did not only ritually cleanse their army but also "sacrificed perfect hecatombs to Apollo, of bulls and goats at the shore of the sea" (*Il.* 1.316); and Apollo cured Orestes' madness by purifying him of the murder of his mother with the blood of a piglet (figure 8). But in Greek myth, gods routinely purify humans of murder: it is thus no prerogative of Apollo; and the Greeks in Troy may simply have wanted to placate Apollo because, after all, they had provoked his anger. The best we can say is that purification forms part of the entire nexus of divin-

Figure 8 Apollo purifies Orestes in Delphi. Apulian red-figure bell-krater by the Eumenides Painter, 380–370 BC. Musée du Louvre, Paris. Reproduced after A. Furtwängler and K. Reichhold, *Griechische Vasenmalerei* (Munich, 1904).

ation, illness, and cure around Apollo, without turning the god into a specialist for ritual purification. The colonial city of Cyrene in North Africa received a very long and detailed law on purification from Apollo, not because he was specially concerned with purifications, but because the Cyrenaeans had asked him what institutions would mostly benefit their colony. The god answered as he did because ritual purity guaranteed good relations between humans and their gods.

In the second cosmology, disease is different from other evils. It is a problem of the body that can be healed by special knowledge and experience. This is the cosmology that underlies the claims of the author of *On Sacred Disease*. The learned doctor based his thinking on a radical and enlightened theology that drew on contemporary philosophy rather than religious traditions: gods are by their very nature essentially good, and thus they are unable to harm mankind. Temple-medicine in the sanctuaries of Asclepius basically shared this cosmology, with the one difference that it was less optimistic about human capabilities of healing: it is Asclepius who has this knowledge and who is the supreme physician and surgeon. This was more modern, if compared to the other cosmology. Over time, the different spheres that belonged to this older cosmology were not unaffected by this modernization. The healing priests of the fifth and fourth centuries BCE, objects of polemic and ridicule by the more modern-minded, represent a narrowing down of older forms. Whereas formerly sacrifices and hymns were the main ritual means of healing and purifying, these specialist focussed on ritual acts that used the gestural language of washing and cleaning, and they broke the connection with Apollo.

SUMMARY

Apollo the healer continues the tradition of a Bronze Age god of healing, Paiawon, who survived in Apollo's epithet and song, Paiean and the paean. We cannot tell whether Homer still kept the two gods apart, but if he did so, this need not reflect religious reality of his own age. Apollo's cult as a healer spread to the Black Sea colonies and to Rome far away in the West, and despite the ascent of his son Asclepius, Apollo remained a healer especially in Rome's Western provinces where he was identified with local healing divinities. Apolline healing is narrowly connected with the god's ability to remove disorder and to keep evil away, whereas his son is much more of an active healer: the intriguing miracle stories from Epidaurus and other Asclepian sanctuaries portray him as an actual physician who intervenes with drugs and surgery in a hands-on approach utterly alien to his more aloof and speculative father. Two millennia later, Apollo the Healer surfaces again, this time in a work of fiction: he is the kindly and competent, but also somewhat sinister Doc Appleton in John Updike's novel *The Centaur* (1961) whose wife Corinne (Coronis) disappeared after she was suspected of adultery.

APOLLO, THE YOUNG, AND THE CITY

THE YOUNG GOD AND THE YOUNG MEN, 1:
CUTTING ONE'S HAIR

Towards the end of the *Iliad*, Achilles finally gives the order to prepare the burial of Patroclus. The pyre is ready, the body is put on it, but then "Achilles thought of something else." He steps aside, cuts his "blond hair that he had grown for the river Spercheius," and "looking over the wine-dark sea," he addresses Spercheius, the main river of his father's realm, far away in Thessaly. Peleus vowed to offer his son's hair to the river together with fifty sheep, should his son return from the foreign war. Now that Achilles knows that he will find his grave near Troy, he offers his hair instead to his dead friend. "Thus said, he put the hair into the hands of his dear friend, and all felt the urge for a lament." The poet leaves it open who it is they are lamenting: the dead Patroclus – or Achilles whose gesture makes plain his imminent fate (*Il.* 23.138–157).

The ritual Achilles speaks about is strangely ambiguous, to Homer's audience no less than to us. In a first understanding, he seems to talk about a customary vow Greeks and Romans alike used to make when departing into danger: they promised a sacrifice and a gift, if the god would provide a safe return. The river, the powerful local god who was sometimes the ancestor of a royal dynasty, seems an appropriate pro-tector of the king and his heir; and hair offerings were often associated with the rescue from the dangers of a sea voyage. When Ptolemy III returned from a dangerous campaign in Asia, his young wife Berenice offered a lock of her hair to the gods; when it vanished from the sanctu-ary, the court astronomer was quick to find it in a hitherto unnamed constellation, still known to today's astronomers as the Lock of Berenice. There is, however, a second layer of meaning, elucidated by the learned archbishop of Thessalonica, Eustathius (ca. 1115–1195 CE), in his some-what rambling commentary on the scene:

In antiquity, the young men had the custom to let their hair grow until adulthood, then to cut it for the local rivers. . . . They regarded the rivers as nourishers of the young (*kourotróphoi*) because of their humidity, as they did with Apollo the sun because of his warmth.

Achilles was a young man in transition between adolescence and social maturity; his return from war would have marked his adulthood.

Already Hesiod, in his genealogy of Oceanus in the *Theogony*, connects Apollo with this rite: his daughters "all over the earth make men out of adolescents, together with Lord Apollo and the rivers" (v. 346f.). Hesiod uses a rare word for what I translated with "make out of adolescents," *kourízein*. The underlying noun, *koûros*, is one of the terms for "adolescent," and it belongs to the root *ker-*, "to shear, to cut (hair)." Hair-cutting, that is, defined adolescents. The custom of cutting one's hair at the moment of social maturity lasted through most of pagan antiquity and was an ritual act of prime social importance. The "ostentatious man," in Theophrastus' collection of character sketches, takes his son to Delphi for the ritual hair cut: the hair would stay in the sanctuary, displayed for all of Greece to see (*Characters* 21). He follows a prestigious example: already Theseus, the role model for all young Athenians, is said to have offered his hair to Apollo in Delphi; or he did so on Delus when sailing home from Crete with his lover Ariadne, before becoming the new king of Athens.

The divine recipients of this dedication varied from place to place. The local rivers and the nymphs, sometimes called *koûrai*, "girls," often appear in our sources. In the epoch of the Roman emperors, even Asclepius, Apollo's son, would receive such a hair offering. One emperor did so in a variation of Theophrastus' ostentatious man: when Domitian's favorite boy Earinus came of age, the ritual, performed in the world-famous sanctuary of Asclepius at Pergamum, was duly celebrated by the court poets, Statius (*Silvae* 3.4) and Martial (*Epigram* 9.16).

But all over Greece, Apollo was as central to the rite as the nymphs and rivers. Apollo's image mirrors the appearance of Greek adolescents. He is always shown with long and untrimmed hair, and a common epithet from Homer onwards is "He of the Uncut Hair," *akersekómēs*. Like Achilles or Theseus, Apollo is a *koûros* or ephebe. And since the favorite ephebe's pastime in Greece was athletics, exercised in the nude, Apollo's favorite statuary dedication in Archaic Greece was the nude, long-haired young male, what the archeologists aptly call a kouros. The archaeological debate on whether this image represents the god or a young man – as it certainly does when a kouros marks the grave of a youth – seems somewhat pointless in this context. But Apollo was not just any ephebe:

he was the most beautiful ephebe, the very ideal of male attractiveness in Greek society. And in a society such as the society of Classical Athens where beauty was male and eroticism was articulated in homoerotic terms, adolescent Apollo turned into the bench-mark for all aesthetic perfection. Athens' cultural achievements meant that this view was transported through the ages, to Rome and beyond. In eighteenth-century Europe, J.J. Winckelmann, the founder of classical art history, again fell under the spell of Apollo's adolescent beauty (see chapter 7).

It is not just his long hair that marks out Apollo as an ephebe. Like the ephebes, he is a singer and dancer, and sometimes he is not "Leader of the Muses" (*Mousagétēs*) but "Leader of the Nymphs" (or "Brides," *Nymphagétēs*). We remember that in Archaic Greece the song-dance of young men and maidens was the main occasion for courtship and matchmaking (chapter 2). And like ephebes, Apollo did not fight with the sword, the citizen's weapon; he fought with bow and arrow. In combat, the young archers fired from behind the front lines. Only the adult citizen fought in the front; they had to be strong enough to carry heavy armor and wield a sword.

THE YOUNG GOD AND THE YOUNG MEN, 2: A HAPLESS LOVER

Unlike other gods, Apollo is a rather unlucky lover. Just one of Apollo's love stories is entirely satisfactory, the story of Cyrene, probably his first conquest. Cyrene was a nymph, and no ordinary girl. Instead of staying home and making wool, she guarded her father's flocks in the mountains of Thessaly. When he saw her valiantly wrestle down a mighty lion, young Apollo fell in love with her. He made a queen out of a wild maiden: the couple moved to Libya, where Cyrene founded the town that was named after her and became its first ruler. Their son was Aristaeus; his father turned him into a god, protector of cattle and bees. The story, told at length by Pindar in his Ninth *Pythian Ode* commissioned by one Telesikles of Cyrene, resonates with ephebic themes. The world of the ephebes – the males "in the prime of youth, *hébē*" – was the mountains and the wilderness along the border of the city's territory. Here, they served as border guards and advance reconnaissance corps; only marriage civilized them and brought them back into the city. In myth, however, marriage concerns Cyrene only; Apollo did never settle down. Nor did his son Aristaeus; he grew up in the wild as yet another pupil of the centaur Chiron, and his lust caused the death of Orpheus' newly wed wife.

Apollo's other love stories turned out much less happily. Daphne, the daughter of the river Peneius, tried to escape his impetuous wooing, but the god raced after her and, since he was so much faster, rape seemed inevitable, had not her father turned her into a laurel tree. This explains why the laurel is sacred to the god. Marpessa, daughter of another river god, was abducted by the mortal Idas; Apollo spotted her and tried to take her away from him. In the ensuing fight between the two rivals, Idas disarmed Apollo, and Zeus had to intervene to restore the hierachy between mortals and gods. With Zeus's backing, Marpessa chose the mortal husband, a true marriage over a transient pleasure (if pleasure it would have been) – immortal Apollo would never have aged, as she, a mere mortal, inevitably did. He was somewhat more successful with Coronis, at least at first; but when pregnant with his son, Coronis took a mortal husband, and the cuckolded god killed them both and almost lost his unborn child. Ephebes might sire sons, but they do not marry.

Other stories of Apollo's erotic entanglements have somewhat less unfortunate outcomes. But these are all much more concerned with the sons than with the mothers whose names change from source to source, whether she is the mother of the musician and poet Philammon, of the hero Linus, or the shadowy hero Delphus whose mother remains anonymous. These are not love stories, but genealogies that express some connection with Apollo. The same is true for Apollo's seduction of Creusa, the daughter of the Athenian king Erechtheus, and their child Ion. As a love story, it is tragic: intercourse with a god always resulted in pregnancy, and Creusa, the unmarried mother, in desperation exposed her baby; Apollo saved it. The main thrust of the myth is genealogical and political: Apollo is the ancestor and protector god of the Ionians, Ion's people. But between Apollo and Ion, there is an Athenian princess: among the Ionians, the Athenians are supreme, or at least claim to be so. But beyond such political claims, the story could also be read, as in Euripides' *Ion*, as an example of how a powerful god could refuse to take responsibility for his actions. Then it becomes disquieting: what are we to make of a god who denies paternity of his own child? We can read the play as an inquest into the deficiencies of traditional gods, the theological defects of mythical narratives, or as an insight into the socially problematic nature of male adulthood.

GROUPS AND INSTITUTIONS

Ancient gods were not just protecting individuals. Their power penetrated every aspect of life, the political life of a community no less than the private life of a family; personal religion, some scholars thought, was a late development. Thus, Apollo is not only a protector of young adolescents whom he helps to become adults; his worship is connected with many groups, not the least the group of citizen that made up an ancient city-state (*polis*).

Citizenship in a Greek polis concerned only a small number of people; at least in a large city such as Athens, or later Rome, free residents and unfree slaves must have outnumbered the citizens. The citizen body of any given city, furthermore, was organized in subdivisions and subgroups; in many Greek cities, there were, in descending order, tribes (*phýlai*), phratries, and clans (*génē*) and citizens were defined not only by citizenship in their city but also by membership in a subgroup, and by genealogy. In democratic Athens, the key group was the phratry: phratries were mainly concerned with questions of family, descent, and citizenship, and it remained necessary for every Athenian citizen born in Athens to Athenian parents to become a member of the phratry. The main phratry rituals concerned the introduction of the male children of their members into the group; the performance of these rituals was seen as the ultimate proof of belonging. The introduction took place in several steps, and each step was marked with a sacrifice performed together with all the phratry members: at birth, at age three, and at social maturity. This final sacrifice was called *koúreion*, since it was connected with the ritual cutting of the adolescent's hair.

These sacrifices could be part of the annual festival of the Apaturia which was held in the month of Pyanopsion, in late autumn. The festival, whose name means "Festival of Common Fathers," was shared by all Ionians, and defined what it meant to be an Ionian. At the beginning of the Iron Age Ionians had spread from Athens through the Aegean Islands to Asia Minor: since they all share the festival, it must precede this expansion and date back to the Bronze Age. In Athens, the third day of the festival was called *Koureôtis*, "Day of the *koúreion*": this was the customary day for the introduction of the adolescent males into the phratry.

In Classical Athens, Apollo had no role to play in the Apaturia: its main sacrifices were offered to the divinities that represented the Athenian state, Zeus Phratrios and Athena Phratria. Apollo, however, was not far; after all, the month Pyanopsion was named after his festival that was set on its seventh day, the Pyanopsia or Pyanepsia, "Festival of the Vegetable Stew." Legend has it that on his return voyage from Crete, Theseus made a vow to Apollo on Delus: if he and his twice seven companions returned safely home to Athens, they would make an offering in Apollo's honor. They landed on Athenian soil on the seventh day of Pyanopsion, and to fulfill their vow they took whatever was left of their provisions, put it into one big pot, and cooked it into a stew that they then ate together. The

myth of Theseus' return from Crete was an image for the Athenian ephebes who turned into adult citizens, and this rite was both concerned
with new citizenship and with the community of the citizen body. There
are other familiar themes present as well. The unusual sacrifice of veget-
ables instead of an animal could be read as reflecting a time prior to the
sacrifice of animals, and is certainly a marker of a marginal phase of
transition, as is the theme of community. The transition is a double one,
to the next festival day and, underlying it, from adolescence to adulthood; the next day was the main festival day of Theseus, king of Athens,
with a large animal sacrifice and a meal where meat was now plentiful.
At the same time, the festival was an occasion for carrying the *eiresiône*,
as was the Thargelia: this laurel branch that was adorned with wool, the
first fruits of the season, and with small honey pots was a symbol of
plenty; it makes as much sense in the context of citizenship and community as it did after the driving out of the scapegoat. In Greek thought,
it is harmony among the citizens that guarantees the well-being and
wealth of the city. Thus, the main Apolline festival of the month centered
on themes that were ritually present again in the phratries' *koureotis* day
and that were very important for Apollo all over Greece.

ANCESTRAL APOLLO

At least one phratry in fourth-century Athens introduced the small boys
at the Thargelia, not the Pyanopsia, with a sacrifice to Apollo Patroos,
Ancestral Apollo (literally "He of the Fathers") (Isaeus, *Oration* 7.53).
Apollo Patroos had a sanctuary on the Athenian agora, not far from the
seat of the Council, the State Archive in the Sanctuary of the Mother, and
the Hall of Zeus Eleutherios, "Liberator": the sanctuary and its god were
central to the political life of the democratic city. The first temple of
Apollo Patroos on the agora was built in the sixth century BCE. There are
no earlier traces, perhaps for good reasons: to replace the many small
clan sanctuaries with one central sanctuary of Apollo Patroos gave the
democratic city better control over clan cults that could harbor aristocratic resistance against democracy.

The cult also makes a more far-reaching ideological claim. The epithet "Ancestral" had a double meaning. All over Greece, divinities that
protected clans or similar associations were designated as ancestral,
patrôos: the epithet referred to the divine protection of a common ancestry, not necessarily to a divine ancestor. Not so in Athens, however: here,
Apollo was the father of Ion, the name-giving ancestor of the Ionians.
Ion's mother was the Athenian princess Creusa: Ion was an Athenian,

and through him the Athenians claimed leadership among all the cities of Ionia. This myth has political resonances, and it cannot be older than Athens' claim to leadership in the sixth century BCE. This fits the date the first temple of Apollo Patroos was built.

APOLLO DELPHINIOS

This does not exhaust the ways Athenian Apollo was connected with Theseus, his arrival in Athens, and the ephebes. A short distance outside the city walls, in the green valley of the river Ilissus, lay the sanctuary of Apollo Delphinios. Although the epithet was perhaps connected with the root in the Greek word for brother, *a-delphós*, "having shared the same womb," Greeks read it as "Dolphin-Apollo." A story narrated by Pausanias focusses on the moment young Theseus arrived in Athens from Troizen where he was born and brought up, unknown to his father, the Athenian king Aegeus; in a drunken night, the visiting Aegeus had sired a son with the local princess Aethra. Aegeus never had intended to do so: Aethra's father, desperate to have a grandson from the king of Athens, had slyly pushed his young daughter into his drunken guest's bed. About sixteen years later, Theseus came to Athens, to seek out his father. He was wearing long hair, as epehebes did, and the long Ionian robe that befitted a prince of the past (the dress only survived with Apollo's servants, the professional lyre players). When he passed the construction site of the Delphinion in his curls and frock, the workers teased the youth and called him a lovely maiden. Theseus, angry and eager to prove his manliness, unyoked two oxen that by chance were waiting at the yoke of a construction chariot; in one move, he hurled them over the yet unfinished roof of the sanctuary.

The story again leads to Athens' ephebes. This time, it explains a specific ritual that they were performing during the one year they were serving the city, as Theseus had as Athens' crown prince: they carried a bull on their shoulders to the altar, imitating Theseus' mighty throw of two oxen; and like Theseus, they had untrimmed hair and were wearing a black cloak reminiscent of Theseus' black sail when he sailed back from Crete. Myth, however, is never tidy: in the mythical chronology of events, Theseus' arrival at the Delphinion preceded his departure for Crete.

Another Theseus story also belongs to this first arrival, and it too is connected with the Delphinion. When Theseus arrived from Troizen, his fame as a powerful hero was preceding him (whatever the oafs constructing Apollo's temple might have heard or imagined). On his way, he had killed no less than six monsters and highwaymen who endangered the busy route that led from the Isthmus of Corinth to Athens. When he entered Athens, he cautiously disguised his identity; this almost led to disaster. His father, fearful of what he assumed was a dangerous stranger, was talked by Medea, his lover, into poisoning him. Medea had recognized Theseus but, devious as ever, feared for the future of sons she and the elderly king might still have; she wanted to make sure that she would become Queen Mother. Aegeus invited Theseus to a sacrifice in the Delphinion to celebrate the foreigner's arrival, and, in a signal honor, he asked his guest to cut the meat. To perform this task, Theseus drew the sword he was carrying. The sword had its story: Aegeus had left it in Troizen after that fateful night, hidden under a huge boulder, with the instruction to Aethra that the sword should be Theseus' as soon as he was strong enough to lift the rock. Aegeus immediately recognized the sword as his own, and with it his son. And he saw the imminent danger: Medea was about to offer to Theseus a poisoned welcome drink. In a quick movement, he knocked the cup out of Medea's hand. The spilled wine stained the floor; centuries later, the Athenians still showed the red mark to tourists. Aegeus then formally recognized his son as his future heir. This story, told by Plutarch (*Life of Theseus* 12), perhaps following a lost play of Euripides, is yet another etiological myth: the Delphinion, Apollo's sanctuary, was the place of a law court that decided on questions of paternity and citizenship.

MOLPOI AND CURETES

Apollo Delphinios does not belong to Athens only, nor is his cult in Athens as important as in some other Greek cities, such as Miletus and some of its colonies. Although his Milesian sanctuary was very simple – an open court with a central altar – the political importance of its cult cannot be overrated; this is visible already in the fact that the sanctuary doubled as public archive of Miletus. It was the cult center for a small religious body, the six Molpoi, "singer-dancers." Their leader was also the political head of the city, at least in archaic and classical times, called the *aisymnḗtēs*, "ruler." An inscription from about 475 BCE regulates their ritual duties. Most of their sacrifices were addressed to Apollo Delphinios, and they usually accompanied them by drinking and the performance of a paean, with its combination of song and dance. Their main ritual, however, was a day-long procession from Miletus to Didyma, with many sacrifices and paeans along the Sacred Way: it is a ritual assertion that the Didymaean sanctuary and the vast territory between Miletus and Didyma belonged to Miletus. We know much less about Apollo Delphinios at Olbia, Miletus' important colony on the Crimea. The god is attested there since the Archaic Age; his sanctuary was the center for Molpoi as well, and formed part of the agora, the commercial and civic center of the colony. It is thus a reasonable assumption that the religious and political function of the Olbian Molpoi was very similar to the one the god had in their metropolis.

Molpoi are known only from Miletus and Olbia; but they have a close parallel in Ephesus, another Ionian city, some forty miles north along the coast from Miletus. Here, inscriptions attest to an association of *Kourētes*, a group of six leading citizens, and their assistants, mainly musicians. At the time of the inscriptions (first to third centuries CE), this group of ritual performers was associated with the prytaneion, the City Hall, its cult of Hestia on the city's common hearth on which an eternal fire was burning, and with the worship of the Roman emperors; in these cults, they performed sacrifices and sang hymns. However, the association is older than the Imperial age. A fourth-century BCE text connects them with the main sanctuary of the city, the Artemision, and a local myth, attested in Strabo (14.1.20), tells how their mythical ancestors danced around baby Artemis to protect her from the wrath of Hera, as the Cretan Curetes had danced around the Zeus baby to protect him against Cronus. In memory of this rite, the Ephesian Curetes were holding a banquet and performed a dance in a small sanctuary outside the town where Leto gave birth to her daughter. To a modern mind, it seems somewhat strange to imagine the stately and perhaps somewhat portly gentlemen of Ephesus's upper class performing an armed dance; but music and dance must have been part of their performance. Their name links them not only with the mythical dancers of ancient Crete, but also with the *koûroi*, the long-haired adolescents of Archaic Greece, although at the time we meet them, they certainly had outgrown adolescence, as had the six Molpoi, the similarly upper-class "singer-dancers" at Miletus.

The two bodies that we find in two neighbouring Ionian cities, at a distance of four centuries, are close enough to allow us to understand changes and transformations of a body that originally must have had very similar functions and roles. At the heart of these archaic cities, there was a small group of men who combined ritual performance in the city's main cults with strong political power; these singers-dancers were running the city as an aristocratic group, and they managed to preserve much of their power in more democratic times. But the modernization of society that accompanied democratization slowly led to a separation of religious and political power; in the Imperial epoch, their ritual role had become predominant, although there remained vestiges of political influence and power.

APOLLO, INITIATION, AND "MÄNNERBUND"

The archaic instiution of the Molpoi has a resonance that one has to explore further. Ordinarily, the complex of musical and dance performance, one of the main provinces of Apollo, is not associated with the leading citizen of a city, but rather with adolescents on the verge of adulthood. The link is old: already in *Iliad* 1, the paean that appeases Apollo is performed by the *koúroi Akhaíōn*, the young men who form the Greek army. The Milesian and the Ephesian groups are phenomenologically too close not to excite curiosity about just how they are related to each other, beyond the transformations just sketched.

The model past scholars used to explain this connection was developed in late nineteenth- and early twentieth-century ethnology and anthropology. Interest in the social structures of tribal cultures led to work on secret societies, tightly knit groups of men whose coherence was guaranteed by secret rituals and who wielded considerable political power. In other societies, including those of early modern Europe, adolescent males were found to form comparable bands with a more or less closed structure; members of such groups would wear masks and disguise themselves as, or at least call themselves after fearsome predators such as leopards in Africa or wolves in Europe. German scholars who were among the first to pursue the topic, called them *Männerbünde*, a term that has become somewhat invidious after its adoption by Nazi ideologists; but ideological misuse of a concept does not necessarily prove the concept wrong. In a more hypothetical evolutionary theory, these secret societies were understood as having developed out of tribal initiation rites. Such rites concern either gender and are intended to turn adolescents into adult members of society, equipped with all the ritual and social knowledge that the tribe's tradition provides and that tribal leaders regard as essential for the tribe's self-definition. More often in the case of young men than of young women, adolescents were organized in age groups that underwent the rituals together, secluded from the village in a place in the forest or on a remote island where they were introduced into the ritual traditions as well as into the activities of hunting, fishing, and warfare; the return to the village was celebrated by an impressive performance of dancing and singing that displayed bodily abilities and showed readiness for marriage and procreation.

If one locates the Milesian Molpoi and the Ephesian Curetes on such an ethnographic background, one is tempted to see them as phenomenologically related to male secret societies, the German scholars' "Männerbünde." Like these, the Greek associations were small groups of adult males; their identity and coherence resulted from common rituals, and they wielded power in their cities. But they lacked one essential characteristic, secrecy: the Molpoi and the Curetes were highly visible in their cities, and no ancient text talks about mysteries or other secret rites in connection with them. There was another group in late Archaic Greece that would come much closer to the phenomenology of secret societies: the Pythagoreans who were organized as a ritual society, had their secrets, and ruled for a while the city of Croton. And it is worth noting that Apollo is connected with the Pythagoreans as well: Pythagoras, the leader of the group, was seen as a human form of Hyperborean Apollo.

Thus, comparativism goes only so far. If we confine our perspective to the Greek world, both Molpoi and Curetes are rooted in the song-dance culture of Archaic Greece and the central role it played in society. In two cities, for reasons unknown to us, these ritual and performative forms associated with Apollo and the young men were transformed into a much more selective institution of aristocratic governance. The Milesian group retained its connection with Apollo, the Ephesian one was tied to his sister – Ephesus, after all, was Artemis' city; there is a possibility that in other cities, such as Pergamon or Halicarnassus, similar groups were connected with Zeus.

ARCHAIC INSTITUTIONS IN IONIA AND CRETE

Milesians preserved another venerable institution that points to archaic social structures. According to Herodotus, they were dining among themselves, without their wives; he explains it as a memory of the fact that the celibate colonizers married native women. This is local mythology: Miletus was settled about a millennium before the time of Herodotus, and it is unlikely that historical memory stretched so far.

More importantly, the Milesians shared this radical gender segregation with two other Greek regional cultures, Crete and Sparta. Sparta prided itself on the institution of the *pheiditia*, the common meals of all its adult warrior citizens. Later philosophers understood it as a moralizing reform by Lycurgus, the Spartan law-giver, to prevent the Spartans from succumbing to luxury dining. The same custom was preserved in Crete: in their cities, "the adult men dine together in what they call the men's houses (*andreîa*) so that the poor would eat the same portions as the rich, since all are fed at public expense" (Ephorus F 149). No wonder that Cretan authors believed that Lycurgus had also come to their island to introduce his way of life. Single cities usually had several men's houses, presumably according to the subdivisions of the population, and they served not only as dining halls but also as a place for political decision-making: during their meals, the assembled men discussed politics, both day-to-day matters and larger issues, in a set agenda.

In both cultures, this institution goes together with a strict stratification of male society according to age, with elaborate rites of passage between the stages. The Spartan educational system was very complex, embraced all free-born Spartan boys, lasted over many years, and trained the boys in order to turn them into members of the most successful army in Greece before Alexander. The Cretan system was looser and contained three stages: pre-*agela* age (boyhood), age of the *agela* ("herd": adolescence), and adulthood. All age classes were closely connected with the men's house. Young Cretan boys were present in the men's house as servers; only after this service would they become members of the "herds." Each house had an adult official who was responsible for the training of the adolescents. He trained them in archery and in the armed dances "which the Curetes had introduced," and in combat techniques: "On stated days, the herds attack each other and fight to the rhythm of flutes and lyres."

When Strabo wrote that the Curetes had introduced armed dancing, he was alluding to the well-known myth of the armed dancers who protected newly born Zeus; singing and hitting their shields with their swords, they drowned the baby's wailing that could have given him away to his evil father Cronus. Behind this myth and the armed dances it explains already native observers noticed the same background of a society whose main educational instrument was the dance of the adolescents, and where adult men, organized as a close community, ruled the city-state. Crete was the one region where these customs survived best. In Sparta, they were turned into an instrument of a militarist state with an almost professional citizen army. In Ionia finally – in Miletus and in Ephesus – some elements survived in new forms that had close connections both with the administration and with the ritual life of the city.

Where does Apollo enter all this in Crete and Sparta? One would expect him to be the divinity who was firmly associated with the complex of singing and dancing. We saw him in this role in Miletus, as Apollo Delphinios, the god of the Molpoi. Apollo Delphinios loomed large in Eastern Crete as well, and he had an important political function; the god's main festival was so important that some cities had a month named Delphinios after it. Some archaeological contexts are especially impressive. In the small city of Dreros, his archaic sanctuary has been excavated. It is a small building with one room only, with a central hearth and, in the far right corner, a hollow altar filled with the (mostly left) horns of sacrificial goats; on a stone table nearby, there stood three very archaic bronze images of Apollo, Artemis, and Leto. The altar recalls the more famous horn altar on Delus: we must be dealing with a sacrificial practice that may be as old as the Bronze Age, when Ionian Delus and Dorian Dreros were part of the same Aegean culture. The outer walls of the temple were inscribed with the city's constitution, dated to about 650–600 BCE: this again emphasizes the political importance of the sanctuary. The god continued to be important after the Archaic Age, and the Drerians counted him among their main deities in oaths of Hellenistic times. Another temple of Apollo Delphinios, in the town of Hyrtakina, contained the "common hearth" (*hestía koiné*) of the city. Such a hearth with its eternal fire was characteristic of the City Hall, as we saw in Ephesus. In these Cretan cities, then, Apollo Delphinios appeared in the same key position as he did in Miletus, as guardian of the city's political traditions.

The common hearth is of special interest. Its eternal flames had not only symbolical importance: in an age without matches, the common altar was also the source of all the fires on the public altars of a city, and presumably of those on private altars and in private hearths as well. At the same time, one might tentatively connect the central hearth with the Cretan men's house: after all, this house needed a central hearth, for cooking as well as for the sacrifices that were connected with the activities of the adult citizen. Thus, Cretan temples with central hearths in the archaeological record were thought to be the men's houses known from the literary record. The sanctuaries of Apollo Delphinios in Dreros and Hyrtakina, however, seem too small for such a function: they are central sanctuaries of the city, not meeting halls of its subgroups. The temple with one room and with a central hearth, however, might still mirror the men's houses. Thus, we would better understand the role Apollo Delphinios played in Crete as well as in Ionia. The Milesian Molpoi and Ephesian Curetes appear to be citizen groups whose ancestors were the men's dining associations as we know them from Archaic Crete and early Miletus, transformed under the conditions of political change through the centuries. The Athenian Delphinion attests to yet another transformation: under more democratic circumstances, the old men's house turns into a sanctuary closely connected with safeguarding citizenship. The myth of Theseus' recognition by his father in the Delphinion fits well: the Cretan men's houses, after all, were the places where the sons were promoted into the position of adult citizen, not unlike Theseus.

We begin to see, even if somewhat dimly, developments in the role of Apollo Delphinios. (We will explore these somewhat hypothetical alleys further in the next chapter.) In the most Archaic Cretan communities with their direct participatory state, the sanctuary of Apollo was the focus of civic life and mirrored the men's houses of the city's subdivisions. Given the importance of armed dancing in Crete, the cult did not only consist of goat sacrifices to Apollo, to his mother, and to his sister, but also of dances and songs, presumably paeans for which the Cretans were famous, performed by the choirs of adolescent boys and of adult men. Miletus shared the institution of common meals of its adult citizens with Crete; but in a less participatory political system, a small group of leading aristocrats, the six Molpoi, took over the cult of Apollo with its sacrifices and its dances and songs. In the more developed democracy of fifth-century Athens finally, political power was devolved upon the organs of the citizens' assembly, and the sanctuary of Apollo Delphinios was reduced to a place where litigation about citizenship took place.

SPARTAN FESTIVALS AND THE ADOLESCENTS

In Sparta, three festivals of Apollo were especially imporant: the Hyacinthia, the Gymnopaidia, and the Carneia. During all three festivals, the Spartans avoided warfare as far as possible. I have already treated the Hyacinthia as an example of a festival that opposed music and war (see Chapter 2). The same holds true for the other two festivals that connected Apollo with the Spartan age groups and with singing and dancing.

Dancing naked: the Gymnopaidia

The Gymnopaidia – "a festival that the Spartans took extremely seriously," according to Pausanias (3.11.9) – was very much a festival of dance and song; it gave its name to a special dance, the *gymnopaidikè órkhēsis*, or "boy's dance that is performed naked." It was a summer festival whose main feature was dances executed by three choirs, of boys, of adult citizens, and of old men. The choirs performed on the Spartan agora, under the eyes not only of their fellow Spartans, but of images of Apollo Pythaeus, Artemis, and Leto, with the boys always performing in the center, the adults to their left, and the old men to their right. The leaders of the three choirs wore wreaths made of palm leaves, one of

Apollo's sacred plants (the victor in the Delia got a palm branch); the wreaths were called *thyreátis*, a name that recalled a major Spartan battle in the sixth century BCE. This battle, a Spartan victory over its main rival Argos that led to considerable gain in territory, was also recalled in another detail: the boys were said to sing paeans in honor of the Spartans fallen in that battle. The addressee of these paeans was Apollo Karneios, the most Doric Apollo, and a major form of the god in Sparta. Already to dance in the summer heat could be seen as a test of endurance of all Spartan men: while the boys danced naked, adults and old men were wearing full armor. Other contests, this time confined to the adolescents only, concerned boxing, playing ball games, and fighting ritual battles. The boxing recalls the same contest on Delus during the main festival of the Ionians, the regular and ritualized battles between the Cretan *agelai*.

Apollo the Ram and the Carneia

Whereas the Gymnopaidia was Spartan only, the Carneia was one of the most characteristic festivals of all Dorians. It named a month in the calendar of many Dorian cities, from Acragas and Syracuse in Sicily to Rhodes and to Cnossus on Crete, and added the epithet *Karneios* to Apollo's name. Ancient grammarians tell us that in the Dorian dialect *kárnos* meant "ram": Apollo Karneios thus is "Ram Apollo." A coin from the Spartan colony Metapontum (ca. 400 BCE) figures the beautiful head of the god with ram's horns inscribed in his lush hair (figure 9): this confirms the grammarians' notice and helps to understand archaic pillars with a ram's head from Sparta as images of their Apollo. The ram is a rare sacrificial animal, but he is also the leader of the flock – and the symbolism of the flock is well present in Spartan and Cretan society where the adolescents were organized in *agelai*, "herds." In a common metaphor, ancient societies understood the socialization of the young as turning animals into humans: Apollo the Ram, then, evokes the image of leadership in a band of adolescents. At the same time, he can be connected with the center of political power: his is the undying fire in the colony of Cyrene where the Carneia was the main city festival. The founders of Cyrene brought it from Thera, whose founders had brought it from Sparta.

In his *Hymn to Apollo*, Callimachus describes the Cyrenaean Carneia. It was a joyful spring festival where many bulls were sacrificed and where the altars were adorned with the first flowers. The Spartan festival looks gloomier. Demetrius of Scepsis, a writer of the third century BCE, calls it

Figure 9 Apollo Karneios. Silver coin (*stater*) from Metapontum, ca. 425 BC. Author's drawing.

"an imitation of their military education," since the banquet followed a strict order:

> There are nine spots that . . . look somewhat like tents. In each tent, nine men are dining, and everything is done according to the orders of a herald. Each tent holds three brotherhoods (*phratríai*), and the festival is held for nine days.

"Brotherhoods" is Demetrius' term for the traditional three Dorian tribes, the Hyloi, Dymanes, and Pamphyloi, the old subdivisions of every Dorian state and city, including Sparta. Each tent held three representatives of each tribe: the common banquet was a mirror image of the Dorian state in its overall structure. Tents, or rather sunshades, replace solid buildings not only in the army: in many Greek rituals, the underlying opposition between permanent house and temporary tent is used to indicate the suspension of ordinary time during the extraordinary period of the festival. The presence of a herald giving orders for everything may tie into this: the spontaneity and free will of ordinary life is replaced by the guidance of orders to which the entire group submits itself.

This rather stiff common banquet cannot have been all to keep the Spartans busy through the nine days of their main festival. Dancing and singing, again, was more important, although less unusual and thus less noteworthy. We hear of paeans sung by boys; and the musical contest of the Carneia was already famous in the Archaic Age. For

Cyrene, Callimachus describes how at the first Carneia "the girded warriors of Enyo [a Greek goddess of war] danced with the blond women of Libya," touching again on the topic of celibate settlers taking indigenous wives. Another ritual, less banal than dancing and singing, again caught the attention of ancient writers. "In the festival of the Carneia," according to a Byzantine lexicon,

> a person adorned with ribbons runs and prays for the city. Young men pursue him: they are called *staphylodrómoi*, "grape-runners." Should they catch him, the Spartans expect good things for the city, if not, the contrary.

This again leads away from Demetrius' military interpretation, and points towards New Year rituals: the outcome of ritual races was an omen for the year to come. The runner was symbolically turned into the always rather elusive success of the future year; it might be that the enigmatic reference to grapes (after all, the ritual was performed in early spring, well outside the grape season) is simply another way of alluding to something highly desirable, with the future grape harvest standing in for all the goods one wishes for the coming year. As often in ancient ritual, agricultural symbolism could be used to designate much broader societal goals.

The myths associated with the festival give conflicting readings; the learned Pausanias collected them all (*Guide to Greece* 3.1.3). In one reading, Carneius was a pre-Dorian divinity in Sparta who received worship in the house of a seer named "Ram"; Ram's daughter helped the Dorians to conquer Sparta. Another story turns Karnos into a local seer whom the invading Dorians killed. Apollo, protector of the seer's art or even his foster father, punished them. In order to placate the god, the Dorians established a cult of the seer. In both stories, the hero is a seer because this explains Apollo's intervention. Both stories connect the festival with the Dorian conquest of Sparta and the foundation of the Spartan state: the festival guaranteed a successful foundation. This is a mythical form of the same concept that was, in Cyrene, ritually expressed in the undying fire of Apollo Karneios. In a third story, the Greeks in Troy cut down a sacred grove of cornel trees (*kráneia*) to build the Wooden Horse; doing this, they called Apollo's wrath upon themselves, and the festival was instituted to appease the god. Here, the foundation of the festival precedes the Dorian conquest. Myth understands the Dorian invasion of the Peloponnese as the return of the grandsons of Heracles who was thought to have conquered Troy a generation before Agamemnon and his army.

The festival, however, is Panhellenic: the Dorians adopted it and by doing so insist on their fundamental Greekness.

WOLF-APOLLO, THE DORIAN INVASION, AND THE EARLY CITY

Apollo the Ram was to the Spartans and their colonies what Apollo the Wolf was to the Argives, their arch-rivals in the domination over the Peloponnesus. "Wolf-Apollo," at least, is the most reasonable interpretation of the epithet Lykeios that Apollo had in many Greek cities, Argos included (see the following chapter); the wolf sometimes appears as Apollo's animal.

Although the cult of Apollo Lykeios is attested in many places all over the Greek world, it clusters around the Corinthian Isthmus and is central in Argos. Here, his sanctuary was built next to the agora, the place of market and citizen assembly. According to local myth, it was founded by Danaus, the mythical king of Argus from the line of Zeus and Io, the daughter of the local river-god, who fled to Egypt. Her great-grandson Danaus returned to Argos and demanded the ancestral kingship. The Argives already had a king; embarrassed, they asked for a day to think about this tricky demand. In the night, a wolf attacked a herd of cows and killed the lead bull. The Argives understood this as an omen (as they better would): the lonely wolf, an outside intruder who killed the much bigger leader of the herd, symbolized the foreigner Danaus who was about to oust the local king. They made Danaus king of Argus, and he thanked Apollo for his help by building his sanctuary in which Pausanias still admired the throne of Danaus.

More importantly, the sanctuary contained the undying fire of the city, kindled (as the Argives claimed) by Phoroneus, the first human who lived in Argos. It also contained an image of Aphrodite, dedicated by Danaus' daughter Hypermestra. When Danaus came to Argus from Egypt, he brought his fifty daughters with him. The fifty sons of his brother Aegyptus cornered them there, and Danaus had to consent to a highly unwanted mass marriage – at least temporarily: he equipped his daughters with daggers and ordered them to kill their grooms in the wedding night. Forty-nine daughters obeyed; Hypermestra, however, had fallen in love with her cousin and saved him. Her father, incensed, put her on trial for treason, but Aphrodite personally defended her: hence the statue. When Danaus died without a male heir, Hypermestra and her husband founded a dynasty that ruled Argos for centuries.

Thus, the sanctuary was not only associated with the re-foundation of the city (after all, the Argives could be called Danaoi, after Danaus), but more specifically with marriage and the foundation of a dynasty: in a democratic city, every citizen belonged to such a dynasty since he had to have parents who were free citizen who had to have parents who were, etc. But there was more. Inside the temple, there was the statue of a famous athlete who carried a bull to the altar of Zeus, and an image of a famous runner. Somewhere else in the sanctuary, there was also the grave of a famous boxer: this is unusual, since graves could be neither in sanctuaries nor inside a city. Running and boxing were not just athletic disciplines in Greece, they were the ritual core disciplines of archaic education; to carry a bull to an altar was the ritual regularly performed by the Athenian ephebes who imitated Theseus' feat at the sanctuary of Apollo Delphinios. The themes surrounding the Argive sanctuary of Apollo Lykeios, thus, had extremely rich resonances. There was the story of the origins of the state and the connection with the undying fire; there was marriage and citizenship; and there was athletics and other ephebic occupations.

Parts of this rich nexus around Apollo Lykeios are visible in other cities as well. In two other cities, the sanctuary of the god was next to the agora – in Metapontum, a South Italian colony of Achaia in the north-west of the Peloponnesus, and in Sicyon west of Corinth. In Epidaurus and in Athens, the sanctuary was next to a gymnasion, a sports field; the Athenian Lykeion was not only a place famous for its running contests (and, in the fourth century, for the school of Aristotle, the ancestor of every lyceum or Lycée); it was also the place for the regular exercises of the Athenian infantry, cavalry, and archers: athletics and warfare are never far apart, not only in Greece. And it may be more than coincidence that the radically democratic reforms of Cleisthenes were debated in an assembly in the Lykeion, or that the city of Eressus on Lesbos, when overturning its undemocratic junta, made the judges who put them on trial take an oath on Apollo Lykeios.

It is tempting to explain this rich nexus of themes around Apollo the Wolf – wolf, war, foundation, and citizenship – by a somewhat hypothetical reconstruction of history. Apollo Lykeios is best attested in the Doric city-states around the Isthmus of Corinth, the natural path for any immigrant or invader to the Peloponnese. When at the end of the Bronze Age the powerful kingdoms of Southern Greece – Mycenae, Tiryns, Pylus, Cnossus – collapsed, the Dorians moved south from their home in Northwestern Greece and took over the land: their dialect, not attested in the Mycenaean texts, became the common dialect of most of the Peloponnese and the Southern Aegean islands, including Crete and Rhodes. Mythology describes this movement as a return of Heracles' descendants and of their armies to their ancestral lands; but the myth of return is a narrative ploy to legitimate a conquest. Historical scholarship in the nineteenth and early twentieth centuries used the template of migration to describe this movement and imagined the one-time influx of an entire new population group from Northwestern Greece. Archaeological research, however, found no trace of such a large-scale immigration and population change; all we have is a new dialect, some new cities, and new political structures. Thus, the template of migration has been replaced by that of a gradual take-over of population centers and fertile land by an invading military elite that slowly trickled into the area attracted by its wealth and no longer kept out by military power. In many early societies, bands of young men put themselves under the sign of some fierce and predatory animal, as we saw above; they sometimes clashed with the authorities or organized military campaigns or rather rampages. It is tempting to imagine young Dorian warriors under the sign of Apollo the Wolf pushing south, taking over former Mycenaean lands and founding new settlements such as Corinth where they dedicated the main city temple to their god.

APOLLO THE HERDSMAN AND TRICKY FRAMES OF REFERENCE

Even the ancient authors, too, understood Apollo Lykeios to mean "Wolf Apollo," but they gave a different explanation. Many stories connect the god with the wolves. We have already seen how the Argive cult of Apollo Lykeios was connected with Danaos and the wolf who symbolized him; but there were other stories. They tell how Leto, pregnant with Zeus' children, was led by wolves from the country of the Hyperboreans to Delus to give birth there; or how wolves led her with her new-born babies from Delus to Xanthus in Lycia, her main shrine in Anatolia; or how Apollo sent a she-wolf to nourish his exposed son, Miletus, the founder of the most powerful Ionian city; or how Apollo slept with the nymph Cyrene in the shape of a wolf. The Delphians narrated that, after Apollo had killed Python, a wolf brought him a laurel twig from the Tempe valley. They also showed the statue of a wolf in their sanctuary and explained how once a thief had invaded it and got away with rich booty; but when he was sleeping, a wolf attacked and killed him, obviously sent by Apollo. In Sicyon near Corinth, Pausanias heard the story that once so many wolves were killing the sheep that the farmers were unable to fend them off; but Apollo showed them how to poison the wolves with the bark of a particular tree, and the grateful herdsmen dedicated a temple to Apollo Lykeios where visitors could still see pieces of the miraculous wood. The Corinthians must have had a similar story that competed with the myth of Danaus and the wolf, since Sophocles calls the Argive Apollo not Lykeios but *lyko-któnos* "wolf-killer," as the protector of the Argive sheep against wolves.

Thus, whatever the story, the connection with the wolf is constant and obvious throughout antiquity; only Servius, the commentator on Virgil in the fourth century CE, offers an alternative, namely that Lykeios derived from the Greek word for white, *leukós*, "because Apollo is the sun." Most scholars disregarded this interpretation as being based on a wrong assumption and followed the wolf interpretation; others derived the god from Lycia where Leto had a major shrine. A few assumed that the wolf connection was a remnant of animal worship, the wolf being a totemic animal. But totemism never really made an impact of Greek religion, and most scholars preferred another angle: among the many ancient stories, they picked the one that explained Apollo as protector of the herds, and jettisoned all other stories. They did so because there is some evidence that, among his many functions, Apollo is a protector of sheep and cattle. In this role, he was called Nomios, "herdsman," whereas the Boeotians, according to Plutarch, called him Galaxios, "Milk-Apollo," because "abundance of milk indicated his helpful presence." Other epithets indicate a similar nature, "wherefore he is recognized as patron of cattle and a true herdsman," as the late Roman Macrobius has it (*Saturnalia* 1.17.43). But already in the *Homeric Hymn* he had his own cattle; and when Zeus punished him by having him serve a human, he guarded the cattle of king Admetus of Pherae. The fact that Apollo was so often connected with *agélai*, "herds" of young men, seemed to confirm this very connection: it was an extension of the original "agricultural" meaning.

Thus, we are confronted with several interpretations of Lykeios. There were three basic ways of understanding the epithet, as deriving from the Lycians, light, or the wolf; among the derivations from wolf, there were again three options: the totemistic interpretation, Apollo as wolf totem; the agricultural one, Apollo as protector of the herds against wolves; and the sociological one, Apollo as leader of adolescent wolf societies. Some theories were more easily refuted than others: the connection with "light" is linguistically unsound, the one with Lycia crumbled as soon as it became clear that Leto was no Lycian goddess, and totemism preceded shamanism as a widely over-used concept; neither should be generalized outside the cultures in which it was found. In the end, we are left with the sociological interpretation, and the agricultural one. Both resonate with the cult of Apollo: he truely is god of cattle and sheep, and he is the leader of young adolescents; the main question was which of these functions was prior or "original," and which was secondary and derived.

This raises an interesting methodological question. There are other instances in Greek religion where these two interpretations oppose each other. The most conspicuous one is the case of Demeter who presides over the crops, and over the fertility of the married women: here too, the priority was at stake, and the answer used to be the same as in Apollo's case: "originally," Demeter was a goddess of agriculture (and Apollo a god of cattle), but then this function was metaphorically transferred onto children, the fruit of women, or upon young men, organized in "herds" and living outside the polis, as cattle and herdsmen did. The only reason for this choice was the assumption that agricultural (or pastoral) concerns were at the core of religion because man was first an agriculturalist and pastoralist and only later turned into a city-dweller.

This frame of reference was challenged by Émile Durkheim, the founder of French sociology. For Durkheim, religion and ritual was not connected with fertility, but with social cohesion and identity: rituals created social unity and established social order, and religion was the main force that shaped early men into a functioning group. Thus, the interpretation depends solely on the frame of reference for the data that we have from antiquity. For the agricultural/pastoral frame, social concerns develop out of agricultural ones and are metaphors of them; for the sociological frame, agriculture/pastoral life is a metaphor for social concerns.

The development of prehistory has made it possible to decide between the two frames of interpretation. Prehistoric research has shown that agriculture and husbandry developed rather late, in about 8000/7000 BCE, in what has been called the Neolithic Revolution. Society preceded agriculture and husbandry for many millennia, already when *homo sapiens* (and even his predecessors) existed in the African savannahs, there were social groups, bands of hunters and gatherers, and they must have developed ritual instruments to hold these groups together. The agricultural interpretation of ritual is secondary, and relatively young.

APOLLO THE LEADER THROUGH THE AGES

This is, of course, prehistory, and like any prehistory, hypothetical. Apollo's close ties with the political life in many cities of historical Greece, however, are undeniable, and not only among the Dorians, and so is his role as the ancestor of entire population groups. At a time late in the sixth century BCE, when the growing antagonism between the two main Greek powers, Sparta and Athens, made them conceptualize Greece in terms of an old and fundamental opposition between Ionians and Dorians, Doric Heracles was opposed to Ionic Apollo, father of Ion, grandson of an Athenian king. In the cities of the Greek world, Apollo competed with Athena for the possession of the most important city sanctuary. Mapping them shows no clear pattern and certainly no Dorian/Ionian dichotomy, thus the distribution must precede this ideological construction. The favorite daughter and the favorite son of Zeus share not only the function of the principal divinity in the city, but also the care for the adolescent citizen-warriors; the two are related. The procession of the Athenian Panathenaia displayed the young horsemen who were the backbone of Athens' army and the protégés of Athena, whereas in Sparta a similar display took place during Hyacinthia, Gymnopaidia and Carneia under the tutelage of Apollo. Only a few other cities selected other divine protectors, such as Hera in Argus where the young warriors marched in the procession from the city out to the sanctuary of the goddess far away at the border of the territory. In myth, Athena is the unswerving protectress of warlike heroes such as Heracles or Theseus, whereas Apollo kills as many heroes as he fathers and protects. Still, the Homeric opposition between Athena, the main patroness of the Greeks, and Apollo, the leading patron of the Trojans, looks as if it is constructed on the background of this functional overlap of the two divinities, although the singer also projected the acropolis temple of Athena, known to him from his own world, onto his imaginary city of Troy.

After Alexander's conquest of the East, Greek cities lost part of their power and independence, becoming part of the kingdoms that succeeded Alexander's conquest. From Alexander onwards, divine kings supplemented the protection the Olympian gods provided for Greek cities: ruler cult is the religious expression of the new distribution of power. But the forms of this cult were surprisingly flexible and ranged from seeking divine protection for the king to outright worship of a divinized ruler. In this world, Apollo appeared as the ancestor and protector of the dynasty of the Seleucids, the rulers of large parts of the Near East. The founder of the dynasty, Alexander's general Seleucus who became king Seleucus I Victor (Nicator; died 281 BCE) invoked Apollo as the Leader (Hēgemōn) of his family. Accordingly, when a city instituted a festival in honor of king Seleucus, the assembly would decree the institution of "contests in music, athletics, and horsemanship, such as we perform for Apollo the Leader of the dynasty"; the same was true for his sons and successors. Over time, Apollo turned from being protector of the dynasty into its very ancestor, and historians could tell exactly how it happened:

> When the mother of Seleucus married Antiochus, a nobleman at the court of king Philip of Macedonia, she had the impression that, when relaxing, she had intercourse with Apollo and became pregnant from him. To thank her for her love, the god gave her a ring with an anchor engraved on its stone, and told her she should hand it over to the son to whom she would gave birth.
>
> (Justin, *Epitome* 15.4, 3–5)

The story, as strange as it sounds to a modern ear, has a rich ancestry: it was also told about Alexander's conception from Zeus Ammon but goes back to the template of Egyptian royal ideology: every pharaoh was conceived by his mother when she slept with the ruling god of Egypt's pantheon.

It seems a small step from the divinization of a mortal and living king to his identification with an Olympian god. No Hellenistic king, and few Roman emperors for that, made this step themselves or allowed a city to do it during their life times. It was a somewhat different matter to do it posthumously and to institute a cult to a deceased king in the guise of a Greek god. In a list of priests that held office in one of the Seleucid foundations, Seleucia in Northern Greece, we find not only a priest of Zeus Olympios and Koryphaios ("He of the Mountain Top") and two priests of Apollo, but also a priest of Seleucus Zeus Nikator and of Antiochus Apollo Soter ("Savior"). Thus, after their deaths, the founder of the dynasty mutated into a form of Zeus, and his son and successor, Antiochus I, into Apollo, the god of the dynasty.

Rome's emperors succeeded the Hellenistic kings, and they adapted these forms of religious representation of earthly power to their own purposes. Apollo thus became also the god of the Roman emperors: hardly the Roman god of healing, but the Greek ancestor of dynasties.

There was an Apollo Augustus, "Imperial" Apollo, on coins of Antoninus Pius in the middle of the second century CE. Less than a century before that, coins portrayed the emperor Nero as Apollo Citharoedus, in a clear allusion to Nero's artistic ambitions. Nero's connection with Apollo, however, was more complex than this and goes back to the ideology devised for him by his advisers. His teacher and secret chancellor Seneca wrote the *Apocolocyntosis*, a satire on Nero's predecessor Claudius which was recited shortly after Nero's accession in 54 CE. In this work a singing Apollo helps the Fates bring forward the ruler of the new Golden Age, Nero, a second Apollo whose "radiant face blazes with gentle brilliance and his shapely neck with flowing hair." The identification of Apollo and Helios/Sol, the Sun God, is common in this epoch: when he traveled in Greece many years later, the Greeks addressed Nero specifically as "New Sun God," Neos Helios; and when he returned from this trip where the Greeks celebrated him as their liberator and a most gifted singer and lyre-player, the groups of young noblemen that he had organized into the Augustanei hailed him as another Apollo.

Nero's self-definition as Apollo, however, as outrageous as it seemed even to his senators, rested firmly on the adoption of Greek Apollo by the founder of the dynasty, Augustus. After Caesar's death and yet another civil war, the young heir of Caesar, Octavian, who later was to call himself Augustus, and Caesar's most faithful lieutenant Marc Antony had divided the world among themselves: Marc Antony took over the splendid and fabulous East, including the sexy and wily queen of Egypt Cleopatra, while his junior partner Octavian got the West with its big problems created by decades of civic unrest and civil war. In the ensuing propaganda war between the former allies, Marc Antony offered himself to the world as the new Dionysus, divine conqueror of the East and god of an easy life. Octavian first wavered about his own divine symbol, leaning towards calling himself Novus Romulus, a new founder of the state; this too had many Greek parallels. But his advisers pointed out that Romulus was an ambiguous figure not too well suited for the purpose of projecting a positive image since, after all, he had killed his brother; Augustus thus opted for Apollo as the god whom he would follow – not so much the Roman god of healing as the Greek youthful warrior and Averter of Evil. The first step had been done already in the battle of Philippi in 42 BCE: here, both sides had used Apollo's name as military password, building on a tradition that associated Apollo, the oracular god, and his symbols with the hope for a better future. Once he had become ruler of the West, Octavian slowly adopted this symbolism: he made the sphinx, an Apolline creature, into his seal symbol and was wearing a laurel wreath in public ceremonies. In 36 BCE he attributed a resounding naval victory to the help of Apollo and Artemis, whose sanctuary was not far from the Sicilian coast where the battle occurred. He did the same on a grander scale when the propaganda war with Marc Antony turned into a real war: he attributed his victory over Marc Antony and Cleopatra in the sea battle of Actium (31 BCE) to the intervention of Apollo whose sanctuary, again, was not that far away; it seems that it was not too difficult to find a sanctuary of Apollo close by wherever in Greek lands one was. It does not surprise that in 17 BCE, when he inaugurated a new epoch, a *saeculum*, he put himself again under the protection of Apollo and his sister and had the poet Horace compose a hymn in their honor (*Carmen Saeculare*).

The association with Apollo was a brilliant move. Apollo the youthful god and warlike patron of young men was a fit protector for a ruler who was in his early twenties when he came to power. Apollo, the Averter of Evil, the god of music, of harmony, and of prophecy, promised solace from the ravages of a century of civil war and punishment for all arrogance, as he and his sister had punished arrogant Niobe by killing her seven sons and seven daughters: not by chance, this myth was represented more than once in the official art of Augustan Rome. The restrained harmony of Apollo was opposed to the excesses of Dionysus-Marc Antony, the Roman who had become a dissolute Oriental and sexual slave of a foreign queen: this exploited all the negative associations that could be read into Dionysus, especially in a Rome that was prone to associate Dionysiac rites with sex and crime. It was almost inevitable that Augustus, too, was inserted into the by now almost traditional royal mythology: even before Actium, a story was current about how his mother Atia became pregnant from a divine snake, another form of the god Apollo. Like Alexander, and like Seleucus, the new king of Rome was the physical son of his divine protector.

Augustus, unsurpassed master of political propaganda, did more than just foster these rumors. In a move that inscribed his closeness to the god Apollo into the center of Rome to be seen by all, he built a temple of Apollo on the Palatine, next to his own house and easily accessible from it, so that his house and the god's temple were in fact one single palatial complex. Whoever looked up to the Palatine from the Forum or gazed at it from the top of the Capitolium would see and perceive the house and the temple, Octavian and Apollo, as a close unit. His own house door was guarded by symbols of the god, two laurel trees and two pillars of Apollo Agyieus, the Guardian of the House Door. United with Apollo, Augustus would finally bring back the Golden Age that the Cumaean Sibyl, another servant of Apollo, had prophesied, according to a celebrated poem of Virgil (*Eclogue* 4).

SUMMARY

Apollo's connection with communal and political life covers a wide area. At its center is the role he played for the young men: himself an eternal ephebe, he was their main protector, and his myths reflect their triumphs and problems. Groups of young men – perhaps the most dynamic, but also the most unstable part of the social body – have always been crucial in power politics, down to the role they play in today's Islamic terrorist movements: hence Apollo's involvement with the power of the city and with ruling bodies whose strange combination of music, dance, and power looks back to early forms of Greek political life. His political power, however, remained unbroken and transformed itself even into the protection of Roman emperors, starting with Augustus. The last Roman emperor to tie himself to Apollo was no other than Constantine, the first Christian emperor, whose image on top of a porphyry column in his new Rome, Constantinople, may well have started out as an image of Apollo.

6

ORIGINS

THE QUEST FOR ORIGINS

Nowadays, scholars on Greek religion want to know how ritual and myth functioned in Greek society, how religion and institutions interacted, or how the single divinities defined each other in the pantheon of a city or in Panhellenic religion (if Panhellenic religion existed as a system and not just as a loose aggregate of myths and cults). This interest is relatively new, and it results from a radical paradigm shift that happened in the 1960s and 1970s. This shift in turn depended on two earlier paradigm changes in social anthropology and religious studies, from evolutionism to functionalism and from an interest in individuals and their thoughts to an interest in groups and their needs. Somehow connected with these earlier paradigms was an emphasis on origins: to understand a cultural phenomenon meant to find its origins; later developments only complicated, overlaid, and darkened the true original meaning. These paradigms had their root in historicism and evolutionism, the two approaches that dominated much of nineteenth-century thought but go much further back, to ancient interpretations of religion. In the case of Greek divinities with their multiple and often heterogeneous functions, this meant to find the original core out of which this confusing reality had developed: the historical divinities were seen as the result of manifold transformations, accretions, and sometimes incorporations of other divinities, in what was generally understood as early "syncretism." Thus, in this approach, the logical operation of ordering a confusing and heterogeneous plurality was conceived as the reconstruction of its past history: heterogeneity, scholars thought, resulted from developments over time, and one had to go back step by step in order to reach the first and original core that was simple and coherent.

The first example of cultural evolutionism was the reconstruction of an Indo-European language as the common origin of most languages between India and Ireland, as it was formulated in the late eighteenth and early nineteenth centuries. In this reconstruction, a set of sometimes complex phonetic laws reduced the confusing diversity of the individual extant languages to the one reconstructed Indo-European *Ur*-language. Meaning was seen as developing in the same way, from a hypothetical Indo-European meaning to the many different meanings a word would have in the single languages; in semantics, however, it was less easy to formulate laws. A very simple example may demonstrate the approach. The English word *father*, the German *Vater*, French *père*, Italian *padre*, Latin *pater*, Sanscrit *pitar* (and a host of words in other languages) lead back to the Indo-European root *$p\vartheta_2$tr- (where the asterisk warns that this is a hypothetical word that was nowhere spoken, and ϑ_2 is the conventional sign for the short vowel that is supposed to be the starting point for the different vowels in the extant words). The word's basic meaning is surprisingly constant in all Indo-European languages and must correspond to a very elementary social structure. But there are additional meanings, developed over time and under specific social circumstances: in some languages, the word is also used to designate a Christian priest or an authority figure in society. The founders of Indo-European studies were convinced that they were reconstructing a language that was at one time spoken by a group of people whose habitat they could more or less reconstruct, and this view still exists, but it competes with the more sophisticated view that the reconstructed language exists on the plane of reconstructive logic only but not necessarily on that of history – which curiously coincides with Dante's view that Latin, the common origin of all Romance languages, was a hypothetical language only, never spoken by any human being.

I did not choose the comparison with Indo-European linguistics by chance. In religious studies, linguistic reconstruction has often become the main tool with which to reconstruct Indo-European religion, the assumed origin of many phenomena of historical religions, including the divinities and their functions. The most convincing case is still the god whom the Greeks called Zeus. He had namesakes among the Germans (*Tiu/Tyr*) or the Indians (*Dyaus*), or in Rome, where his name was combined with the honorary title "father" to *Iu-piter*. Linguists derived these names from the root that appeared in Latin as *dies*, "day(-light)," and defined the underlying god *Dyaus as the Indo-European god of the sunny day-light sky. This led to complex theories to explain how such a god turned into the Greek god of clouds and tempests who resided on mountain tops but who also ruled the pantheon, oversaw the marketplace, and protected justice, friendship, and personal possessions. These reconstructions all were understood as reconstructed history; but it is worth keeping in mind that the Indo-European god *Dyaus, the divinity of the clear sky, is as much a logical construct as the underlying linguistic root. Even more importantly, with the exception of Zeus and the goddess Hestia, no major Greek divinity has such an undisputed Indo-European etymology.

This has not deterred scholars from proposing etymologies for these divine names as well, in order to find who a Greek divinity "really" was; if one found the true meaning of a divine name, one would know the original function, and sometimes the original home, of the divinity. Given the complexities of the Eastern Mediterranean world, scholars speculated not only on Indo-European origins, but on Anatolian and Ancient Near Eastern loans or influences as well. The problem with this approach is that etymology, like anything else that concerns language, has no sharp and clear-cut rules. Thus, it can become circular: the selection of the "correct" etymology depends on a frame of reference that is situated outside linguistics. The different attempts at etymologizing Apollo's epithet Lykeios, as discussed in the last chapter, show this clearly. Scholars who assumed that Apollo was a sun god connected Lykeios with the Indo-European root for light that is preserved in Latin *lūx*, genitive *lūc-is*; to them, this was an instance supporting their general theory that myths had their origins in natural phenomena. Others rejected this general theory and objected specifically that the identification of Apollo and the sun was late; moreover, the word *Lykeios* had a short first vowel and not the long *ū* of *lūx*: thus, this etymology could be falsified in linguistic terms (this does not mean that it has lost its defenders). This left two other linguistic connections, with Lycia, and with the wolf. Scholars who assumed that Apollo was an Anatolian god, opted for Lycia: they took Apollo's protection of the Trojans in Homer as confirmation of this derivation. Others followed the already ancient connection with the wolf, Greek *lykós*; depending on their frame of reference, they offered two explanations. Those who saw agricultural concerns at the roots of early religion understood the god as averter of wolves and protector of sheep and goats; those who understood, with Émile Durkheim, religion as the bond of society and its institutions, connected the wolf with archaic warrior groups. Linguistically, neither etymology is falsifiable; the Lycian hypothesis has been rejected because the reading of recently found Lycian inscriptions has made clear that Apollo had a radically different name in this language (see Chapter 6). Falsification had to concern the respective frames of reference.

The decipherment of Linear B, the writing system for Greek in the late Bronze Age, did not change the overall methodology, but added new data and expanded the chronological framework. Before this decipherment, evolutionary theories of Greek religion started with Homer and Hesiod as the earliest attestations of a divine name. In the late nineteenth and earlier twentieth centuries Heinrich Schliemann excavated Troy, Mycenae, and Tiryns, and Sir Arthur Evans Minoan Crete, especially its capital, Cnossus. This revealed the two splendid – and absolutely unexpected – Greek cultures of the late Bronze Age, the earlier Minoan culture in Crete and its adjacent islands, and the later Mycenaean culture centered on mainland Greece; Minoan culture heavily influenced the Mycenaeans who conquered Crete at some point after 1500 BCE. In about 1150 BCE, the Mycenaean world collapsed, due to huge earthquakes followed by the attack of enemies who destroyed cities and fortresses already weakened by the forces of nature. For about half a century after their discovery, both cultures, the Minoan and the Mycenaean, remained mute. Although the excavators found a large number of texts inscribed on clay tablets, their writing systems eluded linguistic understanding. Scholars quickly saw that they were dealing with two different systems, called Linear A and Linear B, and that both had too many signs for an alphabetic script and not enough for a system that assigned a different sign to each word. It thus had to be syllabic, each sign usually denoting the combinations of a vowel and a consonant; but its language remained enigmatic. Only after World War II did Michael Ventris, an architect and language buff, succeed in cracking the code: he understood that the language written in Linear B, by far the better attested system, was Greek: suddenly the Aegean Bronze Age had a voice.

The other main system, Linear A, stilll remains elusive, not the least because the number of texts is much smaller. The only certainty is that Linear B developed from Linear A, and that Linear A cannot be Greek: the system was not invented for the complex phonology of Greek: Linear A thus attests a non-Greek culture that preceded a Greek take-over. Somewhat disappointingly to some, the tablets turned out to be financial notes, not historical records or poetical texts. They were slips of clay that contained the expenses of the palace during a very few days only, temporary notes that regularly were consolidated in a master ledger, after which they were destroyed – only that, during the catastrophe that destroyed the Mycenaean palaces, there was no time for such a consolidation: the same conflagration that destroyed the palaces burnt the slips of clay and preserved them for posterity. Even so, the Linear B tablets changed our understanding of late Bronze Age Greece, a country ruled by warrior lords who were living in impressive fortresses like the ones at Mycenae or Tiryns, or in the airy palace of Cnossus. Suddenly, we had highly specific data on the daily routine in these centers of local power. Part of this routine was to send offerings to outlying sanctuaries: the tablets meticulously noted the location of the sanctuaries, the divine recipients, and the nature of the offerings, preserving for us a somewhat random but impressive number of divine names. Many of them are known and familiar, even more are otherwise unknown.

APOLLO'S PREHISTORIES

Apollo's name has no clear parallels in other Indo-European languages, and he is the only Olympian god whose name does not figure on the Linear B tablets (a word fragment on a Cnossus tablet has been read as a form of his name, but the reading is highly conjectural and has convinced few scholars). The absence may well be significant. We possess well over a thousand texts that come from the palaces of Thebes in Boeotia, Mycenae, and Pylus in the Peloponnese, Cnossus and Chania on Crete, that is from practically the entire geographical area of the Mycenaean world, with the exception of the west coast of Asia Minor. Only a fraction contains information on religion, not only the names of gods and their sanctuaries, but also month names that preserve a major festival and personal names that contain a divine name (so-called theophoric names); but the sample is large enough to preserve almost all major Greek divine names. Thus, there is enough material to make an omission seem statistically significant and not just the result of the small size of the sample. But the absence creates a problem: if Apollo did not exist in Bronze Age Greece, where did he come from?

Scholars have attempted several answers. None has remained uncontested. There are four main possibilities: Apollo could be an Indo-European divinity, present although not attested in Bronze Age Greece, or introduced from the margins of the Mycenaean world after its collapse; or he was not Greek but Near Eastern, with again the options of a hidden presence in Bronze Age Greece or a later introduction. Scholars who accepted the absence of Apollo from the Mycenaean pantheon had two options. If he had no place in Mycenaean Greece, he had to come from elsewhere, at some time between the fall of this world and the epoch of Homer and Hesiod, that is during the so-called "Dark Age" and the following Geometric Epoch. During most of this period, Greece had isolated itself from Near Eastern influences but was internally changed by population movements, especially the expansion of the Dorians from the mountains of Northwestern Greece, outside the Mycenaean area, into what had constituted the core of the Mycenaean realm, the Peloponnese, Crete, and the Southern Aegean. Thus, a Dorian origin of Apollo was an almost obvious hypothesis; but since the Dorians were

Greeks, albeit with a different dialect, one had to come up with a Greek or at least an Indo-European etymology for his name to make this convincing. If, however, scholars could find no such etymology, they assumed an Anatolian or West Semitic origin: in Western Anatolia, Greeks had already settled during Mycenaean times but arrived again in large numbers during the Dark Age, and contacts with Phoenicia became frequent well before Homer, as the arrival of the alphabet around 800 BCE shows. Finally, if one did not accept Apollo's absence in the Linear B texts as proof of his historical absence in the Mycenaean world (after all, the argument was based on statistics only), or if one accepted the one fragment from Cnossus, there was even more occasion for Anatolian or Near Eastern origins, in the absence of an Indo-European etymology.

A Bronze Age Apollo of whatever origin could find corroboration in Apollo's surprising and early presence on the island of Cyprus. Excavations have found several archaic sanctuaries, some being simple open-air spaces with an altar, others as complex as the sanctuary of Apollo Hylatas at Kourion that may have contained a rectangular temple as early as the sixth or even late seventh century BCE. Inscriptions in the local Cypriot writing system attest several cults of Apollo with varying epithets, from Amyklaios to Tamasios, and a month whose name derives from Apollo Agyieus.

In a way, Apollo should not exist on Cyprus, or only in later times, if he was Dorian or entered the Greek world after the collapse of the Bronze Age societies. Cyprus, the large island that bridged the sea between Southern Anatolia and Western Syria, was inhabited by a native population; Greeks arrived at the very end of the Mycenaean period. They must have been Mycenaean Greeks who were displaced by the turmoil at the time when their Greek empire was crumbling. They brought with them their language, a dialect that was akin to the dialect of Arcadia in the Central Peloponnese to where Mycenaeans retreated from the invading Dorians, and they brought with them their writing system, a syllabic system closely connected with Linear A and B that quickly developed its own local variation and survived until Hellenistic times; then it was ousted by the more convenient Greek alphabet. The long survival of this system shows that, after its importation in the eleventh century BCE, Cypriot culture was very stable and only slowly became part of the larger Greek world. There was no later Greek immigration, either large-scale or modest, during the Iron Age: when Phoenicians immigrated in the eighth century, Cypriot culture, if anything, turned to the Near East. It is only plausible to assume that the Mycenaean settlers also brought their cults and gods with them: thus, the gods and festivals attested in the Cypriot texts are likely to reflect not

Iron Age Greek religion but the Mycenaean heritage imported at the very end of the Bronze Age.

This leaves room for many theories and ideas that followed the pattern I outlined above. Only two attempts have commanded more than passing attention, a derivation from the Hittite pantheon in Bronze Age Anatolia and a Dorian hypothesis that made Apollo the main divinity of the Dorians who pushed south from their original home in Northwestern Greece, once the fall of the Mycenaean Empire let them do so.

Apollo and the Hittites

In 1936, Bedřich Hrozný, the Czech scholar who deciphered the Hittite language, claimed to have read the divine name Apulunas on several late Hittite altars inscribed in Hittite hieroglyphs, together with the name Rutas. He immediately understood them as antecedents of Apollo and Artemis and defined Apulunas' function as that of a protector of altars, sacred areas, and gates. He thus added, as he thought, proof to the idea that Apollo, his sister, and, implicitly, their mother Leto were Anatolian divinities: after all, had not Homer insisted on their protection of Troy, and did not all three have a close conection with Lycia? The reading has been rejected by other specialists – but Hittite Apollo did not disappear: he surfaced as Appaliunas, a divinity in a (damaged) list of oath divinities invoked by the Hittite king Muwattalis and king A, and king Alaksandus of Wilusa; the text immediately preceding Appaliunas is broken. Since scholars identify Wilusa with Ilion, Apollo seems to appear in Troy, and Manfred Korfmann, the German archaeologist who impressively changed the accepted archaeological image of Bronze Age Troy, immediately adopted the idea and helped popularize it: Homer's Apollo, the protector of the Trojans, seemed well established in Aegean prehistory, in the very city Homer was singing about.

Problems remain, besides Apollo's absence from Linear B and the thorny question of how the *Iliad* relates to Bronze Age history, even after the rejection of Hrozný's reading. Contemporary proponents of an Anatolian Apollo still follow Hrozný and point to Apollo's Lycian connection that is already present in Homer; they feel encouraged by Wilamowitz, the most influential classicist in Hrozný's time, who had concurred. But Lycian inscriptions found since then in Xanthus, where Leto had her main shrine, have cast severe doubts on whether Wilamowitz was right. Neither Leto's nor Apollo's name is attested in the indigenous texts, among which pride of place belongs to a text dated to 358 BCE, written in Lycian, Greek, and Aramaic. As in a few other indigenous texts, Leto is

"The Mother of the Sanctuary" (meaning the one in Xanthus), without a proper name. Only in the Aramaic text has what one would call the Apolline triad, Lato (*l'tw'*), Artemus (*'rtemwš*) and a god called Hšatra-pati, the Iranian Mitra Varuna as the equivalent of the young powerful god whom Greeks called Apollo. In the Lycian text, the Greek personal name Apollodotus, "given by Apollo" was rendered in Lycian in way that made clear that the Lycian equivalent of Apollo was Natr-, a name of uncertain etymology but one that has no linguistic relation whatsoever with Apollo. No member of the Apolline triad, then, had a Lycian name that sounded like Leto, Apollo, or Artemis: the names were Greek, not indigenous to Lycia. Lycia may have been Apollo's country in myth (and in Homer), but not in history. The sanctuary of Xanthus does not trans-form Hittite cults into the Iron Age, and a Bronze Age Anatolian Apollo seems far-fetched, to say the least. This directs our quest back to Greece.

Apollo and the Dorian assembly

In different Greek dialects, Apollo's name took several forms. Ionians and Athenians called him *Apollōn*, Thessalians syncopated this to *Aploun*; many Dorians used the form *Apellōn* that resonated with the Cypriot *Apeilōn*. Several scholars, most authoritatively Walter Burkert, pointed out that there was a Greek dialectal word with which the Dorian form of the god's name, *Apellōn*, was already connected in antiquity: whereas most Greeks called their assembly *ekklesia*, the Spartans used the term *apella*. In their dialect, then, Apellon would be "the Assembly God." In the Dorian states, the assembly of all free adult men was the supreme political instrument: at least once a year, these men assembled to decide on all central matters of politics. Apollo as its god would fit his role in the archaic city-states that I worked out in the last chapter. To make this work, we have to assume that *apella* was already the term for this institution among the early Northwestern Greeks, before the Dorians entered the Peloponnese. This assumption can be backed by the fact that most Dorian cities had a month named Apellaios. Greek month names derive from the names of festivals, not from the names of gods: Apellaios leads to a festival named Apellai. Such a festival is attested in Delphi, outside the Dorian dialectal area but within the West Greek area: it is the main festival of a Delphian brotherhood, a phratry. As we saw in the last chapter, phratries are closely connected with Apollo as their protector and with citizenship: this again connects the god and the festival with the same archaic political and cultic nexus.

In this reading, Apollo arrived in Greece with the Dorians who slowly moved into the Peloponnese and from there took over the towns of Crete, after the fall of Mycenaean power. Four centuries later, at the time of Homer and Hesiod, the god had become an established divinity in all of Greece, and a firm part of the narrative tradition of epic poetry. Such an expansion presupposes some degree of religious and cultural inter-penetration and exchange throughout Greece during the Dark Ages. This somewhat contradicts the traditional image of this period as a time when the single communities of Greece were mostly turned towards themselves, with little connection with each other. But such a picture is based mainly on the rather scarce archaeological evidence; communica-tion between people, even migration, does not always leave archaeo-logical traces, and cults are based on myths and narratives, not on artifacts. And well before Homer, communications inside Greece opened up again, as shown by the rapid spread of the alphabet or of the so-called Proto-Geometric pottery style that both belong to the ninth or early eighth centuries BCE.

The main obstacle to this hypothesis is Apollo's well-attested pres-ence on Cyprus, in a form, *Apeilon*, that is very close to the Dorian *Apellon*: would not Apollo then be a Cypriot? Burkert removed this obs-tacle with the assumption of a very early import to Cyprus from Dorian Amyclae; Amyclae, we remember, had an important and old shrine of the god. Another scenario is possible as well: the Mycenaean lords who fled to Cyprus did so only after their society integrated a part of the Dorian intruders and their tutelary god Apollo. After all, the pressure of the Dorians must have been felt for quite a while, and their bands that were organized around the cult of Apollo could have started to trickle south even before the fall of the kingdoms, and blended in with the Mycenaeans.

Overall, then, I am still inclined to follow Burkert's hypothesis that is grounded in social and political history, rather than to accept some-what vague Anatolian origins – even if I am aware that the neat coinci-dence of etymology and function might well be yet another of these circular mirages of which the history of etymologizing divine names is so full. And it needs to be stressed that the picture of a simple diffusion from the invading Dorians to the rest of Greece is somewhat too neat. Things, as often, are messier, for two reasons: there are clear traces of Near Eastern influence in Apollo's myth and cult, and there are vestiges of a Mycenaean tradition that cannot be overlooked.

MYCENAEAN ANTECEDENTS

The most obvious Mycenaean antecedent of Apollo is the god Paiawon who is attested in two Linear B texts from Cnossus on Crete. One text is too fragmentary to teach us much, the other is rather laconic and presents a list of recipients of offerings: "to Atana Potinija, Enyalios, Paiawon, Poseidaon" – that is "Lady Athana" (the Mycenaean form of Athena), Enyalios (a name that Homer uses as a synonym of Ares, whereas local cult distinguishes the two war gods), Paean, and Poseidon. The list cannot inform us on any function besides the fact that Paiawon seems to be a major divinity, on the same level as the other three who from Homer onwards appear among the twelve Olympian gods. In the language of Homer, the Mycenaean *Paiawon* develops to *Paiēōn*; in other dialects this double vowel is simplified to *Paiān* or *Paiōn*. All three forms are attested in extant Greek texts; and we dealt with the problem that, in Homer, Paeon seems an independent mythological person, the physician of Olympus, whereas in later Greek, Paean is an epithet of Apollo the Healer to whom the paean was sung and danced. It should be pointed out that the refrain of any paean always was "ie Paean," regardless whether it was sung for Apollo or Asclepius or even, in a rare case, to Dionysus. I feel tempted to see this as a vestige of the god Paean's former independence and even to imagine that the paean as a ritual form goes back to the Bronze Age as well. Proof, of course, is impossible. But maybe it is no coincidence that Cretan healers and purifiers were famous in later Greece: Bronze Age remnants survived better in Crete, and the paean was connected with healing and purification. This does not mean that Apollo as such was a Mycenanean god; if anything, it rather suggests the contrary, that a non-Mycenaean Apollo absorbed the formerly independent Mycenaean healing god Paiawon, perhaps including one of his rituals, the song-and-dance paean.

NEAR EASTERN INFLUENCES

Greece was always at the margins of the ancient Near Eastern world; it has always been tempting to look for Oriental influences in Greek culture and religion. In the case of Apollo, theories went from partial influences to wholesale derivation. Wilamowitz, at one time the leading classical scholar in Germany, derived Apollo from Anatolia, stirring up a controversy whose ideological resonances are unmistakable; after all, from the days of Winckelmann, Apollo seemed the most Greek of all the gods. Others went even further, stressing the god's absence in Linear B, and made him come from Syria or Phoenicia. This is wildly exaggerated; but there can be no doubt that partial influences exist. They are best visible in two areas: healing and the calendar.

In the past, arguments from the calendar were paramount. In the calendar of the Greeks, a month coincides with one cycle of the moon: the first day thus is the day when the moon will just be visible, the seventh day is the day when the moon is half full and as such clearly visible. Apollo is connected with both days. The seventh day is somewhat more prominent: every month, Apollo receives a sacrifice on the seventh day, all his major festivals are held on a seventh, and his birthday is on the seventh day of a specific month. But already in Homer, he is also connected with new moon, *noumēnía*: he is Noumenios, and his worshippers can be organized in a group of noumeniastai. Long ago, Martin P. Nilsson, the leading scholar on Greek religion in the first half of the last century, connected this with the Babylonian calendar where the seventh day is very important. He went even further. Every lunar calendar will, rather fast, get out of step with the solar cycle that defines the seasonal year; to remedy this, all systems invented intercalation, the insertion of additional days. Greek calendars introduced an extra month every ninth year, to cover the gap between the solar and the lunar cycle. According to Nilsson, they did so under Babylonian influence that was mediated through Delphi: Delphi's main festivals were originally held every ninth year, and only Delphi would have enough influence in the Archaic Epoch to impose such a system upon all Greek states. However, this is very speculative; Nilsson certainly was wrong in his additional assumption that Delphi also introduced the system of months: month names are already attested in the Greek Bronze Age. Still, the connection of Apollo's seventh day with the prominence of the same day in the Mesopotamian calendar is interesting.

As to healing, it seems by now established that itinerant Near Eastern healers visited Greece during the Archaic Age and left their traces. The most tangible trace is the role the dog plays in the cult of Asclepius: the dog is central to the Mesopotamian goddess of healing, Gula, two of whose statuettes were dedicated in seventh-century Samos. In Akkadian, Gula is also called *azugullatu*, "Great Physician": the word may be at the root of Asclepius' name, and it resonates in a singular cult title of Apollo on the island of Anaphe, Asgelatas. Later, Greeks turned the epithet into Aiglatas, from *aigle* "radiance," and told the story that Apollo appeared to the Argonauts as a radiant star to save them from shipwreck. This looks like the later rationalization of a word that nobody understood anymore and that may be a trace of an Oriental healer who instituted this specific cult. Another Oriental detail is the plague arrows Apollo shoots in *Iliad* 1, as we saw, and his role as an armed gatekeeper to keep away pestilence that is attested in several Clarian oracles.

Yet another area of Oriental influence is Apollo's role in divine genealogy. To Hesiod and, to a lesser degree, to Homer, Apollo is the oldest son of Zeus: Zeus is the god who controls the present social, moral, and natural order, Apollo is his crown prince and, so to speak, designated successor, if Zeus were ever to step back. This explains, among other things, Apollo's direct access to Zeus' plans and knowledge. A similar constellation recurs in West Semitic and Anatolian mythologies. Here, the god most closely resembling Zeus in function and appearance is the Storm God in his different local forms; he is also the god of kings and of the present political and moral world order. In Hittite mythology, his son is Telepinu, a young god whose mythology talks about his disappearance in anger and whose rituals may have been be connected with the New Year's festival to secure the continuation of the social and natural order. In some respects, the young and tempestuous Telepinu reminds one of Apollo.

In narratives from Ugarit in Northern Syria, the Storm God is accompanied by Reshep, the plague god or "Lord of the Arrow." In bilingual inscriptions from Cyprus, his Phoenician equivalent, also called Reshep, becomes Greek Apollo. In iconography, Reshep is usually represented as a warrior with a helmet and a very short tunic, walking and brandishing a weapon with his raised right arm; these images are attested in the Eastern Mediterranean from the late Bronze Age to the Greek Archaic Age. In Cyprus, such a god appears in a famous bronze image from the large sanctuary complex at Citium; since he wears a helmet adorned with two horns, some scholars understood him as the Bronze Age version of the later Cypriot Apollo Keraïtas, "Horned Apollo."

Greek Apollo, most of the time, looks very different. But a very similar statuette has been found in Apollo's sanctuary at Amyclae in Southern Sparta. Here, it must reflect Apollo's archaic statue in this sanctuary that we know from Pausanias' description:

> I know nobody who might have measured its size, but I guess it must be about thirty cubits high. It is not the work of Bathycles [the sculptor who made the base for the image], but old and not worked with artifice. It has no face, and its hands and feet are added from stone, the rest looks like a bronze column. On its head, it has a helmet, in its hands a lance and a bow.
>
> (*Description of Greece*, 3.10.2)

An image on a coin shows not only that the body could be dressed in a cloak to soften the strangeness of its shape but also that it brandished the lance with its raised right hand: the coincidence with the Reshep iconography seems perfect, and the Oriental influence almost obvious. It has even been suggested that the place name Amyclae is Near Eastern: there is a Phoenician Reshep Mukal, "Mighty Reshep," whom the Cypriot Greeks translated as Apollo Amyklos. The Greek epithet cannot derive from the place name (it would have to be *Amyklaîos*), but it shares the same verbal root; its basic phonetic structure is the same as that of *mukal*. Thus, one wonders whether it was Phoenician or Cypriot sailors who first founded a sanctuary on this lonely promontory on one of the trade routes to the west.

SUMMARY

Apollo's origins are complex and not fully explained. He is not attested in the Mycenaean Linear B texts (with a very uncertain exception), but well established in Greek religion at the time of Homer and Hesiod, and central in fundamental political and social institutions of the Archaic Epoch. There are obvious Near Eastern influences in his myths and even in some aspects of his cult; but neither a West Semitic origin nor an Anatolian origin of the god are convincing, and his protection of the Trojans needs not to reflect such an origin. The absence of Linear B documents is intriguing and puzzling; but his early presence in Cyprus does not necessarily invalidate the conclusion drawn from this absence, that he was unknown in Mycenaean religion. It is possible that he was not present here, whereas the Northwestern Greeks worshipped him already in the Bronze Age as the protector of their *apéllai*, the warriors' assemblies. As protector of warriors, he entered, with them, the former Mycenaean area at the very beginning of the Transitional Period between the Bronze and the Iron Age (the Greek "Dark Age"): this allows for several centuries of transformations and adaptations, and it is not inconceivable that Apolline warriors even sailed to Cyprus among the Mycenaean refugees and settlers.

APOLLO AFTERWARDS

APOLLO'S FLOURISHING AFTERMATH

Apollo's history did not end with his second adoption in Rome, as Augustus' personal deity after the battle of Actium (31 BCE), or with the myth that he had been born on a British island. During the Imperial Epoch, the god received worship in many sanctuaries throughout the Roman provinces. Many centuries before the city became the capital of Charlemagne's renewed Roman Empire, Aachen in Germany had a famous healing sanctuary of Apollo Grannus: the emperor Caracalla, always in search of cures for his many ailments, spent some time there. At the other end of the Empire, the god had a splendid sanctuary in Daphne, a suburb of Antioch (Antakya) in Syria; it was famous for its colossal cult image made of gold and ivory (chryselephantine). Julian, the last pagan emperor, had the temple restored for his own visit to the city in the fall of 362 CE; following the lead of Augustus, he stylized himself as a new Apollo. The Antiochean cult had been brought by Greek settlers; the cult in Aachen continued the worship of an indigenous god who had been identified with Apollo. This was very common: all over the ancient world, local gods could be regarded as the native forms of Apollo, such as Phanebal in Ascalon, Reshef in Palmyra, Grannus in Gaul, or Maponos in Britain. The reasons varied: Phanebal "Messenger of Ba'al" was a young and warlike god, Reshef was the local variation of the Ugaritic and Phoenician plague god Reshep, and Grannus and Maponos presided over healing springs.

Julian's restoration of the sanctuary of Daphne was an act of defiance, aimed at the Christian hostility to pagan cults. It strikes one as highly symbolic that the sanctuary burned down shortly after Julian's arrival, and presumably it was meant that way; certainly this was how Julian understood the blaze. In the last decade of the fourth century CE, the emperor Theodosius promulgated several edicts in which he declared the performance of pagan ritual as unlawful. Bands of fanaticized monks swarmed out to destroy major and minor sanctuaries that were still operative despite the adverse conditions during much of the century. Books of magic – the label magic had been tagged on all sorts of pagan ritual – went up in flames in many places; and eager bishops kept their congregations from lapsing into forbidden rites. Pagan cult went underground, and slowly died out over the course of the following century. But the gods survived, although somewhat precariously sometimes, not in the prayers of their worshippers, but on the pages of books and in works of art. Crucial for Apollo's survival in Christian times was his identification with Helios/Sol, parallel to Artemis' identification with Selene/Luna. Stoic and Neoplatonist philosophers adopted this interpretation of the twin gods: this secured them a prestigious place among the planets. This survived into the Middle Ages and beyond: Renaissance painters regularly depicted Apollo as the sun-god, riding in a chariot, his head surrounded by rays. Throughout the Middle Ages and the Renaissance, another important aspect of Apollo was his patronage and inspiration of music and poetry; early modern poets stressed his association with Orpheus, the Muses and the Graces. In the mid-eighteenth century, the beauty of youthful Apollo, alluded to occasionally in earlier epochs, became essential for Winckelmann's classicist reading of Greek art; a marble statue of Apollo in the Vatican, the Belvedere Apollo, was emblematical for this new view of the Greeks that blended aesthetic and sexual attraction (figure 10). Apollo's "noble simplicity and restrained greatness" ("edle Einfalt und stille Grösse," in Winckelmann's often quoted German phrase) became influential again more than a century later when Friedrich Nietzsche emphasized the tension between Apollo and Dionysus that had, in his reading, created Athenian tragedy and Wagnerian opera.

In this final chapter I will sketch the history of the god Apollo through these centuries, from the Roman Empire to modern times. Although the territory is by no means uncharted, there exist no comprehensive accounts of all the works that Apollo has inspired and of all the learned pronouncements about the god during almost two millennia. What follows, then, can only be a preliminary sketch, dictated more by the author's idiosyncrasies and predilections than by historical evidence.

LATE ANTIQUE ALLEGORY AND OTHER LEARNED INTERPRETATIONS

Greek gods came under scrutiny and attack long before the Christians came to power. Philosophy, late in the Archaic Age of Greece, fostered the expectation that gods would behave ethically. They were, as Plato

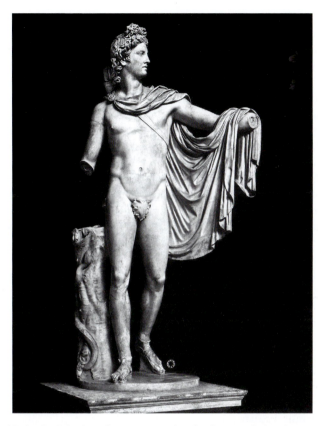

Figure 10 Apollo Belvedere, Roman copy of a Greek original, fourth century BCE. Museo Pio Clementino, Vatican Museums. Copyright Alinari/Art Resource, NY.

argued, supremely good, so why should stories make them do evil? Thus, philosophers rejected traditional stories as unethical and inadequate for an age of refined moral standards. At the same time, the singers of the Homeric poems, the rhapsodes, turned more and more into interpreters of the texts they were performing. Their audiences needed explanations, and not only of the many obscure details of life at the time of the poems, but also of the problematical myths narrated or alluded to in them. In response, the singers developed an interpretative instrument that later scholars called allegory. Greek *allegorízein* means "to say or mean something else": the myths, their expounders claimed, meant something different from what they seemed to say on their narrative surface. This underlying meaning could be moral, or physical, or historical. Heracles' twelve labors could symbolize the moral struggle of a virtuous man;

Zeus' hanging Hera on a chain in the sky, with an anvil dangling from the chain, could mean the layering of elements in the cosmos, from weightless fire (sky) to heavier air (Hera whose name was read as an anagram for air, *aêr*, in a language without a letter for "h") to heavy earth (the iron anvil); the Minotaur threatening Athens could mean an admiral of king Minos of Crete attacking the Athenian fleet. Over time, the method became more sophisticated and was widely used as a hermeneutical tool; Jewish philosphers used it in order to reconcile Torah and Platonism, and Christian theologians interpreted the Bible in whatever sense time and society needed and even to introduce the prestigious pagan mythology into Christian education, literature, and figurative art.

Apollo did not escape allegorization. In rare cases, he was Christianized, or Christ was seen as the real Apollo, as in a hymn by an anonymous Christian poet of perhaps the fifth century. The text hails Christ as

> true Apollo, famous Paean, victor over the infernal snake. Sweet is the quiver of your testimony that comprises four men. Your arrow is steeped in the honey of prophecy, feathered with the oracles of the fathers. Your bow sounds strong with your father's virtue, its string is powerful with miracles: they have killed the old snake through their own death.
>
> (Pseudo-Paulinus of Nola, *Poem* 2 [Patrologia Latina 41])

> *Salve, o Apollo vere, Paean inclite,*
> *Pulsor draconis inferi.*
> *Dulcis tui pharetra testimonii*
> *Quod quatuor constat viris;*
> *Sagitta mellis tinctilis prophetico,*
> *Pinnata patrum oraculis;*
> *Arcus paternae forte virtutis sonans,*
> *Miraculis nervus potens:*
> *Stravere veterem morte serpentem sua.*

Apollo the killer of the Pytho dragon is turned into a Christ killing the snake of Hell, detail by detail. Echos of such a reading of Apollo reverberate through the ages, to Michelangelo's triumphant Christ presiding over the Last Judgement in the Sistine Chapel, or to Catholic mythography of the seventeenth century. After Winckelmann, however, and even more so after Nietzsche's rejection of Christianity, Apollo could again stand for paganism in opposition to Christianity, as in the small and otherwise unremarkable book on a Christian literary theory with the suggestive title *Christ and Apollo* by the Jesuit father F. Lynch (1960) where Apollo stands for the rejected "neo-pagan" reading of literary works.

But mostly, allegorization of Apollo was physical, and it was rather uniform, from antiquity to modern times. As Macrobius puts it in his *Saturnalia*, a treatise written at about 420 CE : "Apollo's names refer in manifold interpretation to the sun." This statement introduces chapter 17 of book I of the *Saturnalia* which is written to confirm this derivation and its antiquity. Besides other ancient authors, Macrobius' learned speaker, the aristocrat Vettius Agorius Praetextatus, cites the dramatist Euripides, the philosopher Plato, and Chrysippus, the main philosopher of early Stoicism. He proves his case with a wealth of details: the etymology of Apollo's name and of his epithets, the iconography of his image, single myths, and facts of cult. The etymologies are fanciful, as is to be expected, and again prove my point that etymologies in religion tend to be circular. Apollo's name means "sending (Greek *apopállein*) the rays"; Apollo is called Delphios because the sun manifests things (*délei*), Phoibos because "he comes violently" (*phoitâi bíai*), "He of the Golden Hair" because the golden rays of the sun are his hairs; and "He who is not Shorn . . . because the rays of the sun can never be cut off from their source." If even single epithets receive somewhat complex explanations, entire myths do even more so. Macrobius narrates Apollo's childhood story, albeit in a somewhat different version from the *Homeric Hymn*: when Leto had given birth to him and his sister against the fierce resistance of the step-mother Hera, the snake Pytho invaded the god's cradle, but the baby boy killed it with his arrows. This, the learned interpreter contends, is a symbolic representation of how the cosmos with its sun and its moon was born from chaos. Leto is earth, Hera is air: cold and hostile air prevented earth from growing anything, until she gave birth first to the moon, then to the hot sun. The sun heated up the air, and its moisture turned into vapors that threatened the new life, until the rays of the sun could overcome it. The interpreter then adds yet another explanation for the snake: it symbolizes the winding way of the sun through the year, "and when the sun has finished its course, it has finished off the snake." Multiple explanations are typical for this way of thinking: they do not contradict each other but prove that the same story can contain several levels of meaning. Sometimes, the symbolism is more straightforward than this: images of Apollo, Macrobius explains, carry an image of the three Graces in their right and the bow and arrows in their left hand "because the god is reluctant to harm humans, and much more eager to hand out health": the right hand is active and stretched out, the left passive and hanging down.

In Macrobius' long chapter on Apollo, Praetextatus presents a synthesis of the god and his myths as it was developed over almost a millennium of Greek and Roman literature, art, and philosophy. In many ways, the chapter is almost a digest of pagan philosophical theology. It demonstrates how two philosophical schools, Plato's Academy and the Stoa of Zeno and Chrysippus, shaped this approach to the divine. Both schools cultivated an ethically purified theology, without altogether rejecting the traditional gods and their myths, but reading them instead as allegories. Whereas Academic philosophers read the myths as moralistic tales, the Stoics perfected physical allegory: to them, the gods and all their mythical narratives were symbols for natural processes.

Macrobius was an author widely read in medieval times. His *Saturnalia* is a rather long-winded and selective commentary on Virgil, a key author of medieval schools; his other preserved work is an allegorical commentary on Cicero's *Dream of Scipio*, another key text in medieval teaching. Both works preserve ancient learning for the medieval world and transmit its allegorical mode of reading pagan mythology.

Equally important was another work written not very much later, the *Mythologies* of a certain Fulgentius, presumably the African bishop Fulgentius who died in 532 or 533 and became a saint. The *Mythologies* are short allegorical explanations of Greek myths, narrated mostly after Virgil and Ovid, the main texts for Greek and Roman mythology in the West for many centuries to come. Fulgentius agrees with Macrobius on Apollo as the sun (book 1, chapters 12–17), and he proves it with the etymologies of his name and of selected epithets, and with mythical details. Both the details and the epithets are entirely different from what Macrobius selected: both authors thus were independently drawing on a much wider pool of knowledge. Like Macrobius, or even more so since it was a handbook, the *Mythologies* of Fulgentius were widely read and used by Medieval scholars and poets. The Apolline myths that Fulgentius explains are mostly the ones found in Ovid's *Metamorphoses*, such as the story of the Raven, of Daphne, of Phaeton. He adds explanations of the tripod, the arrows, and the snake Python; the nine Muses together with Apollo symbolize the ten organs of speech: four front teeth, two lips, tongue, palate, throat, and lungs. It seems hopeless to assign a specific organ to a specific divinity; what counts is the number of ten on both sides. We find the same allegorization in Greek writers of later antiquity and Byzantine times, such as the commentaries of Eustathius of Thessalonica on Homer, written in the twelfth century (see Chapter 1). Eustathius has no doubt that Apollo is the sun and applies an almost alchemical key to this interpretation: his priest Chryses has a golden sceptre "because the ancients dedicated this metal to the sun, as they dedicate silver to the moon and other metals to other planets" (on *Il.* 1.15).

APOLLO THE SUN

The identification of Apollo with the sun goes back to fifth-century BCE Greece, and it persisted through the centuries. *Phoîbos*/Phoebus is often a poetical way of denoting the sun, as Artemis/Diana is used for the moon: this is a rhetorical device as old as Homer (who uses Demeter for bread, Dionysus for wine) that later was called metonymy, "noun change." Learned poets turned this on its head and used physical elements to describe the respective gods. In his *Dionysiaca*, Nonnus of Panopolis (fifth century CE) narrates a series of duels between the Olympian gods: Athena fights against Ares, Hera against Artemis, Poseidon against Apollo. This last duel is described as a fight between fire and water: Apollo, "the fiery chief," fights with a "branch of Delphic fir" against an enemy who sends his high waves (36.83–87). More complex descriptions use divine names for riddling accounts of seasonal patterns. In a parody of such poetical conceits, Seneca describes the onset of autumn: "Phoebus had already drawn in the arc of his light in a shorter path; dark Sleep's time was growing, and triumphantly Cynthia extended her reign." Or, as he adds: "I think this is better understood if I say: the month was October" (*Apocolocyntosis* 2): Cynthia is Artemis/ Diana the moon goddess, as Cynthius is Apollo, named after the one mountain of Delus; here, she stands for the night. Almost one and a half millennia later, an unknown poet used the same conceit to open a poem in honor of Joanna queen of Naples (1414–1435). He is often more enigmatic: "With his shining chariot Cynthius had left behind the Thessalian quivers, aiming for the Capricorn and the path that leads back" – the sun, that is, is moving from Sagittarius (represented as a Thessalian centaur who is also an archer) to Capricorn; winter is coming (*Carmen Bucolicum Gaddianum* 1). Compared with this overly learned text, Milton's evocation of Spring with its returning sunshine is almost straightforward, and in much more elegant Latin:

> *Delius ipse venit, video Peneïde lauro*
> *implicitos crines: Delius ipse venit!*

> The Delian god himself is coming: I see him, his hair wreathed in laurel from Peneus –
> the Delian god himself is coming!

> (Elegy 5.13, written in 1628)

The only name a contemporary needs to have explained is Peneus, a river that runs through the Tempe valley and who as a river-god is the father of Daphne, Apollo's victim turned into laurel.

The identification of Apollo and the sun has several consequences. A minor one is that Apollo is now inserted into the myths of Helius/Sol, the Sun God: in Fulgentius, Phaëthon, in Ovid the son of Sol, turns into the son of Apollo. More important is that Apollo took a place – the preeminent place – among the planetary gods, as did his sister Artemis/Diana. This was a bookish development in a Christian world that had conveniently forgotten that Helios/Sol and Selene/Luna were "real" deities who once had their own cult, distinct from Apollo and Artemis. Since all the other planets, from Mercury to Saturn, were named after major pagan gods, sun and moon, or Sol and Luna, did not fit the system, whereas Apollo and Artemis/Diana did. (One has to keep in mind that to ancient and medieval astronomers, Sun and Moon were planets circling around a stable Earth; Earth alone did not need a divine name.) This development took some time. In his *Etymologies*, Isidore, the learned bishop of Seville (died 636 CE), still called the respective planets *Sol* and *Luna*, as do many later texts that are strictly astronomical: they preserve the conventions of their Greek and Roman predecessors. Outside these technical texts, however, the identification of god and celestial body spread fast. It became so popular that Apollo even entered Christian churches in planetary guise: frescoes in many churches in Italy and elsewhere depict the seven planetary gods, among them Apollo and Diana, as sitting or standing persons.

Isidore had good reasons for not turning Apollo into a planet. Following a different school of allegorists, he understood the gods as human rulers of old whom posterity elevated to gods. We call this school Euhemerism, after Euhemerus of Messene who, at about 300 BCE, wrote the most influential book on the topic; its roots, however, are older. The Christian fathers eagerly adopted the theory: it helped to deflate the pagan gods by turning them into humans. Isidore, a bishop and an influential theologian, followed established Christian traditions. In his chapter on the pagan gods ("De diis gentium," *Etymologies* 8.11), he gives a long list of "humans of old whom they began to worship, each after his respective merits, such as Isis in Egypt, Jupiter on Crete, . . . or Apollo on Delus." In his treatment of Apollo, he mentions the identification with Sol, without commenting on it. To him, Apollo's functions are divination and medicine alone, in a purely Roman perspective. Greek Apollo, however, is not entirely forgotten: "The same god [he writes] is called Phoebus because he is an ephebe, that is a young man; therefore they sometimes depict the sun as a boy, because he is born every day and shines with new light." We should not expect too much intellectual cohesion in Isidore's work: it is essentially an encyclopedic collection of Greek and Roman knowledge, put together at the threshold of the

Middle Ages. Although Isidore's Apollo is not a planetary god, the identification with the sun was so commonplace in his time, and so strong, that he simply could not overlook it.

Outside the world of the learned clergymen, Apollo could survive in a very different guise. In his first letter to the Corinthians, Paul had demoted the pagan gods to demons, *daimonia*. This became commonplace in later Christian thinking: the pagan gods had not disappeared, they continued to live as demons. In a sermon, Martin bishop of Praga in Portugal (sixth century) gives a long list of these demons from which only Apollo is curiously absent, as he is in a much later list in Walter Mapes' entertaining *Courtiers' Trifles* (*De Nugis Curialium*, twelfth century). Martin's list is very serious: as long as pagan cults were alive, pagan gods were a menace to Christians. Every Christian who entered a "sanctuary of Juppiter, Apollo or Diana" feared that the contact with the cult image polluted him (*Patrologia Latina* 4, 898D); and Christian nightwatchmen had routinely to undergo an exorcism after their rounds, lest they would become possessed by one of these demons. Once the cults died out, fear became entertaining: now we hear stories about Jupiter the magus, Apollo the devil or Venus the beautiful sorceress.

MEDIEVAL AND RENAISSANCE INTERPRETERS

Pagan traditions survived not only in Isidore. A considerable corpus of medieval mythography was nurtured by them; these books in turn kept the mythological tradition alive in medieval teaching. Three anonymous treatises from manuscripts in the Papal Library, the so-called *Vatican Mythographers*, summarize mythology as it was taught in medieval schools. Whereas the oldest text simply retells the stories, the two later provide rich allegorical explanations and systematization, such as the following (*Mythographus Vaticanus* 2.28):

> It is well known that Apollo's powers are threefold: in the sky, he is the Sun, on earth, he is Dionysus, in the underworld, he is Apollo. Hence, we see his image accompanied by three attributes: the lyre which is the image of celestial harmony, the chariot which shows him as a terrestrial divinity, the arrows which indicate his nature as underwordly and pernicious (which is why he is *Apollon* in Greek which means "destroying").

The materials found here can all be traced back to antiquity. The derivation of Apollo's name from Greek *apóllymi* "to destroy" is as old as Aeschylus; the lyre is a symbol of the harmony of the spheres in the

Pythagorean and Platonic traditions. Only systematization and the didactic purpose are new. And it is easy to see how the explanation of his attributes could serve to guide medieval artists in their iconographical choices.

In many respects, the Renaissance followed medieval thinking about Greek and Roman gods, even if its authors were much better acquainted with ancient literature and could draw on Greek texts as well as on Roman ones. The *Genealogia Deorum* of Giovanni Boccaccio (1313–1375) is a mythographical handbook that defined for almost two centuries how poets and artists saw the gods of antiquity. But far from breaking away from medieval traditions, Boccaccio continues them. Like Isidore's, Boccaccio's explanations are strictly euhemeristic: like all gods, Apollo was once a powerful king and a benefactor of humanity. For his theological interpretations, Boccaccio relied heavily on Cicero's *On the Nature of the Gods* (*De Natura Deorum*). In this lengthy work, the Roman orator and philosopher presented the theological thinking of the three major philosophical schools of his time, skeptical Platonism, Stoicism, and Epicureanism, and exemplified their interpretations with a wealth of mythological details. Boccaccio was somewhat less interested in philosophical theology than Cicero: to a Renaissance Christian, ancient gods had become the topic of erudition, not of belief and worship. Accordingly, he focussed on Cicero's mythographical facts: often, he repeated them faithfully, although in Apollo's case he radically cut Cicero's list of four different Apollos (*De Natura Deorum* 3.23) down to two. In a good euhemeristic reading, the first Apollo was "a fiery man of inexhaustible fervor . . . . He invented medicine and acquired knowledge of herbs." The second was the son of Jupiter and Latona, and on him Boccaccio concentrates: "Although Cicero writes that besides him there were three others, everything has to focus on this one god, since all the poets concentrate their efforts on this Apollo, as if he were the only one." The use in poetry determines Boccaccio's choice; after all, he was a celebrated poet himself.

Good handbooks last long. It was not until two centuries later that Boccaccio's book was replaced by the *Mythologiae* of Natale Conti (1520–1581, from Milan; he latinized his name as Natales Comes). Its first edition appeared in 1551; the substantially enlarged edition of 1561 remained the standard text on Greek and Roman gods, heroes, and their myths for the next two centuries or so. Conti's treatment of individual gods, such as the lengthy chapter on Apollo, seems first and foremost a collection of what ancient authors from Homer and Hesiod to Ovid and Plutarch were saying about a specific god, with systematic information about cult places and epithets; in Apollo's case, the epithets range from

Abaeus to *Zosterius*. All this is not very different from what our contemporary encyclopedias still present to their readers. The final paragraph of the lengthy chapter on Apollo, however, goes far beyond the encyclopedic presentation of data and facts. It begins with an address to his reader: "Let us now investigate what they meant by all this." The answer, not surprisingly, is simple: he is the Sun, and all the details that were so meticulously presented find their lenghty explanation in this one truth.

Conti's handbook was destined not only for scholars and other learned users, but also for artists. For this very reason, many editions included lavish images that were taken over from another famous work, Vincenzo Cartari's *Le Imagini degli Dei Antichi* ("The Images of the Ancient Gods"). When its first edition appeared in 1609, it quickly became fundamental to the way artists represented ancient gods. But it was much more than a collection of images. Cartari collected even more ancient sources than any of his predecessors; his list of authors stretches from Homer to the Neoplatonist philosophers. He is a resolute physical allegorist: "The poets, who were the first to write about the gods, invented stories about them . . .: they turned the elements, the stars, the sun, and the moon into divinities." This programmatic sentence opens his chapter on Apollo. The god is, not surprisingly, the Sun: this is the master key to most things Apolline that Cartari discusses with iconography in mind – iconography understood not simply as image-making, but as visual expression of philosophical, moral, and theological concepts. He gives many descriptions of ancient images, apparently following the motto "the stranger the better": foreign, Oriental images express more numerous and more complex concepts than the plain images of the Greeks. He also describes all the attributes of a given divinity and explains them allegorically; plates add the necessary visual illustration (figure 11). In Apollo's case, there is the lyre with its seven strings, symbol of harmony among the seven planets (Sun and Moon included); or the nine Muses who correspond to the nine "celestial bodies," Earth plus the seven planets and the sphere of the stars. Similarly, he explains Apollo's sacred animals. The wolf belongs to Apollo because the rays of the sun devour all humidity, or because the wolf sees even in the night and thus overcomes darkness. The swan shines in pure whiteness; the rooster announces the rising sun; the crocodile is holy to Apollo because "the theologians of Egypt put the Sun in a ship carried by a crocodile." But even Cartari's learning and ingeniosity cannot explain everything from Apollo's solar nature. The raven is Apollo's animal because he foretells the weather and thus participates in his divinatory powers, as does the laurel, his sacred tree. Apollo's preferred sacrificial animal, the male goat, is explained with

Figure 11 The many aspects of Apollo, from Vincenzo Cartari, *Le imagini degli dei antichi* (Venice 1571), p. 60.

reference to Pausanias' account of Delphi (*Description of Greece* 10.11.5). The people of Cleonae, Pausanias wrote, dedicated a bronze goat in Apollo's sanctuary after he had helped them to defeat an epidemic disease by advising them to sacrifice a male goat to himself at sun-rise (another reason for Cartari to equate Apollo and sun). The image of Apollo with the Graces in his right and bow and arrows in his left hand comes directly from Macrobius' description more than a millennium before: such is the force of the medieval tradition even in the Renaissance. The same solar key that explained images and attributes worked for the myths: Apollo killed Python because the sun dries humidity (again from Macrobius), the Cyclopes because the sun drives away the clouds: the Cyclopes fabricated the thunderbolts, as the clouds produce lightning. Apollo Lykeios is Wolf Apollo, and the wolf again is solar;

Apollo Smintheus drives mice away because these and other pests symbolize the bad and humid parts of the air. Cartari adds an illustration that contains as many details as possible, and that derives from earlier illustrated books, such as the *Libellus de imaginibus deorum* (ca. 1400): this *Booklet on the Images of the Gods* contains an image of Apollo with all his symbolical attributes that is almost as rich as Cartari's and combines several literary sources, from Servius' commentary on the *Aeneid* and Martianus Capella's *Wedding of Mercury and Philosophy* to a medieval commentary on the poet Martial. The *Booklet* in turn goes back to the *Book on the Images of the Gods*, the *Liber de imaginibus deorum*, written by one Albricus Londoniensis (perhaps a pseudonym of the famous scholar Alexander of Neckham, 1157–1217) at the end of the twelfth century; it already combined many of these literary sources.

The importance of these early modern mythological handbooks should not be underrated. They perpetuated the knowledge of Greek and Roman gods and contributed to it by collecting a steadily increasing number of ancient texts; and they offered models for a "modern" interpretation of these gods that had nothing to do with their former role in pagan ritual and cult. The gods and their myths were understood as embodiments of philosophical and theological insights that appealed to a contemporary audience. This is valid not only for texts, but equally for artistic representations. A mythical scene painted or sculpted by an early modern artist – who relied most often on Ovid's *Metamorphoses* – could simply evoke aesthetic pleasure; but to a better informed viewer it meant also philosophical and even spiritual insights. Already the Middle Ages justified the reading of Ovid's *Metamorphoses* by turning the poem into a vast store house of edifying tales; the late medieval *Ovide Moralisé* that makes all these moral teachings explicit was a huge success, as its many surviving manuscripts show. Early modern scholars followed suit, offering a wide array of interpretations that could draw on any handbook such as Cartari's or Conti's; but it could also draw on other allegorizations, such as those of the Florentine Neoplatonists (on whom Cartari heavily depended anyway). Whatever an artist such as Paolo Veronese or Gian Lorenzo Bernini meant when they painted or sculpted the transformation of Daphne escaping Apollo's pursuit, his patron or any other contemporary viewer could feel free to read it in any of the keys provided by the learned literature.

THE DAWN OF MODERN SCHOLARSHIP

After the Renaissance and its open-minded ways, the pressure of the Counter Reformation added a new urgency to finding ways to make pagan myths acceptable to Catholic thinking. In a remarkable and very successful book, the *Proofs from the Gospels* (*Demonstratio Evangelica*) published for the first time in 1672, Pierre-Daniel Huet (1630–1721), bishop, member of the French Academy and educator of the French crown prince, tried a radical reconciliation between Christian faith and the pagan stories cherished in general culture. To Huet, Apollo was none other than Moses; his demonstration used the full register of possible and impossible parallels, from Biblical prophecy to the Muses as images of the Israelite women dancing around Moses in the desert, and even to a Euhemerist identification of Python with the Pharaoh, Moses' victim. Using a tradition that is attested already in ancient mythography, it also identified Apollo with Dionysus and read the death and dismemberment of baby Dionysus as a distorted account of Moses' exposure on the Nile. The book was very successful in its time and still read in the eighteenth century. With the rise of the Enlightenment, however, Huet's book began to be seen as an outmoded way of looking at the pagan gods that was superseded by enlightened skepticism and the beginnings of scholarship in a modern sense, guided by a consciousness of historical distance and the concomitant necessity for encyclopedic data collection.

Fifty years after Huet, Benjamin Hederich (1675–1748: "former headmaster at Grossenhain," as he introduced himself) published the first edition of his "exhaustive lexicon of mythology," the *Gründliches Mythologisches Lexicon* (1724). He wanted to create a dictionary that would offer the facts of ancient mythology to any educated person and prevent artists from "making mistakes." The work was wildly successful and went into many printings, and in 1770, the librarian and professor of philosophy Johann Joachim Schwabe published a heavily revised second edition. Hederich's entry "Apollo" presents the god as any of our dictionaries would: the lexicon has created the template for all of us. Hederich leads his reader through etymology, mythology, ancient worship, and iconography, and he sums all this up with the modern interpretations. Additional lists give Apollo's epithets and his (female) lovers and children: there is no hint of Apollo's many male lovers, in a rare instance of moral censorship. As an interpreter of myth, Hederich is vaguely euhemerist, but he faithfully reproduces biblical, physical, and ethical interpretations. He insists on the identification of Apollo with the sun, but points out that this is recent: he is among the first to do so, and many of our contemporary popular books have yet to realize this. In his preface to the second edition, Schwabe take his distance to Hederich's interpretations: "I have undertaken not ... to excise the physical and moralistic interpretations of the fables. I do not like them, but they may please others, as they have pleased many." Eighteenth-century scholarship moved towards a purely historical reading of Greek mythology, even if this meant to acknowledge the growing distance in time and world view. The nineteenth century would continue in this historicization that meant to reject allegorical and symbolical readings. Apollo, however, resisted the scholarly efforts to be turned into a historical exhibit, as we shall see presently.

APOLLO, GOD OF POETRY

From its earliest appearance in Greek culture, *mousikē*, "song-dance," belonged to Apollo, as did the Muses. This did not by itself turn the god into a patron of writers and their art; this happened only in Hellenistic times when the unity of archaic *mousikē* was divided into its two constituent parts, literary writing and musical performance. This was the result of what I would call the privatization and individualization of poetry: poetry was no longer written only for public performance, but for recitation or silent reading in the narrow circle of the *cognoscenti* who could enjoy its refined details, and for the lonely reader. The introduction to Callimachus' *Aetia* features the god who sternly admonishes the budding poet to adhere to new aesthetic ideals (see Chapter 2). Unlike his classical predecessors, the lone Alexandrian poet has to follow his own inspiration; he cannot rely on collective traditions. Callimachus somewhat playfully justified this new poetic program as the choice to which the poet had been compelled by Apollo, against his own wishes. Latin authors, from Virgil in his *Eclogues* onwards, adopted the scene to their own ends, and they made Apollo their protector and inspirator, as in Ovid's short prayer (*Amores* 1.15.35):

> *mihi flavus Apollo*
> *pocula Castalia plena ministret aqua.*

May blond Apollo offer me a cup, full to the brim with water from Castalia.

It is in his Latin guise that Apollo the patron of poetry began his career in the Western tradition, and he remained a literary creation. In Roman life, not Apollo but Minerva presided over the poets' organization, the guild of *scribae*, "public scribes" – Roman Apollo had started his career as a doctor, not a poet.

It is impossible to give here more than the bare outline of Apollo's later career as the patron of poetry and music. The paintings that depict Apollo with the lyre or the violin, alone or among the Muses, are legion, and poets and composers put him on stage long before Igor Strawinski and George Balanchine staged *Apollon Musagète* as a modern ballet in 1928. Here, Apollon "leader of the Muses" takes center stage, as he did in some earlier works such as Bach's secular cantata "The Contest between Phoebus and Pan" (1731) or in Mozart's delightful *singspiel* "Apollo and Hyacinthus" (1767). More often, however, the god remained off-stage. European opera began with his son Orpheus: Angelo Poliziano's *Favola d'Orfeo* was performed in 1480 at the court of the Gonzaga in Mantua; Claudio Monteverdi's *L'Orfeo* of 1607 set the standard for the genre to come. The tragic destiny of Orpheus made a much more powerful story for early modern opera, conceived by its promoters as a renewal of the ancient genre of tragedy; gods are unsuitable tragic heroes, since they cannot die. But Apollo remained the patron of the artists. Following ancient custom, poets continued to invoke him as their guide; Academies and Music Schools were adorned with his image; theaters and movie theaters still bear his name as a testimony to their cultural aspirations. And even his divinatory powers occasionally inspired the use of his name: *Apollo Anglicanus*, Richard Saunder's almanac that was first published in 1664, remained a bestseller for almost a century. The almanac promised

> to assist all persons in the right understanding of this year's revolution, also of things past, present, and to come: with necessary tables plain and useful . . . to which is added a short discourse of comets, and what accidents have succeeded them for some years past.

It followed William Lilly's *Merlinus Anglicanus* that began to appear in 1644: in the long run, the Greek god of prophecy outlived the Saxon sorcerer, and even spawned off a short-lived *American Apollo*.

But however entertaining, these are side-tracks. What I want to do here, and what I am able to do, is different and less ambitious: it is to present some passages from European literature in which Apollo, the patron god of poetry, is highly visible, passages that not infrequently set the tone for some time to come.

One of these works is Dante's *Divina Commedia*, written after 1307. At the beginning of each of its three parts, Dante (1265–1321) invokes different helpers for his poetical undertaking. In the first book of the

Inferno, the helper offers himself – the Roman poet Virgil, who had traveled through the Underworld when he created the sixth book of the *Aeneid*. At the beginning of *Purgatorio*, Dante invokes the Muses (*o sante Muse* 1.8) and especially one of them, Calliope, and he does so in a surprisingly polemical spirit: the poet is prepared to defend himself and his work, as did the Muses when they were challenged by the arrogant Pierides and turned them into magpies (Ovid, *Metamorphoses* 5.295–678). Things get even more surprising in the prologue to *Paradise*. For the crowning third part of his vast poem, Dante cannot rely on the Muses alone any more, he needs a more divine helper, the god Apollo himself:

> O buono Apollo, all'ultimo lavoro
>   fammi del tuo valor sì fatto vaso
>   come dimandi a dar l'amato alloro.
> Infino a qui l'un giogo di Parnasso
>   assai mi fu; ma or con amendue
>   m'è uopo intrar nell'arringo rimaso.
> Entra nel petto mio, e spira tue
>   sì come quando Marsia traesti
>   della vagina delle membra sue.

> O good Apollo, for this last labor
> make me into a vessel worthy
> of the gift of your belovèd laurel.
> Up to this point, one peak of Mount Parnassus
> has been enough, but now I need them both
> in order to confront the struggle that awaits.
> Enter my breast and breathe in me
> as when you drew out Marsyas,
> out from the sheathing of his limbs.

(*Paradiso* 1.13–21)

Inspiration, both prophetic and poetic, is the only way to succeed in this task, and Apollo alone can provide it. Apolline inspiration is able to separate the soul as far from the body as possible, and this separation is needed to describe Paradise, a purely spiritual place radically separated from the material body. If read correctly, the story of Marsyas demonstrates this power of Apollo: it does not talk of Marsyas killed by being flayed alive, but of Marsyas forced by Apollo to leave his body, in an agonizing rite of purification. Dante's interpretation of the Ovidian story takes Ovid's playfulness and cleverness seriously. As the Roman poet tells the story, Marsyas' final outcry to Apollo was "Why do you tear me from myself, *qui me mihi detrahis?*" (*Metamorphoses* 6.385) – a grim witticism that invited deeper speculation: Dante's understanding was followed by the Florentine Neoplatonists whose philosophy aimed at a separation from corporeality. Only when he is separated from his body can the poet be crowned with Apollo's laurel wreath, taken from Apollo's first love, Daphne:

> *O divina virtù, se mi ti presti*
> > *tanto che l'ombra del beato regno*
> > *segnata nel mio capo io manifesti,*
> *venir vedra' mi al tuo diletto legno,*
> > *e coronarmi allor di quelle foglie*
> > *che la matera e tu mi farai degno.*

> O holy Power, if you but lend me of yourself
> enough that I may show the merest shadow
> of the blessèd kingdom stamped within my mind,
> You shall find me at the foot of your belovèd tree,
> crowning myself with the very leaves
> of which my theme and you will make me worthy.

> (*Paradiso* 1.22–27)

For Dante, such a coronation has become very rare indeed in his time, compared to what used to be:

> *Sì rade volte, padre, se ne coglie*
> > *per triunfare o Cesare o poeta,*
> > *colpa e vergogna dell'umane voglie*
> *Che parturir letizia in su la lieta*
> > *delfica deità dovria la fronda*
> *Peneia, quando alcun di sè asseta.*

> So rarely, father, are they gathered
> to mark the triumph of a Caesar or a poet –
> fault and shame of human wishes –
> anyone's even longing for them,
> those leaves on the Peneian bough, should make
> the joyous Delphic god give birth to joy.

> (*Paradiso* 1.26–33)

As many centuries earlier in Callimachus, the invocation of Apollo is a poetical program. Poetry, Apollo's gift, must return to an excellence worthy of its ancient models. The Renaissance is just around the corner.

A generation later, with Francesco Petrarca (Petrarch) (1304–1374) Italian poetry has officially arrived at this stage: on Easter Sunday 1341, on the Capitole of Rome, a Roman senator crowned Petrarch with Apollo's sacred wreath, conveying upon him the dignity of a *Poeta Laureatus*, "poet crowned with laurel." Very few poets had preceded him in past centuries, many more were to come, such Conrad Celtis, the first German laureate (crowned in 1487 by the emperor Maximilian I), or Ben Jonson, the first English Poet Laureate (crowned in 1616 by James I). But it was only with John Dryden (crowned in 1668 by Charles II, to mark the end of the Civil War) that an uninterrupted line of laureate poets begins, leading up to Andrew Motion (crowned in 1999 by Elizabeth II) and attesting to the secret presence of Apollo in the contemporary world.

Petrarch's coronation did not come by chance. Once he had made the girl Laura into the intimate subject of much of his poetry, his work (and perhaps his life) was connected with Apollo's sacred tree: Laura, as he knew well, is the feminine form of the Latin word for laurel, *laurus*. After Dante's passionate plea for Apollo's help, this is so neat that already some of Petrarch's contemporaries doubted the existence of the girl that, as he claimed "first appeared to my eyes in my youth, in the year of our Lord 1327, on the sixth day of April, in the church of St. Clare in Avignon, at matins." However that might have been (and however futile it might be to separate a life from the texts in which the poet narrated and relived this very life), the god's love for Daphne (Greek for Laura – in Greek, unlike Latin, a feminine noun) gave a template for the poet's love. This was not without danger, since Apollo was a jealous lover, and the poet's constant sighs for Laura could arouse his anger:

se non che forse Apollo si disdegna
ch' a parlar de' suoi sempre verdi rami
lingua mortal presuntuosa vegna.

Except perhaps that Apollo is scornful
that mortal tongue should be presumptuous
to speak of his eternally green boughs.

(*Rime Sparse* 5.12–14)

But overall, the poet is confident, even sometimes cocky, as in *Rime Sparse* 43 where Apollo is both the lover of Laura and the sun looking down onto earth to find her, but disappointed hides himself in bad weather and thus misses her:

Il figluol di Latona aveva già nove
volte guardato dal balcon sovrano
per quella che alcun tempo mosse in vano
i suoi sospiri et or gli altrui commove.

Poi che cercando stanco non seppe ove
s'albergasse da presso o di lontano,
mostrossi a noi qual uom per doglia insano
che molto amata cosa non ritrove.

Et così tristo standosi in disparte,
tornar non vide il viso che laudato
sarà, si io vivo, in più mille carte,

Latona's son had already looked down nine times from his high balcony, seeking her who once in vain moved his sighs and now moves those of another.

When, tired with searching, he could not discover where she was dwelling, whether near or far, he showed himself to us like one mad with grief at not finding some much-loved thing.

And thus sadly remaining off by himself, he did not see that face return which shall be praised, if I live, on more than a thousand pages.

A century later, in another reign, another poet claimed Apollo as the leader of his entire life:

Le jour que je fus né, Apollon qui préside
aux Muses, me servit en ce monde de guide,
m'anima d'un esprit subtil et vigoureux
et me fit de science et d'honneur amoureux.

The day I was born Apollo, who presides
over the Muses, served as a guide in this world,
animated me with a subtle and vigorous spirit
and made me fall in love with learning and with honor.

Thus begins the *Hymn to Autumn* by Pierre Ronsard (1523–1585), poet to the court of France. The Hymn, first published in 1563, begins with a long account of Ronsard's early poetry, starting with an initiation by the Muses modeled on Hesiod's ("l'Ascréan"), but evoking also the memory of Callimachean poetics that aims for the rare and the exquisite:

Car la gentille Euterpe ayant ma dextre prise
pour m'ôter le mortel par neuf fois me lava
de l'eau d'une fontaine où peu de monde va.

Gentle Euterpe, taking my right hand,
to take away my mortality bathed me nine times
in the water of a fountain to which few people go.

But it was not the Greek poet from Ascra whom Ronsard admired and followed most, it was the poet from Florence. In Ronsard's understanding of the recent history of poetry, Petrarch had overcome the night of Dante and other medieval poets and brought the beauty of Apollo's gifts to Italy ("les dons d'Apollon dont se vit embellie, quand Pétrarque vivait, sa native Italie"). And thus, he claimed the laurel wreath as much as the Florentine had done – he too saw himself crowned with Apollo's laurel, "un laurier sur le front" (*Dialogue du Poète et des Muses*, 1556).

To invoke Apollo and the Muses when beginning a work of poetry did not remain a custom of Greek and Roman poets and of their Renaissance followers. But already in late antiquity, this invocation had changed its nature. As long as it was written by a pagan poet and read within a polytheistic world, any reader could perceive its religious implications: these invocations usually followed the established form of prayer and hymn. In a world turned Christian, however, Apollo and his Muses became symbols and metaphors for poetry and poetic inspiration. Some religious coloring, however, could persist even in this new guise. When Dante addressed Apollo as "father," he uses a predominantly Christian form of divine address. No pagan would have done so; pagan Apollo was too young for such an address. In the new religious world, strong emotions for a pagan god who is at the same time Poetic Inspiration capitalized can coexist with a wide-spread disregard for the literal meaning of a myth. This explains why Dante could so easily refer to the allegorical meaning of Marsyas' flaying, or why Petrarch sometimes almost blended Apollo's and his own poetic persona.

Over time, the conventionality of such an invocation became more obvious, and poets reacted by discarding these traditional forms; one does not have to wait for the Romantic movement to see this happen. But it is not so easy to get rid of gods, even after the Enlightenment. In the early twentieth century, one of the leading German poets again opened two of his books of poetry with Apollo. The way he does so, however, tells us that the times have changed since Dante, Petrarch, and Ronsard.

In 1907 and 1908 respectively, Rainer Maria Rilke published the two books of his *Neue Gedichte*, "New Poems." At the time, Rilke was at the zenith of his fame and one of Germany's leading poets. Both books are introduced by a sonnet about Apollo – not an invocation anymore, but the description of a work of art.

The earlier poem, the first of the new collection, is entitled "Early Apollo" ("Früher Apollo").

Sometimes a morning that is sheerest spring
may peer through twigs still bare of foliage:
nothing obscures his head and nothing screens
us from this almost fatal radiance

of all poems ever, of all poetry.
For there is yet no shadow in his gaze,
his brow is still too fresh for laurel wreaths
and time must pass before the long-stemmed rose

can flourish at his eyebrows and put out
and open, one by one, its tender leaves
to touch and to caress the trembling mouth

that is still shining-new, still motionless;
lips smiling, open as if drinking
as if to drink the liquid of his song.

Wie manches Mal durch das unbelaubte
Gezweig ein Morgen durchsieht, der schon ganz
im Frühling ist: so ist in seinem Haupte
nichts was verhindern könnte, dass der Glanz

aller Gedichte uns fast tödlich träfe;
denn noch kein Schatten ist in seinem Schaun,
zu kühl für Lorbeer sind noch seine Schläfe
und später erst wird aus den Augenbraun

hochstämmig sich der Rosengarten heben,
aus welchem Blätter, einzeln, ausgelöst
hintreiben werden auf des Mundes Beben,

der jetzt noch still ist, niegebraucht und blinkend
und nur mit seinem Lächeln etwas trinkend
als würde ihm sein Singen eingeflösst.

The poet explores the concept of being early on several levels. Early first means "early in the history of Greek art": we are to see an archaic image of Apollo, such as one of the kouroi who had become famous at this very time. But it is also an Apollo "early in his life": he is not yet wearing his olive wreath, his gaze is still modest, and he is not yet producing poetry that is being poured into him as a liquid into a young child's mouth. At the same time, the concept of being early is expressed in two images, early in the morning, and early in the year. There is the "not yet" of a spring morning that promises the full splendor of the day and the full splendor of the year: trees do not yet carry leaves that would prevent the morning sun from hitting us, but they certainly will one day, and there will be rose-gardens that bloom and later will shed their petals rich in color and scent. But the main promise, expressed already by the position of the poem, is metapoetical. It is the promise of perfect poetry to come; the opening poem promises an aesthetic experience such as the reader has not yet had so far.

The second poem is markedly different. It again looks at an archaic Apollo, but this time at a torso only. A torso implies distance and reflexivity; accordingly, the poem's title uses the technical term "archaic" instead of "early."

We never knew his legendary head
nor saw the eyes set there like apples ripening.
But the bright torso, as a lamp turned low
still shines, still sees. For how else could the hard

contour of his breast so blind you? How could
a smile start in the turning loins and settle
on the parts which made his progeny?
This marble otherwise would stand defaced

beneath the shoulders and their lucid fall;
and would not take the light
like panther-skin; and would not radiate

and would not break from all its surfaces
as does a star. There is no part of him
that does not see you. You must change your life.

Wir kannten nicht sein unerhörtes Haupt
darin die Augenäpfel reiften. Aber
sein Torso glüht noch wie ein Kandelaber,
in dem sein Schauen, nur zurückgeschraubt,

sich hält und glänzt. Sonst könnte nicht der Bug
der Brust dich blenden, und im leiseren Drehen
der Lenden könnte nicht ein Lächeln gehen
zu jener Mitte, die die Zeugung trug.

Sonst stünde dieser Stein entstellt und kurz
unter der Schultern durchsichtigem Sturz
und flimmerte nicht so wie Raubtierfelle;

und bräche nicht aus allen seinen Rändern
aus wie ein Stern: denn da ist keine Stelle,
die dich nicht sieht. Du musst dein Leben ändern.

This is a very different Apollo, and a different poem. Its entire focus is on visuality, starting with the missing head and its imagined eyes that ripen like fruit. But even without eyes, the entire body does not only shine, it looks; its active beauty is so immense that it generates the appeal to change the addressee's, our, life. At the same time, this body has a powerful sexual attraction. Its loins ("*Lenden*" in German, with clear sexual connotation) move seductively, and its center that focuses the viewer's gaze is the active male sex ("*Zeugung*" in German is the generative act). Metapoetically, it promises the reader sensual pleasures. But unlike the earlier text, this poem does not strongly invite a metapoetical reading. It stands on its own, creating a powerful image of male bodily presence even in the torso of this Apollo.

The poetic voice, writing at the beginning of the early twentieth century, is unable to invoke Apollo as a guide in these two poems as it did in earlier poems. The only access to the god is through a concrete image preserved from Archaic Greece. Between the times of Petrarch and Ronsard and the epoch of Rilke, the pagan gods have receded as an immediate presence; they are firmly anchored in past history and experienced aesthetically only, as part of one's cultural training. We already saw this process reflected in the development of mythological handbooks, with the second edition of Hederich's *Encyclopedia* (1770) initialing this historicization.

This does not mean that the gods could not be evoked any more as persons; but this often sounds ironical. W.H. Auden's poem "Under

Which Lyre" was written in 1946 for Harvard's Phi Beta Kappa. Occasion and audience call for traditional learning, and the poem's subtitle "A Reactionary Tract for the Times" marks the poet's ambivalent and ironical stance. The theme is the return of academic normalcy after the war, after "Ares at last has quit the field," as the first line states. The young warriors have returned to fight other battles, and they have turned to new gods:

> Let Ares doze, that other war
> is instantly declared once more
>   'twixt those who follow
> precocious Hermes all the way
> and those who without qualms obey
>   pompous Apollo.

The lyres of the title are the improvised lyre of Hermes and the stately lyre of Apollo. The two divine brothers stand for two ways of life: Apollo's is the middle-class seriousness of the achievers who have returned from the war and are eager to lay the groundwork for a respectable career during their college years, Hermes' a more ironical and disrespectful *joie de vivre*. Auden seems to miss this *joie* in his audience and in a society at large that he sees entirely dedicated to Apollo's pursuits.

> Today his arms, we must confess,
> from Right to Left have met success,
>
>   his banners wave
> from Yale to Princeton, and the news
> from Broadway to the Book Reviews
>   is very grave.

To this, the poet opposes his "Hermetic Decalogue" – a list of forbidden things that sound almost as banal as Apollo's values and are clearly aimed at undergraduates that to Auden seem in need to relax and wind down.

APOLLO AND DIONYSUS

Auden's "pompous Apollo," the symbol of well-mannered adjustment, is not entirely his own creation. His dichotomy of Apollo and Hermes is intimately connected with the opposition between two principles, the

Apolline and the Dionysiac that we associate with the work of the German classicist and philosopher Friedrich Nietzsche (1844–1900). In his *Birth of Tragedy* (*Die Geburt der Tragödie*, 1872), Nietzsche analyzed the emotions at the root of art. He insisted on "the deep opposition . . . between the art of the sculptor, the Apolline, and the non-figurative of the music, being Dionysiac." He understood both as fundamental forces that he saw at work in any artistic creation. Apollo, the god of light, stood for the rationality of distinct figures, Dionysus, the patron of ecstasy, for the loss of self during the inspirational experience. Only two movements in all art history were able to fuse the two opposite principles into a single work of art, Attic tragedy in Greek antiquity and the operas of Richard Wagner in contemporary Germany.

Nietzsche was far from being the first to see an opposition between the two gods. In antiquity, the sacred year in the sanctuary of Delphi was distributed between Apollo and Dionysus. During the winter months, Apollo was away in the Far North, among the Hyperboreans. During this time, Dionysus reigned in Delphi: his festivals and those of his menads were all held in winter whereas Apollo was celebrated from spring to autumn. Even Apollo's temple showed this division of divine presence: Apollo and the Muses were figured on the east pediment, over the entrance of the temple, Dionysus with his ecstatic female followers, the Thyiades, on the west pediment, in the "back" of the temple. The opposition was even expressed in terms of mortality and immortality: the Delphians were convinced that there was a grave of Dionysus in Apollo's temple.

The opposition between the two gods must have expressed a Greek perception of both gods; in many ways, the Greeks saw them as opposed and complementary to each other. Both were sons of Zeus, Apollo from an almost Hera-like mother, Dionysus from a mortal princess who died before she could give birth. Both were eternally young; although Archaic Greece represented Dionysus as bearded, he later was often viewed as an almost girlish young god. Dionysus married Ariadne and was strictly heterosexual (with one obscure exception where he was the passive partner), while Apollo remained decidedly bisexual. Both were connected with altered states of mind, Apollo with prophetic possession, Dionysus with the ecstasy of dance and drugs. Both had their music, Apollo the stately music of the grand lyre (*kíthara*), Dionysus more often the frenzied sounds of pipes and drums, and of smaller string instruments. The opposition between the two gods became pronounced in Rome and under the pressure of political image spin, when two competing Romans, Marc Antony and Augustus, had recourse to the two gods to express their contrasting political programs as we saw above (Chapter 5).

The powerful god of luxury and peaceful exuberance who had conquered the entire Orient, from Anatolia to India, seemed an apt symbol for Marc Antony's ambitions. Caesar's heir Octavian – who would become the emperor Augustus – answered by turning Apollo into his very personal god. To the Italians who were still suffering from the pains of a long series of civil wars, Apollo the god of healing and of counsel seemed more appropriate and acceptable than the frivolous luxury of Dionysus.

The modern opposition, however, draws on another source, the difference between Dionysiac and Apolline music; Greeks regarded the *kíthara* as the serious and grand instrument that was exclusively played by men, whereas flute and drums belonged to an ectstatic kind of music, often connected with women such as the menads, or the *hetairai*. Ancient theoreticians of music elaborated on this opposition, as we saw, and so did their modern successors. In the 1830s, German classical scholarship insisted on the fundamental contrast between Apolline and Dionysiac music; this theory went far beyond what the ancient authorities had said. Nietzsche, an expert on Greek musical theory, knew this, and he appropriated it for his own construction. But he went much further than the theoreticians of music: he expanded their contrast between two fundamentally opposed types of ancient Greek music into two modes of artistic expression and experience. By applying the same contrast to Wagner's music, he exported it into his own contemporary culture. In the years to come, Nietzsche's followers took the final step and projected these two modes of artistic experience onto general culture or even life styles. This watered the principles down to the rather commonplace opposition between rational and irrational or even between traditional and iconoclast. More importantly for twentieth-century Europe, this banalization helped to give irrationalism a legitimacy that proved utterly distructive to German culture and society. It was no coincidence that, when the Italian fascist dictator Benito Mussolini looked for a fitting donation for the recently founded Nietzsche Archive in Dresden, he presented Hitler with a Greek head of Dionysus. Dionysiac frenzy, not Apolline rationality, was dominant in European politics of the age.

APOLLO, ART, AND ARCHAEOLOGY

The loss of immediacy that we found in Rilke's two poems reflected changes in cultural outlook that had begun during the Enlightenment. Unlike Renaissance intellectuals and artists, their successors in nineteenth- and twentieth-century Europe no longer regarded Greeks and Romans as direct ancestors whose values they emulated and hoped to perpetuate. In a time that saw the rise of the university and of scholarship as we know them, it was no longer the poets and artists but the historians who studied Greek texts and artifacts, even when the sheer beauty of these artifacts was able to provoke the personal response of Rilke's second poem.

The change that lead to this new appreciation of ancient art began in the eighteenth century when Greek art began to be recognized and valued as something of its own. Ancient works of art, almost exclusively statuary, had been known long before. Chance finds and intentional excavations in the expanding city of early modern Rome had produced a large number of ancient statues, most of them marble copies of earlier Greek works; aristocrats, cardinals, and popes vied with each other to create their own collections of ancient sculpture. Many statues were recognized in the descriptions found in Pliny's *Natural History* and Pausanias' *Description of Greece*. Early modern Europe slowly began to see the real works of the great sculptors of old, or at least copies of them. These sculptures, however, did not stimulate research into the history of Greek art but served as models for contemporary artists. Their presence mattered, not their history.

This changed in the eighteenth century. The change is mainly due to one man, Johann Joachim Winckelmann (1717–1768). Winckelmann became interested in ancient art when he was a librarian with count Bünau in Saxony; this gave him access to the rich collections of antiquities in the capital, Dresden (1748). Seven years later, he moved to Rome, the center of the study of antiquity. Here, he wrote his seminal *Geschichte der Kunst des Alterthums* (*History of the Art of Antiquity*, 1764) that marked the beginning of scholarly understanding of Greek and Roman art. Apollo played a very personal role in Winckelmann's view of Greek art. To him, Greek art was the unsurpassed concretization of beauty in human history, Greek sculpture the pinnacle of Greek art, and images of Apollo the apogee of Greek beauty:

> With Apollo, the highest conception of ideal male youth has been made into an image; he combines the strength of a perfect age with the tender forms of the most beautiful spring of youth. His forms are youthfully simple and not those of a darling

who prefers cool shadows and whom Venus, as Ibycus said, brought up on roses; they are fit for a noble young man, born to great destiny; therefore, Apollo was the most beautiful among the gods.

Beauty is not perceived in aesthetical but in ethical terms. The image of Apollo is beautiful because the god embodies a specific form of human existence. In this respect, Winckelmann saw the Greeks as timeless ideals. But to him, this ideal did not take form in a philosophical or poetical text or in myths that could be read allegorically, but visually in a work of art.

Winckelmann found the perfect image of Apollo in a celebrated marble statue that he saw in Rome, the so-called "Belvedere Apollo." It was found in the late fifteenth century; in 1511, its owner, Pope Julius II, transferred it from the garden of his former residence to the Vatican's Belvedere Court. It is a copy of a lost Greek bronze original, created by the Athenian sculptor Leochares in the years around 320 BCE; the copy was made in the reign of the emperor Hadrian. It does not represent a specific moment of Apollo's mythology but conveys a general impression of the god's appearance and nature. Extremely lightfooted, he is swiftly walking forward, bow and arrow in his oustretched left hand; a short cloak is draped over his shoulder, otherwise he is naked. Winckelmann imagined that he was setting out on his first exploit, to kill the snake Pytho; this made him see in the statue the "noble young man, born to great destiny." And although he was aware of the historical development of Greek art, he did not recognize the character of the statue as a copy, but regarded it as a work of pure Greek workmanship. Apollo's body is perfect, he noted:

> There is nothing mortal here, nothing which human necessities require; neither blood-vessels nor sinews heat and stir this body, but a heavenly essence, diffusing itself like a gentle stream, seems to fill the whole contour of the figure. . . . My breast seems to enlarge and swell with reverence, like the breasts of those who were filled with the spirit of prophecy, and I feel myself transported to Delos and the Lycaean groves.
>
> (*History of Ancient Art* 11.3.11)

Winckelmann was not the first to admire this Apollo. Ever since the statue had become easily accessible in its Vatican location, it influenced artists, not the least Michelangelo, whose patron was Julius II. But Winckelmann's praise turned the Belvedere Apollo into the Vatican's main attraction for travelers to Rome, and casts of the copy became prestigious and treasured north of the Alps. The Royal Academy of the

Arts in London owned such a cast in the late eighteenth century (it is lost now), and it commanded high attention. In a group portrait of 1795, painted by Henry Singleton, the Academicians posed in front of two ancient sculptures – a huge cast of the Laocoon, the other famous Vatican sculpture, in the center, the Belvedere Apollo to the right. When the young Johann Wolfgang von Goethe (1749–1832) saw another cast of Apollo at the princely court of Mannheim in 1771, he was blown over. "My entire being is shaken, as you can imagine," he wrote to his mentor Johann Gottfried Herder. But unlike Rilke, this earlier German poet felt no impulse to change his life. The statue showed him the unchangeable limits of his own physicality: "Belvedere Apollo, why do you show yourself naked, so that we have to be ashamed of our nakedness?" No young man matches the bodily perfection of the Greek god. Nonetheless, a year later, in his *Wanderers Sturmlied* ("Wanderer's Storm Song"), the memory of the statue inspired Goethe to the portrait of a human whom his genius carries through life to new exploits:

Wandeln wird er
wie mit Blumenfüssen
über Deukalions Fluthschlamm,
Python tötend, leicht, gross,
Pythius Apollo.

He will wander/, as with flowery feet/ over Deucalion's muddy flood/, slaying Python, light, splendid/ Pythius Apollo.

With Winckelmann, Goethe understood the Belvedere Apollo as an image of the young god attacking Python, immediately after the flood had receded and left its traces on Mount Parnassus near Delphi where Deucalion was thought to have landed in his ark.

This is not the only presence of Apollo in Goethe's poem. It is entirely about inspiration and refers to the two Greek gods of inspiration, Apollo and Dionysus. True to the spirit of the epoch that prepared the Romantic age, the genius that inspires the poet is Dionysus, the god of unruly ecstasy. Goethe construed an opposition between Dionysus and Apollo, an inspirational god who to him was more measured and accessible for the many, but as haughty as the Belvedere Apollo: "his regal look over thee will swiftly glide" ("kalt wird sonst / sein Fürstenblick / über dich vorübergleiten").

Goethe was not the first nor the last to be inspired by the Belvedere Apollo. For generations of educated Europeans, the statue – seen through the eyes of Winckelmann – remained the unmatched epitome of Greek art. Disagreement began when general taste moved away from the soft forms of Greek fourth-century art to the harder shapes of fifth century Athens, and from Baroque and Rococo art to European classicism. A commentary by William Hazlitt (1778–1830), in his time a famous journalist and *arbiter elegantiae*, highlights this change. When traveling in Italy, he visited the Apollo, and complained: "There is great softness, sweetness, symmetry and timid grace – a faultless tameness, a negative perfection." Compared to the Parthenon sculptures that Lord Elgin had sold to the British Museum in 1806, "the Belvedere Apollo is positively bad, a theatrical coxcomb." Although one senses, as an underrcurrent, an Anglo-Saxon opposition to the soft Latins, there is more at stake than contemporary political self-definition: we perceive a universal change of taste, articulated in the appreciation of Greek sculpture. The fluid forms of fourth-century sculpture, so beloved to eighteenth-century viewers, yielded to the sterner and more articulated forms of the fifth century, of Phidias and Polyclitus, even of pre-classical art. At the end of the nineteenth century, the German excavators of Olympia found and restored the Apollo from the west pediment of the temple of Zeus: he soon replaced the Belvedere statue as the most admired image of Apollo, despite its fragmentary state.

Who once has seen Apollo from the east pediment of Zeus' temple in Olympia, will never forget him. The artist represented him in a moment of overwhelming grandiosity: in the midst of a tumultuous action, the god appears suddenly, and his outstretched arm commands quiet. His face radiates magnificence, and his wide eyes command through the sheer power of looking; the melancholy of higher knowledge, however, plays around his strong and noble lips. One can not imagine a more exciting appearance of divinity amidst the chaotic savagery of our world.

Thus the German classicist Walter F. Otto in 1929, elevating this statue into the most convincing representation of divinity he could think of, a commanding god who would fulfill his longing for harmony in the chaotic and savage present times. Little did he know how much more savage and chaotic these times would become less than ten years later.

Still, the fame of the Belvedere Apollo persisted. In 1914, the Italian painter Giorgio de Chirico painted Apollo's head, clearly a cast taken from the Vatican statue, at the center of his enigmatic *Canto d'Amore*, together with a red glove and a green ball (now in the Museum of Modern Art in New York City). Much more recently, the same head figured in the badges of NASA's Apollo XVII mission of December 1972. And Winckelmann's feelings are still hiding in the verses that the American

Robert William Service (1874–1958) put into the mouth of his "Idaho pumpkin" who late in life and far from education spent a week in Rome (*Rhymes of a Roughneck*, 1950):

> Abut as I sought amid them sights bewildered to steer,
> The king-pin was the one they called Appoller Belvydeer.
> Say, I ain't got no culture an' I don't know any art,
> But that there statoo got me, standin' in its room apart,
> In an alcove draped wi' velvet, lookin' everlastin' bright,
> Like the vision o' a poet, full o' beauty, grace an' light;
> An' though I know them kind o' words sound sissy in the ear,
> It's jest how I was struck by that Appoller Belvydeer.

If Service does not give his game away already in this poetical appreciation that smacks more of William Blake than of an Idaho pumpkin, he certainly does so in the final verses:

> So I'll go back to Pumpkinville an' to my humble home,
> An' dream o' all the sights I saw in everlastin' Rome;
> But I will never speak a word o' that enchanted land
> That taks you bang into the Past – folks wouldn't understand;
> An' midmost in my memories I'll cherish close an' dear
> That bit o' frozen music, that Appoller Belvydeer.

If we still are under the impression that, somehow, Apollo is the most Greek of all Greek gods, this derives not the least from the spell of the Belvedere Apollo. We know now that Winckelmann elevated to such symbolic height a statue that was merely a Roman copy of a lost original. This might surprise the scholar who was the first to map out the development of ancient art, from its beginning to the end of antiquity. But it is one of the many ironies of history that, in the end, perception has proved to be more powerful than historical reality.

SUMMARY

This has been a trajectory that is as sketchy as it is wide; it does not offer itself to easy summarizing. Gods are as immortal as poets are: they live as long as their stories are told and affect people's emotions and imagination. Apollo has played many roles even after the rise of Christianity – image of the sun in the Middle Ages and beyond, of poetic inspiration in the Renaissance, symbol of Greekness to Winckelmann and his followers, expression of male erotic desire in more recent times. And he still lives on: in her 2007 book *Gods Behaving Badly*, Marie Philips has him living in contemporary London, an eternally lusting, bored, and unkempt adolescent who wonders about getting a tattoo, but who is powerful enough to kill a mortal lover or to turn off the sunlight, for the worst possible reasons of course.

EPILOGUE

It has not been by chance that during this discussion of Apollo, I have so often relied on Homer's *Iliad* and *Odyssey*. Homer's construction of divine personalities has exercised its suggestive power through the ages, and Herodotus was not the first to say so explicitly. The two sculptural images of Apollo that, in the last few centuries, have been standing out from a crowd of statues are ample testimony to this. The alluringly beautiful male arrogance both of the Apollo from the west pediment of the Zeus temple in Olympia and of the Belvedere Apollo are unthinkable without the Homeric portraits, and few scholarly discussions of the god could bypass them. The historian of Greek religion, however, has to resist this powerful pull. Walter F. Otto succumbed to it and wrote his splendidly one-sided *The Gods of the Greeks. The Spiritual Significance of Greek Religion* (*Die Götter Griechenlands. Das Bild des Göttlichen im Spiegel des griechischen Geistes*, 1929). His Greek gods are exclusively the gods of Homer: Homer is the "mirror of the Greek spirit," and his gods are the almost sole incarnation of the divine in Greece. He can do so because, in the end, he did not propose to write a history of Greek religion but to present his readers with his very special view of Greekness and of the divine.

One-sided pictures, however powerful they may be, never capture historical reality. Apollo was always complex and contradictory, in the myths and cults of the Greek and Roman world as much as in his later reception. As each epoch produced its sculptural image of the god, from the small metal statuette in early Archaic Dreros to the chryselephantine statue in Julian's Antioch, in the same way each Greek city had its own Apollo in the various functions that were determined by tradition and desire. The foregoing chapters tried to bundle these many roles of the god into a few main functions and to give them historical depth. Music and dance, divination, healing, the young, and the polis denote areas where Apollo played a major and sometimes a unique role, different in importance from city to city. The historian feels an intellectual pull to construct these fields into an underlying unity. Such a construction might satisfy a thinker's need of neatness; but it sacrifices so much historical diversity that it loses all value for the historian of religion. The same is true for the endeavor to present a convincing prehistory of Apollo. When the Greek world becomes better visible after the collapse of the Bronze Age civilizations and the following "Dark Age," we perceive a complex historical world in which local traditions have had a long time to grow and develop, sometimes isolated from each other, sometimes in contact with other communities and regions and with the civilizations of the Ancient Near East through manifold contacts with Anatolia, Cyprus, Phoenicia, and Egypt: the bewildering multiplicity of local dialects and local writing systems that emerges during the Geometric Age is an indication of these multiple local developments, and a warning against assuming a break-down of communication in the Eastern Mediterranean and Aegean world. Many things might have been recent developments, but some traditions might reach back more deeply into the Bronze Age than we are willing to accept: the Mycenaean civilization as we discern it was a matter of a relatively homogeneous ruling class, and its traces offer only a narrow window into Bronze Age Greece.

The dialectic of the particular and the general, the pull of local traditions and of the desire for the unity of being Greek, is one of the major attractions in the study of Greek religion, and one of the major obstacles to an easy understanding of its history. To this, one has to add the dialectic of a polytheistic system that still defies convincing conceptual analysis. Vernant's metaphor of a closed system is the best approximation available – but this system is not closed but wide open towards the entire Greek world, and to its surrounding civilizations. Religion is a closed system only by force, usually the force of dogma and the power of a centralized priesthood to impose such a dogma. Apollo's many faces are part of this complex system: his image is shaped by the other divinities in the pantheon, most prominently Zeus and Athena, and by the divinities with whom he was identified, inside the Greek world and outside. In astronomy, the force that shapes celestial bodies beyond the force of their rotation is the gravitational pull of all other bodies; in religion, this pull is activated by the manifold desires and needs of societies and individuals to which the polytheistic system responds with its plurality of gods. If this book has succeeded in giving a first impression of the vaster cosmos that shaped Apollo, and of the many shapes resulting from it, then the author feels that he has done his job.

FURTHER READING

There are very few books on Apollo, besides the general histories of Greek and Roman religion and the outdated but still useful L.R. Farnell, *The Cults of the Greek States*, vol. 4 (Oxford: Clarendon Press, 1907). On the Greek side, Marcel Detienne, *Apollon le couteau à la main. Une approche expérimentale du polythéisme grec* (Paris: Gallimard, 1998) is somewhat one-sided but stimulating, as is Philippe Monbrun, *Les voix d'Apollon. L'arc, la lyre et les oracles* (Rennes: Presses Universitaires de Rennes, 2007). Jon Solomon, ed., *Apollo. Origins and Influences* (Tucson and London: University of Arizona Press, 1994) is patchy at best. On the Roman side, Jean Gagé, *Apollon Romain. Essai sur le culte d'Apollo et le développement du "ritus Graecus" à Rome des origines à Auguste* (Paris: Boccard, 1955) is essential; but add some of the essays in Georges Dumézil, *Apollon sonore et autres essais. Esquisses de mythologie* (Paris: Gallimard, 1982).

CHAPTER I

On Apollo in Homer, Emily Vermeule, *Götterkult*. Archaeologia Homerica V (Göttingen: Vandenhoeck & Ruprecht, 1974) is outdated, but has not been replaced. On religion in the *Odyssey*, Hans Schwabl, "Religiöse Aspekte der Odyssee. Zu Götterapparat und Kultgegenheiten," *Wiener Studien* 12 (1978) 5–28 is still useful. On the calendrical and ritual background of Odysseus' return, Christoph Auffarth's chapter (6.3) in *Der drohende Untergang. "Schöpfung" in Mythos und Ritual im Alten Orient und in Griechenland am Beispiel der Odyssee und des Ezechielbuches* (Berlin: De Gruyter, 1991), is stimulating and suggestive.

The *Homeric Hymn to Apollo* is most helpfully discussed by Andrew M. Miller, *From Delos to Delphi. A Literary Study of the Homeric Hymn to Apollo* (Mnemosyne Supplement 93) (Leiden: Brill, 1986).

CHAPTER 2

On the paean, see Lutz Käppel, *Paian. Studien zur Geschichte einer Gattung* (Berlin: De Gruyter, 1992) and Ian Rutherford, *Pindar's Paeans. A Reading of the Fragments with a Survey of the Genre* (Oxford: Clarendon Press, 1996). On Pythagoras, Walter Burkert, *Lore and Science in Ancient Pythagoreanism* (Cambridge, Mass.: Harvard University Press, 1972); on Aristeas, J.P.D. Bolton, *Aristeas of Proconessus* (Oxford: Clarendon Press, 1962), on Empedocles, Peter Kingsley, *Ancient Philosophy, Mystery, and Magic. Empedocles and the Pythagorean Tradition* (Oxford: Clarendon Press, 1995). Among the many books on Orpheus, I single out Charles Segal, *Orpheus. The Myth of the Poet* (Baltimore: Johns Hopkins University Press, 1989), and Martin L. West, *The Orphic Poems* (Oxford: Clarendon Press, 1983).

CHAPTER 3

Divination has long been neglected by scholars. Sarah Iles Johnston, *Greek Divination* (Oxford: Blackwell, 2008) is the first major monograph in many decades; Veit Rosenberger, *Griechische Orakel. Eine Kulturgeschichte* (Darmstadt: Wissenschaftliche Buchgesellschaft, 2001) is useful for the archaeological record only.

Delphi

Among general accounts, I single out H.W. Parke and D.E.W. Wormell, *The Delphic Oracle* (Oxford: Blackwell, 1956) and Joseph Fontenrose, *The Delphic Oracle. Its Responses and Operations* (Berkeley and Los Angeles: University of California Press, 1978). Pierre Amandry, *La mantique apollinienne à Delphes. Essai sur le fonctionnement de l'oracle*, repr. 1975 (Paris: Boccard, 1950) is still helpful; the centenary volume edited by Anne Jacquemine, *Delphes cent ans après la grande fouille. Essai de bilan. Actes du colloque international organisé par l'École Française d'Athènes* (Athens: École Française d'Athènes, 2000) is spotty. On the Pythia's possession, and on possession in general, Lisa Maurizio, "Anthropology and Spirit Possession. A Reconsideration of the Pythia's Role at Delphi," *Journal of Hellenic Studies* 115 (1995), 69–86 is fundamental, as is Christopher Forbes, *Prophecy and Inspired Speech in Early Christianity and its Hellenistic Environment* (Tübingen: Mohr, 1995).

The most recent geological discoveries are summarized in J.Z. De

Boer, J.R. Hale, and J. Chanton, "New Evidence for the Geological Origins of the Ancient Delphic Oracle (Greece)," *Geology* 28 (2001), 707–710.

Clarus and Didyma

We lack a good account of Clarus, despite the French excavations; the known oracles are collected in Reinhold Merkelbach and Josef Stauber, "Die Orakel des Apollon von Klaros," *Epigraphica Anatolica* 27 (1996), 1–53, reprinted in R. Merkelbach, *Philologica* (Stuttgart and Leipzig: Teubner, 1997), 155–218. On Didyma, Joseph Fontenrose, *Didyma. Apollo's Oracle, Cult, and Companions* (Berkeley: University of California Press, 1988) is useful, but not very stimulating. On late antiquity, Aude Busine, *Paroles d'Apollon. Pratiques et traditions oraculaires dans l'Antiquité tardive (IIe–VIe siècles)* (Leiden: Brill, 2005) is learned and thorough.

On the Sibyls, see John J. Collins, *Sibyls, Seers and Sages in Hellenistic-Roman Judaism* (Leiden: Brill, 1997).

CHAPTER 4

Religious healing in general and Apollo the Healer are rather neglected. For details, see Norbert Ehrhardt, "Apollon Ietros. Ein verschollener Gott in Ionien?" *Istanbuler Mitteilungen* 39 (1989), 115–122, on Miletus and its colonies; Walter Burkert, "Olbia and Apollo of Didyma. A New Oracle Text," in *Apollo. Origins and Influences*, ed. Jon Solomon (Tucson and London: University of Arizona Press, 1994), 49–60, 145–147 on Apollo in Olbia; Carsten Schneider, "Apollon Ulias in Velia?" *Archäologischer Anzeiger* (1998), 305–317 on Elea/Velia.

On Asclepius, the two volumes of Emma J. and Ludwig Edelstein, *Asclepius. Collection and Interpretation of the Testimonies* (Baltimore: Johns Hopkins University Press, 1945) are still indispensable. The Epidaurian healing stories are edited and translated in Lynn R. LiDonnici, *The Epidaurian Miracle Inscriptions. Text, Translation and Commentary* (Atlanta: Scholars Press, 1995).

CHAPTER 5

For a critical discussion of initiation in Greece, see Walter Burkert, " 'Iniziazione'. Un concetto moderno e una terminologia antica," in Bruno Gentili and Franca Perusino, eds., *Le orse di Brauron. Un rituale di iniziazione femminile nel santuario di Artemide* (Pisa, 2002), 13–27, and Fritz Graf, "Initiation. A Concept with a Troubled History," in David B. Dodd and Christoper A. Faraone, eds., *Initiation in Ancient Greek Rituals and Narratives. New Critical Perspectives* (London: Routledge, 2003), 3–24; both look at the concept from the distance of a new century. Men's associations, originally debated at the turn of the twentieth century, have been discussed in the context of the symposium, see some of the contributions in Oswyn Murray, ed., *Sympotica. A Symposium on the Symposium* (Oxford: Clarendon Press, 1990), esp. Jan N. Bremmer, "Adolescents, symposium, and pederasty," 135–148. On Apollo Delphinios, see Fritz Graf, "Apollon Delphinios," *Museum Helveticum* 26 (1979), 2–22; on Apollo Lykeios, see Michael H. Jameson, "Apollo Lykeios in Athens," *Archaiognosia* 1 (1980), 213–232. On the Molpoi in Miletus, see Alexander Herda, *Der Apollon-Delphinios-Kult in Milet und die Neujahrsprozession nach Didyma. Ein neuer Kommentar der sog. Molpoi-Satzung* (Mainz: Zabern, 2006). On Apollo in Sparta see Michael Pettersson, *Cults of Apollo at Sparta. The Hyakinthia, the Gymnopaidia and the Karneia* (Stockholm: Åström, 1992).

CHAPTER 6

On the Dorian Apollo, Walter Burkert, "Apellai und Apollon," *Rheinisches Museum* 118 (1975), 1–21. The Anatolian hypothesis has been renewed by Robert S. Beekes, "The origin of Apollo," *Journal of Ancient Near Eastern Religions* 3 (2003), 1–21, and by Edwin L. Brown, "In Search of Anatolian Apollo," in *Essays in Honor of Sara A. Immerwahr, Hesperia* Supplements 33 (2004), 243–257, in both cases mainly for linguistic reasons. Walter Burkert has also done pioneering research on the Oriental connections, see "Rešep-Figuren, Apollon von Amyklai und die 'Erfindung' des Opfers auf Zypern," *Grazer Beiträge* 4 (1975), 51–79; *The Orientalizing Revolution. Near Eastern Influence on Greek Culture in the Early Archaic Age* (Cambridge, Mass.: Harvard U.P., 1992), and *Babylon, Memphis, Persepolis. Eastern Contexts of Greek Culture* (Cambridge, Mass.: Harvard U.P., 2004).

CHAPTER 7

Jean Seznec, *La survivance des dieux antiques* (London: Warburg Institute, 1940; transl. *The Survival of the Pagan Gods. The Mythological Tradition and its Place in Renaissance Humanism and Art*, Princeton:

Princeton University Press, 1953) still deserves a place of honor, but the topic is in need of much more research. A useful starting point is the impressive catalogue of Jane Davison Reid, *Classical Mythology in the Arts, 1300–1990* (New York and Oxford: Oxford University Press, 1993) that covers the literature as well as the figurative arts. On the history of German archaeology since Winckelmann see Suzanne L. Marchand, *Down from Olympus. Archaeology and Philhellenism in Germany, 1750–1970.* (Princeton: Princeton University Press, 1998).

INDEX